Mike Holt's Illustrated

ELECTRICAL APPRENTICESHIP SUPPLEMENT

Extracted from Understanding the National Electrical Code® Volume 1

LEVEL 1

BASED ON THE
2020 NEC®

Mike Holt Enterprises
MikeHolt.com • 888.NEC.CODE (632.2633)

NOTICE TO THE READER

The text and commentary in this book is the author's interpretation of the 2020 Edition of NFPA 70®, the *National Electrical Code*®. It shall not be considered an endorsement of or the official position of the NFPA® or any of its committees, nor relied upon as a formal interpretation of the meaning or intent of any specific provision or provisions of the 2020 edition of NFPA 70, *National Electrical Code*.

The publisher does not warrant or guarantee any of the products described herein or perform any independent analysis in connection with any of the product information contained herein. The publisher does not assume, and expressly disclaims, any obligation to obtain and include information other than that provided to it by the manufacturer.

The reader is expressly warned to consider and adopt all safety precautions and applicable federal, state, and local laws and regulations. By following the instructions contained herein, the reader willingly assumes all risks in connection with such instructions.

Mike Holt Enterprises disclaims liability for any personal injury, property or other damages of any nature whatsoever, whether special, indirect, consequential or compensatory, directly or indirectly resulting from the use of this material. The reader is responsible for understanding what a Qualified Person is and determining safety and appropriate actions in all circumstances based on the applicable safety standards such as NFPA70E and OSHA.

The publisher makes no representation or warranties of any kind, including but not limited to, the warranties of fitness for particular purpose or merchantability, nor are any such representations implied with respect to the material set forth herein, and the publisher takes no responsibility with respect to such material. The publisher shall not be liable for any special, consequential, or exemplary damages resulting, in whole or part, from the reader's use of, or reliance upon, this material.

Mike Holt's Illustrated Electrical Apprenticeship Level 1 Supplement, based on the 2020 NEC®

Second Printing: September 2021

Author: Mike Holt
Technical Illustrator: Mike Culbreath
Cover Design: Bryan Burch
Layout Design and Typesetting: Cathleen Kwas

COPYRIGHT © 2020 Charles Michael Holt
ISBN: 978-1-950431-25-0

Produced and Printed in the USA

For more information, call 888.NEC.CODE (632.2633), or e-mail Info@MikeHolt.com.

NEC®, NFPA 70®, NFPA 70E® and *National Electrical Code*® are registered trademarks of the National Fire Protection Association.

 This logo is a registered trademark of Mike Holt Enterprises, Inc.

If you are an instructor and would like to request an examination copy of this or other Mike Holt Publications:

Call: 888.NEC.CODE (632.2633) • Fax: 352.360.0983

E-mail: Info@MikeHolt.com • Visit: www.MikeHolt.com/Instructors

You can download a sample PDF of all our publications by visiting www.MikeHolt.com/products.

I dedicate this book to the
Lord Jesus Christ, *my mentor and teacher.*
Proverbs 16:3

We Care...

Since the day I started my business over 40 years ago, my team and I have been working hard to produce products that get results and to help individuals learn how to be successful. I have built my business on the idea that customers come first and everyone on my team will do everything they possibly can to help you succeed. I want you to know that we value you, and are honored that you have chosen us to be your partner in training.

I believe that you are the future of this industry and that it is you who will make the difference in years to come. My goal is to share with you everything that I know and to encourage you to pursue your education on a continuous basis. I hope that not only will you learn theory, Code, calculations, or how to pass an exam, but that in the process, you will become the expert in the field and the person others know to trust.

We genuinely care about you and are dedicated to providing quality electrical training that will help you take your skills to the next level. Thanks for choosing us for electrical training.

God bless and much success,

"...as for me and my house, we will serve the Lord." [Joshua 24:15]

TABLE OF CONTENTS

ABOUT THIS TEXTBOOK

Mike Holt's Illustrated Electrical Apprenticeship Level 1 Supplement, based on the 2020 NEC®

Welcome to *Mike Holt's Illustrated Electrical Apprenticeship Level 1 Supplement*, based on the 2020 *NEC*®. This textbook is intended to provide you with the additional training you'll need to be an effective apprentice. Your first level of apprenticeship is primarily focused on understanding the theories behind electricity and the mechanics behind the *National Electrical Code*® rules. Each of these lessons will build on the last to develop a comprehensive knowledge of the *NEC*.

While learning theory is critical, we understand you might be on the job working from the start. Your work will probably start with the mechanical aspects of electrical installation, so you'll need some practical knowledge of the *Code*. You may need to know things like how many wires can fit in a box, the ampacity of a certain size conductor, or how big a conduit needs to be for the conductor you're going to install. With that in mind, we've selected a few *Code*-related skills you can use as you begin your electrical career.

Don't worry if you don't feel like you have these topics mastered the first time you see them. We'll come back and build on what you learn in this level and each subsequent level until you've mastered even the most difficult concepts.

We hope you enjoy studying one of the most exciting trades in the industry. Be safe!

The Scope of This Textbook

This textbook, *Mike Holt's Illustrated Electrical Apprenticeship Level 1 Supplement, based on the 2020 NEC*, covers some of the basic installation requirements contained in the *NEC* from Chapters 1 through 3.

This program is based on 120/208V, 120/240V, or 277/480V, single-phase and three-phase solidly grounded alternating-current systems, using 90°C insulated copper conductors sized to 60°C rated terminals for 100A and less rated circuits, and with 75°C rated terminals for over 100A rated circuits, unless otherwise indicated in the text.

How to Use This Textbook

This textbook is to be used along with the *NEC* and not as a replacement for it. Be sure to have a copy of the 2020 *National Electrical Code* handy. You will notice that we have paraphrased a great deal of the wording, and some of the article and section titles appear different than those in the actual *Code* book. We believe doing so makes it easier to understand the content of the rule, so keep that in mind when comparing this textbook to the *NEC*.

Always compare what is being explained in this textbook to what the *Code* book says. Get with others who are knowledgeable about the *NEC* to discuss any topics you find difficult to understand or join our free *Code* Forum at www.MikeHolt.com/forum to post your question.

This textbook follows the *Code* format, but it does not cover every requirement. For example, it does not include every article, section, subsection, exception, or Informational Note. So, do not be concerned if you see that the textbook contains Exception 1 and Exception 3, but not Exception 2.

Cross-References. Many *NEC* rules refer to requirements located in other sections of the *Code*. This textbook does the same with the intention of helping you develop a better understanding of how the *NEC* rules relate to one another. These cross-references are indicated by *Code* section numbers in brackets, an example of which is "[90.4]."

Informational Notes. Informational Notes contained in the *NEC* will be identified in this textbook as "Note."

Exceptions. Exceptions contained in this textbook will be identified as "Ex" and not spelled out.

As you read through this textbook, allow yourself enough time to review the text along with the outstanding graphics and examples to give yourself the opportunity for a deeper understanding of the *Code*. The articles and rules in this Supplement are extracted from *Mike Holt's Understanding the National Electrical Code Volume 1, based on the 2020 NEC*, and are those rules considered relevant and necessary for Level 1 students. You will notice that the numbering of the graphics in most of the Articles is not sequential. It matches the graphic numbers and references in the Volume 1 textbook to make it easier to cross-reference between the two textbooks. If you want additional information that is not covered in this Supplement, consider getting a copy of *Mike Holt's Understanding the National Electrical Code, Volume 1, based on the 2020 NEC*. Visit MikeHolt.com/Code.

Technical Questions

As you progress through this textbook, you might find that you don't understand every explanation, example, calculation, or comment. Don't become frustrated, and don't get down on yourself. Remember, this is the *National Electrical Code*, and sometimes the best attempt to explain a concept isn't enough to make it perfectly clear. If you're still confused, visit www.MikeHolt.com/forum, and post your question on our free *Code* Forum. The forum is a moderated community of electrical professionals.

Textbook Corrections

We're committed to providing you with the finest product with the fewest errors and take great care to ensure our textbooks are correct. But we're realistic and know that errors might be found after printing.

If you believe that there's an error of any kind (typographical, grammatical, technical, etc.) in this textbook or in the Answer Key, send an e-mail that includes the textbook title, page number, and any other pertinent information to corrections@MikeHolt.com.

Key Features

The layout and design of this textbook incorporate special features and symbols designed to help you navigate easily through the material, and to enhance your understanding.

Code Rule Headers

The *Code* rule being taught is identified with a chapter color bar and white text.

Part I. General Requirements

300.1 Scope

(A) All Wiring Installations. Article 300 contains the general requirements for wiring methods and materials for power and lighting. ▶Figure 300–1

Full-Color, Detailed Educational Graphics

Industry-leading graphics help you visualize the sometimes complex language of the *Code*, and illustrate the rule in real-world application(s). This is a great aid to reinforce learning.

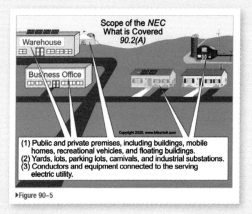

▶Figure 90–5

Author's Comments

These comments provide additional information to help you understand the context.

Author's Comment

▶ An adjustable-speed drive is a piece of equipment that provides a way to adjust the speed of an electric motor. Adjustable-speed drives are often referred to as "variable-speed drives" or "variable-frequency drives (VFDs)."

▶ A variable-frequency drive is a type of electronic adjustable-speed drive that controls the speed of an alternating-current motor by changing the frequency and voltage of the motor's power supply.

Code Change Text

Underlined text denotes changes to the *Code* for the 2020 *NEC*.

(A) Sealing. If a raceway is subjected to different temperatures, and where condensation is known to be a problem, the raceway must be filled with a material approved by the authority having jurisdiction that will prevent the circulation of warm air to a colder section of the raceway. Sealants must be identified for use with cable insulation, conductor insulation, a bare conductor, a shield, or other components.
▶Figure 300–42

Formulas

$$P = I \times E$$

Formulas are easily identifiable in green text on a gray bar.

Examples

These practical application questions and answers are contained in framed yellow boxes.

If you see an ellipsis (● ● ●) at the bottom of the example, it is continued on the following page.

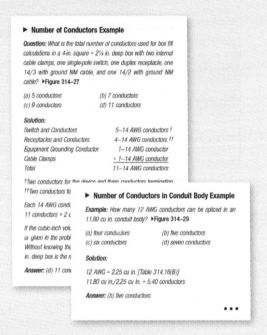

Additional Background Information Boxes

Where information unrelated to the specific rule will help you understand the concept being taught, we include these topics, easily identified in boxes that are shaded gray.

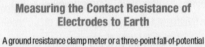

Measuring the Contact Resistance of Electrodes to Earth

A ground resistance clamp meter or a three-point fall-of-potential ground resistance meter can be used to measure the contact resistance of a grounding electrode to the Earth.

Ground Clamp Meter. The ground resistance clamp meter measures the contact resistance of the grounding electrode system to the Earth by injecting a high-frequency signal via the service neutral conductor to the serving electric utility's grounding system, and then measuring the strength of the return signal through the Earth to the grounding electrode being measured. ▶Figure 250–129

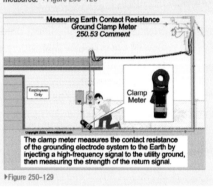

The clamp meter measures the contact resistance of the grounding electrode system to the Earth by injecting a high-frequency signal to the utility ground, then measuring the strength of the return signal.

▶Figure 250–129

Modular Color Coded Page Layout

Chapters are color coded and modular to make it easy to navigate through each section of the textbook. As you can see by the Table of Contents, each Chapter has a unique color.

Caution, Warning, and Danger Icons

These icons highlight areas of concern.

Caution

Caution: An explanation of possible damage to property or equipment.

Warning

Warning: An explanation of possible severe property damage or personal injury.

Danger

Danger: An explanation of possible severe injury or death.

HOW TO USE THE *NATIONAL ELECTRICAL CODE*

The original *NEC* document was developed in 1897 as a result of the united efforts of various insurance, electrical, architectural, and other cooperative interests. The National Fire Protection Association (NFPA) has sponsored the *National Electrical Code* since 1911.

The purpose of the *Code* is the practical safeguarding of persons and property from hazards arising from the use of electricity. It isn't intended as a design specification or an instruction manual for untrained persons. It is, in fact, a standard that contains the minimum requirements for an electrical installation that's essentially free from hazard. Learning to understand and use the *Code* is critical to you working safely; whether you're training to become an electrician, or are already an electrician, electrical contractor, inspector, engineer, designer, or instructor.

The *NEC* was written for qualified persons; those who understand electrical terms, theory, safety procedures, and electrical trade practices. Learning to use the *Code* is a lengthy process and can be frustrating if you don't approach it the right way. First, you'll need to understand electrical theory and if you don't have theory as a background when you get into the *NEC*, you're going to struggle. Take one step back if necessary and learn electrical theory. You must also understand the concepts and terms in the *Code* and know grammar and punctuation in order to understand the complex structure of the rules and their intended purpose(s). The *NEC* is written in a formal outline which many of us haven't seen or used since high school or college so it's important for you to pay particular attention to this format. Our goal for the next few pages is to give you some guidelines and suggestions on using your *Code* book to help you understand that standard, and assist you in what you're trying to accomplish and, ultimately, your personal success as an electrical professional!

Language Considerations for the *NEC*

Terms and Concepts

The *NEC* contains many technical terms, and it's crucial for *Code* users to understand their meanings and applications. If you don't understand a term used in a rule, it will be impossible to properly apply the *NEC* requirement. Article 100 defines those that are used generally in two or more articles throughout the *Code*; for example, the term "Dwelling Unit" is found in many articles. If you don't know the *NEC* definition for a "dwelling unit" you can't properly identify its *Code* requirements. Another example worth mentioning is the term "Outlet." For many people it has always meant a receptacle—not so in the *NEC*!

Many *Code* articles use terms unique to that specific article, and the definitions of those terms only apply to that given article. Definitions for them are usually found in the beginning of the article. For example, Section 250.2 contains the definitions of terms that only apply to Article 250—Grounding and Bonding. Whether definitions are unique to a specific article, or apply throughout the *NEC*, is indicated at the beginning of the definitions (xxx.2) section of the article. For example,

Article 690 contains definitions (in 690.2) that apply ONLY to that article while Article 705 introduces definitions (in 705.2) that apply throughout the entire *Code*.

Small Words, Grammar, and Punctuation

Technical words aren't the only ones that require close attention. Even simple words can make a big difference to the application of a rule. Is there a comma? Does it use "or," "and," "other than," "greater than," or "smaller than"? The word "or" can imply alternate choices for wiring methods. A word like "or" gives us choices while the word "and" can mean an additional requirement must be met.

An example of the important role small words play in the *NEC* is found in 110.26(C)(2), where it says equipment containing overcurrent, switching, "or" control devices that are 1,200A or more "and" over 6 ft wide require a means of egress at each end of the working space. In this section, the word "or" clarifies that equipment containing any of the three types of devices listed must follow this rule. The word "and" clarifies that 110.26(C)(2) only applies if the equipment is both 1,200A or more and over 6 ft wide.

Grammar and punctuation play an important role in establishing the meaning of a rule. The location of a comma can dramatically change the requirement of a rule such as in 250.28(A), where it says a main bonding jumper shall be a wire, bus, screw, or similar suitable conductor. If the comma between "bus" and "screw" was removed, only a "bus screw" could be used. That comma makes a big change in the requirements of the rule.

Slang Terms or Technical Jargon

Trade-related professionals in different areas of the country often use local "slang" terms that aren't shared by all. This can make it difficult to communicate if it isn't clear what the meaning of those slang terms are. Use the proper terms by finding out what their definitions and applications are before you use them. For example, the term "pigtail" is often used to describe the short piece of conductor used to connect a device to a splice, but a "pigtail" is also used for a rubberized light socket with pre-terminated conductors. Although the term is the same, the meaning is very different and could cause confusion. The words "splice" and "tap" are examples of terms often interchanged in the field but are two entirely different things! The uniformity and consistency of the terminology used in the *Code*, makes it so everyone says and means the same thing regardless of geographical location.

NEC Style and Layout

It's important to understand the structure and writing style of the *Code* if you want to use it effectively. The *National Electrical Code* is organized using twelve major components.

1. Table of Contents
2. Chapters—Chapters 1 through 9 (major categories)
3. Articles—Chapter subdivisions that cover specific subjects
4. Parts—Divisions used to organize article subject matter
5. Sections—Divisions used to further organize article subject matter
6. Tables and Figures—Represent the mandatory requirements of a rule
7. Exceptions—Alternatives to the main *Code* rule
8. Informational Notes—Explanatory material for a specific rule (not a requirement)
9. Tables—Applicable as referenced in the *NEC*
10. Annexes—Additional explanatory information such as tables and references (not a requirement)
11. Index
12. Changes to the *Code* from the previous edition

1. Table of Contents. The Table of Contents displays the layout of the chapters, articles, and parts as well as the page numbers. It's an excellent resource and should be referred to periodically to observe the interrelationship of the various *NEC* components. When attempting to locate the rules for a specific situation, knowledgeable *Code* users often go first to the Table of Contents to quickly find the specific *NEC* rule that applies.

2. Chapters. There are nine chapters, each of which is divided into articles. The articles fall into one of four groupings: General Requirements (Chapters 1 through 4), Specific Requirements (Chapters 5 through 7), Communications Systems (Chapter 8), and Tables (Chapter 9).

Chapter 1—General
Chapter 2—Wiring and Protection
Chapter 3—Wiring Methods and Materials
Chapter 4—Equipment for General Use
Chapter 5—Special Occupancies
Chapter 6—Special Equipment
Chapter 7—Special Conditions
Chapter 8—Communications Systems (Telephone, Data, Satellite, Cable TV, and Broadband)
Chapter 9—Tables–Conductor and Raceway Specifications

3. Articles. The *NEC* contains approximately 140 articles, each of which covers a specific subject. It begins with Article 90, the introduction to the *Code* which contains the purpose of the *NEC*, what is covered and isn't covered, along with how the *Code* is arranged. It also gives information on enforcement, how mandatory and permissive rules are written, and how explanatory material is included. Article 90 also includes information on formal interpretations, examination of equipment for safety, wiring planning, and information about formatting units of measurement. Here are some other examples of articles you'll find in the *NEC*:

Article 110—Requirements for Electrical Installations
Article 250—Grounding and Bonding
Article 300—General Requirements for Wiring Methods and Materials
Article 430—Motors, Motor Circuits, and Motor Controllers
Article 500—Hazardous (Classified) Locations
Article 680—Swimming Pools, Fountains, and Similar Installations
Article 725—Remote-Control, Signaling, and Power-Limited Circuits
Article 800—General Requirements for Communications Systems

4. Parts. Larger articles are subdivided into parts. Because the parts of a *Code* article aren't included in the section numbers, we tend to forget to what "part" an *NEC* rule is relating. For example, Table 110.34(A) contains working space clearances for electrical equipment. If we aren't careful, we might think this table applies to all electrical installations, but Table 110.34(A) is in Part III, which only contains requirements for "Over 1,000 Volts, Nominal" installations. The rules for working clearances for electrical equipment for systems 1,000V, nominal, or less are contained in Table 110.26(A)(1), which is in Part II—1,000 Volts, Nominal, or Less.

5. Sections. Each *NEC* rule is called a "*Code* Section." A *Code* section may be broken down into subdivisions; first level subdivision will be in parentheses like (A), (B),..., the next will be second level subdivisions in parentheses like (1), (2),..., and third level subdivisions in lowercase letters such as (a), (b), and so on.

For example, the rule requiring all receptacles in a dwelling unit bathroom to be GFCI protected is contained in Section 210.8(A)(1) which is in Chapter 2, Article 210, Section 8, first level subdivision (A), and second level subdivision (1).

Note: According to the *NEC Style Manual*, first and second level subdivisions are required to have titles. A title for a third level subdivision is permitted but not required.

Many in the industry incorrectly use the term "Article" when referring to a *Code* section. For example, they say "Article 210.8," when they should say "Section 210.8." Section numbers in this textbook are shown without the word "Section," unless they're at the beginning of a sentence. For example, Section 210.8(A) is shown as simply 210.8(A).

6. Tables and Figures. Many *NEC* requirements are contained within tables, which are lists of *Code* rules placed in a systematic arrangement. The titles of the tables are extremely important; you must read them carefully in order to understand the contents, applications, and limitations of each one. Notes are often provided in or below a table; be sure to read them as well since they're also part of the requirement. For example, Note 1 for Table 300.5 explains how to measure the cover when burying cables and raceways and Note 5 explains what to do if solid rock is encountered.

7. Exceptions. Exceptions are *NEC* requirements or permissions that provide an alternative method to a specific rule. There are two types of exceptions—mandatory and permissive. When a rule has several exceptions, those exceptions with mandatory requirements are listed before the permissive exceptions.

Mandatory Exceptions. A mandatory exception uses the words "shall" or "shall not." The word "shall" in an exception means that if you're using the exception, you're required to do it in a specific way. The phrase "shall not" means it isn't permitted.

Permissive Exceptions. A permissive exception uses words such as "shall be permitted," which means it's acceptable (but not mandatory) to do it in this way.

8. Informational Notes. An Informational Note contains explanatory material intended to clarify a rule or give assistance, but it isn't a *Code* requirement.

9. Tables. Chapter 9 consists of tables applicable as referenced in the *NEC*. They're used to calculate raceway sizing, conductor fill, the radius of raceway bends, and conductor voltage drop.

10. Informative Annexes. Annexes aren't a part of the *Code* requirements and are included for informational purposes only.

Annex A. Product Safety Standards
Annex B. Application Information for Ampacity Calculation
Annex C. Raceway Fill Tables for Conductors and Fixture Wires of the Same Size
Annex D. Examples
Annex E. Types of Construction
Annex F. Critical Operations Power Systems (COPS)
Annex G. Supervisory Control and Data Acquisition (SCADA)
Annex H. Administration and Enforcement
Annex I. Recommended Tightening Torques
Annex J. ADA Standards for Accessible Design

11. Index. The Index at the back of the *NEC* is helpful in locating a specific rule using pertinent keywords to assist in your search.

12. Changes to the *Code*. Changes in the *NEC* are indicated as follows:

▸ Rules that were changed since the previous edition are identified by shading the revised text.

▸ New rules aren't shaded like a change, instead they have a shaded "N" in the margin to the left of the section number.

▸ Relocated rules are treated like new rules with a shaded "N" in the left margin by the section number.

▸ Deleted rules are indicated by a bullet symbol " • " located in the left margin where the rule was in the previous edition. Unlike older editions the bullet symbol is only used where one or more complete paragraphs have been deleted. There's no indication used where a word, group of words, or a sentence was deleted.

▸ A Δ represents text deletions and figure/table revisions.

How to Locate a Specific Requirement

How to go about finding what you're looking for in the *Code* book depends, to some degree, on your experience with the *NEC*. Experts typically know the requirements so well that they just go to the correct rule. Very experienced people might only need the Table of Contents to locate the requirement for which they're looking. On the other hand, average users should use all the tools at their disposal, including the Table of Contents, the Index, and the search feature on electronic versions of the *Code* book.

Let's work through a simple example: What *NEC* rule specifies the maximum number of disconnects permitted for a service?

Using the Table of Contents. If you're an experienced *Code* user, you might use the Table of Contents. You'll know Article 230 applies to "Services," and because this article is so large, it's divided up into multiple parts (eight parts to be exact). With this knowledge, you can quickly go to the Table of Contents and see it lists the Service Equipment Disconnecting Means requirements in Part VI.

Author's Comment:

▸ The number "70" precedes all page numbers in this standard because the *NEC* is NFPA Standard Number 70.

Using the Index. If you use the Index (which lists subjects in alphabetical order) to look up the term "service disconnect," you'll see there's no listing. If you try "disconnecting means," then "services," you'll find that the Index indicates the rule is in Article 230, Part VI. Because the *NEC* doesn't give a page number in the Index, you'll need to use the Table of Contents to find it, or flip through the *Code* book to Article 230, then continue to flip through pages until you find Part VI.

Many people complain that the *NEC* only confuses them by taking them in circles. Once you gain experience in using the *Code* and deepen your understanding of words, terms, principles, and practices, you'll find it much easier to understand and use than you originally thought.

With enough exposure in the use of the *NEC*, you'll discover that some words and terms are often specific to certain articles. The word "solar" for example will immediately send experienced *Code* book users to Article 690—Solar Photovoltaic (PV) Systems. The word "marina" suggests what you seek might be in Article 555. There are times when a main article will send you to a specific requirement in another one in which compliance is required in which case it will say (for example), "in accordance with 230.xx." Don't think of these situations as a "circle," but rather a map directing you to exactly where you need to be.

Customizing Your *Code* Book

One way to increase your comfort level with your *Code* book is to customize it to meet your needs. You can do this by highlighting and underlining important *NEC* requirements. Preprinted adhesive tabs are also an excellent aid to quickly find important articles and sections that are regularly referenced. However, understand that if you're using your *Code* book to prepare to take an exam, some exam centers don't allow markings of any type. For more information about tabs for your *Code* book, visit www.MikeHolt.com/tabs.

Highlighting. As you read through or find answers to your questions, be sure you highlight those requirements in the *NEC* that are the most important or relevant to you. Use one color, like yellow, for general interest and a different one for important requirements you want to find quickly. Be sure to highlight terms in the Index and the Table of Contents as you use them.

Underlining. Underline or circle key words and phrases in the *Code* with a red or blue pen (not a lead pencil) using a short ruler or other straightedge to keep lines straight and neat. This is a very handy way to make important requirements stand out. A short ruler or other straightedge also comes in handy for locating the correct information in a table.

Interpretations

Industry professionals often enjoy the challenge of discussing, and at times debating, the *Code* requirements. These types of discussions are important to the process of better understanding the *NEC* requirements and applications. However, if you decide you're going to participate in one of these discussions, don't spout out what you think without having the actual *Code* book in your hand. The professional way of discussing a requirement is by referring to a specific section rather than talking in vague generalities. This will help everyone involved clearly understand the point and become better educated. In fact, you may become so well educated about the *NEC* that you might even decide to participate in the change process and help to make it even better!

Become Involved in the *NEC* Process

The actual process of changing the *Code* takes about two years and involves hundreds of individuals trying to make the *NEC* as current and accurate as possible. As you advance in your studies and understanding of the *Code*, you might begin to find it very interesting, enjoy it more, and realize that you can also be a part of the process. Rather than sitting back and allowing others to take the lead, you can participate by making proposals and being a part of its development. For the 2020 cycle, there were 3,730 Public Inputs and 1,930 comments. Hundreds of updates and five new articles were added to keep the *NEC* up to date with new technologies and pave the way to a safer and more efficient electrical future.

Here's how the process works:

STEP 1—Public Input Stage

Public Input. The revision cycle begins with the acceptance of Public Input (PI) which is the public notice asking for anyone interested to submit input on an existing standard or a committee-approved new draft standard. Following the closing date, the committee conducts a First Draft Meeting to respond to all Public Inputs.

First Draft Meeting. At the First Draft (FD) Meeting, the Technical Committee considers and provides a response to all Public Input. The Technical Committee may use the input to develop First Revisions to the standard. The First Draft documents consist of the initial meeting consensus of the committee by simple majority. However, the final position of the Technical Committee must be established by a ballot which follows.

Committee Ballot on First Draft. The First Draft developed at the First Draft Meeting is balloted. In order to appear in the First Draft, a revision must be approved by at least two-thirds of the Technical Committee.

First Draft Report Posted. First revisions which pass ballot are ultimately compiled and published as the First Draft Report on the document's NFPA web page. This report serves as documentation for the Input Stage and is published for review and comment. The public may review the First Draft Report to determine whether to submit Public Comments on the First Draft.

STEP 2—Public Comment Stage

Public Comment. Once the First Draft Report becomes available, there's a Public Comment period during which anyone can submit a Public Comment on the First Draft. After the Public Comment closing date, the Technical Committee conducts/holds their Second Draft Meeting.

Second Draft Meeting. After the Public Comment closing date, if Public Comments are received or the committee has additional proposed revisions, a Second Draft Meeting is held. At the Second Draft Meeting, the Technical Committee reviews the First Draft and may make additional revisions to the draft Standard. All Public Comments are considered, and the Technical Committee provides an action and response to each Public Comment. These actions result in the Second Draft.

Committee Ballot on Second Draft. The Second Revisions developed at the Second Draft Meeting are balloted. To appear in the Second Draft, a revision must be approved by at least two-thirds of the Technical Committee.

Second Draft Report Posted. Second Revisions which pass ballot are ultimately compiled and published as the Second Draft Report on the document's NFPA website. This report serves as documentation of the Comment Stage and is published for public review.

Once published, the public can review the Second Draft Report to decide whether to submit a Notice of Intent to Make a Motion (NITMAM) for further consideration.

STEP 3—NFPA Technical Meeting (Tech Session)

Following completion of the Public Input and Public Comment stages, there's further opportunity for debate and discussion of issues through the NFPA Technical Meeting that takes place at the NFPA Conference & Expo®. These motions are attempts to change the resulting final Standard from the committee's recommendations published as the Second Draft.

STEP 4—Council Appeals and Issuance of Standard

Issuance of Standards. When the Standards Council convenes to issue an NFPA standard, it also hears any related appeals. Appeals are an important part of assuring that all NFPA rules have been followed and that due process and fairness have continued throughout the standards development process. The Standards Council considers appeals based on the written record and by conducting live hearings during which all interested parties can participate. Appeals are decided on the entire record of the process, as well as all submissions and statements presented.

After deciding all appeals related to a standard, the Standards Council, if appropriate, proceeds to issue the Standard as an official NFPA Standard. The decision of the Standards Council is final subject only to limited review by the NFPA Board of Directors. The new NFPA standard becomes effective twenty days following the Standards Council's action of issuance.

Tentative Interim Amendment—(TIA)

Sometimes, a change to the *NEC* is of an emergency nature. Perhaps an editing mistake was made that can affect an electrical installation to the extent it may create a hazard. Maybe an occurrence in the field created a condition that needs to be addressed immediately and can't wait for the normal *Code* cycle and next edition of the standard. When these circumstances warrant it, a TIA or "Tentative Interim Amendment" can be submitted for consideration.

The NFPA defines a TIA as, "tentative because it has not been processed through the entire standards-making procedures. It is interim because it is effective only between editions of the standard. A TIA automatically becomes a Public Input of the proponent for the next edition of the standard; as such, it then is subject to all of the procedures of the standards-making process."

Author's Comment:

▶ Proposals, comments, and TIAs can be submitted for consideration online at the NFPA website, www.nfpa.org. From the homepage, look for "Codes & Standards," then find "Standards Development," and click on "How the Process Works." If you'd like to see something changed in the *Code*, you're encouraged to participate in the process.

2020 *Code* Book and Tabs

The ideal way to use your *Code* book is to tab it for quick reference—Mike's best-selling tabs make organizing the *NEC* easy. If you're using your *Code* book for an exam, you'll need to confirm with your testing authority that a tabbed *Code* book is allowed into the exam room.

You can order your *NEC* Tabs at www.MikeHolt.com/Code or call 888-632-2633.

ARTICLE 90

INTRODUCTION TO THE *NATIONAL ELECTRICAL CODE*

Introduction to Article 90—Introduction to the *National Electrical Code*

Article 90 opens by saying the *National Electrical Code (NEC/Code)* is not intended as a design specification or instruction manual. It has one purpose only, and that is the "practical safeguarding of persons and property from hazards arising from the use of electricity." That does not necessarily mean the installation will be efficient, convenient, or able to accommodate future expansion; just safe. The necessity of carefully studying the *Code* rules cannot be overemphasized, and the step-by-step explanatory design of a textbook such as this is to help in that undertaking. Understanding where to find the requirements in the *NEC* that apply to the installation is invaluable. Rules in several different articles often apply to even a simple installation. You are not going to remember every section of every article of the *Code* but, hopefully, you will come away with knowing where to look after studying this textbook.

Article 90 then goes on to describe the scope and arrangement of the *NEC*. The balance of it provides the reader with information essential to understanding the *Code* rules.

Most electrical installations require you to understand the first four chapters of the *NEC* (which apply generally) and have a working knowledge of the Chapter 9 tables. That understanding begins with this article. Chapters 5, 6, and 7 make up a large portion of the *Code* book, but they apply to special occupancies, special equipment, or special conditions. They build on, modify, or amend the rules in the first four chapters. Chapter 8 contains the requirements for communications systems, such as radio and television equipment, satellite receivers, antenna systems, twisted pair conductors, and coaxial cable wiring. Communications systems are not subject to the general requirements of Chapters 1 through 4, or the special requirements of Chapters 5 through 7, unless there is a specific reference to a rule in the previous chapters.

90.1 Purpose of the *NEC*

(A) Practical Safeguarding. The purpose of the *National Electrical Code* is to ensure electrical systems are installed in a manner that protects people and property by minimizing the risks associated with the use of electricity. The *NEC* is not a design specification standard nor is it an instruction manual for the untrained and unqualified.
▶Figure 90–1

Author's Comment:

▶ The *Code* is intended to be used by those who are skilled and knowledgeable in electrical theory, electrical systems, building and electrical construction, and the installation and operation of electrical equipment.

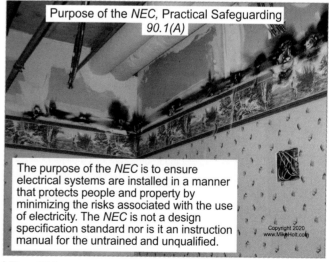

Purpose of the *NEC*, Practical Safeguarding 90.1(A)

The purpose of the *NEC* is to ensure electrical systems are installed in a manner that protects people and property by minimizing the risks associated with the use of electricity. The *NEC* is not a design specification standard nor is it an instruction manual for the untrained and unqualified.

Copyright 2020
www.MikeHolt.com

▶Figure 90–1

(B) Adequacy. The *NEC* contains the requirements considered necessary for a safe electrical installation. If one is installed in compliance with the *Code*, it is considered essentially free from electrical hazards.

The requirements contained in the *NEC* are not intended to ensure an electrical installation will be efficient, convenient, adequate for good service, or suitable for future expansion. ▶Figure 90–2

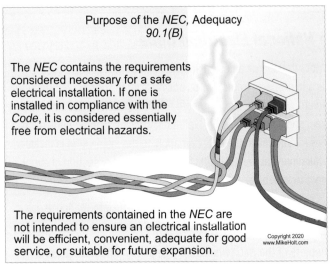

Purpose of the *NEC*, Adequacy
90.1(B)

The *NEC* contains the requirements considered necessary for a safe electrical installation. If one is installed in compliance with the *Code*, it is considered essentially free from electrical hazards.

The requirements contained in the *NEC* are not intended to ensure an electrical installation will be efficient, convenient, adequate for good service, or suitable for future expansion.

Copyright 2020
www.MikeHolt.com

▶Figure 90–2

Author's Comment:

▶ Electrical energy management, equipment maintenance, power quality, or suitability for future loads are not issues within the scope of the *Code*.

Note: Hazards often occur because the initial wiring did not provide for increases in the use of electricity and therefore wiring systems become overloaded. ▶Figure 90–3

Author's Comment:

▶ The *NEC* does not require electrical systems to be designed or installed to accommodate future loads. However, the electrical designer (typically an electrical engineer) is concerned with not only ensuring electrical safety (*Code* compliance), but also that the electrical system meets the customers' needs, both for today and in the coming years. To satisfy their needs, electrical systems are often designed and installed above the minimum requirements contained in the *NEC*.

(C) Relation to International Standards. The requirements of the *Code* address the fundamental safety principles contained in the International Electrotechnical Commission (IEC) Standard.

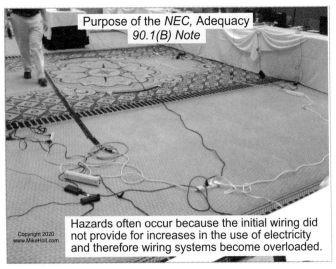

Purpose of the *NEC*, Adequacy
90.1(B) Note

Copyright 2020
www.MikeHolt.com

Hazards often occur because the initial wiring did not provide for increases in the use of electricity and therefore wiring systems become overloaded.

▶Figure 90–3

Note: IEC 60364-1, Section 131, contains fundamental principles of protection for safety that encompass protection against electric shock, protection against thermal effects, protection against overcurrent, protection against fault currents, and protection against overvoltage. All of these potential hazards are addressed by the requirements in this *Code*. ▶Figure 90–4

Purpose of the *NEC*, Relation to International Standards
90.1(C) Note

The *NEC* addresses the safety principles contained in the IEC Standard such as:
• Protection against electric shock
• Adverse thermal effects
• Overcurrent
• Fault currents
• Overvoltage

NFPA 70
National Electrical Code
2020

nec

Copyright 2020
www.MikeHolt.com

▶Figure 90–4

90.2 Scope of the *NEC*

(A) What is Covered by the *NEC*. The *NEC* covers the installation and removal of electrical conductors, equipment, and raceways; signaling and communications conductors, equipment, and raceways; and optical fiber cables and raceways for the following: ▶Figure 90–5

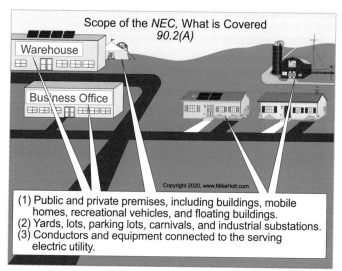

▶Figure 90–5

▶Figure 90–7

(1) Public and private premises including buildings, mobile homes, recreational vehicles, and floating buildings.

(2) Yards, lots, parking lots, carnivals, and industrial substations.

(3) Conductors and equipment connected to the serving electric utility.

(4) Installations used by a serving electric utility such as office buildings, warehouses, garages, machine shops, recreational buildings, and other electric utility buildings that are not an integral part of a utility's generating plant, substation, or control center. ▶Figure 90–6

Author's Comment:

▶ The new item in Article 90's scope, 90.2(A)(5), appears to include the power cable between the pedestal and the boat in the scope of the *NEC*, but there are no specific rules in Article 555 covering that power-supply cord.

▶ The text in 555.35(B) requires leakage detection equipment to detect leakage current from boats and applies to the load side of the supplying receptacle.

(6) Installations used to export electric power from vehicles to premises wiring or for bidirectional current flow ▶Figure 90–8

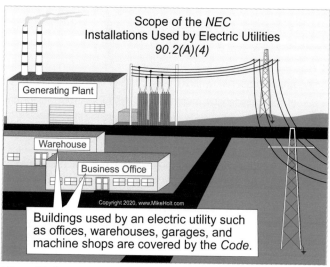

▶Figure 90–6

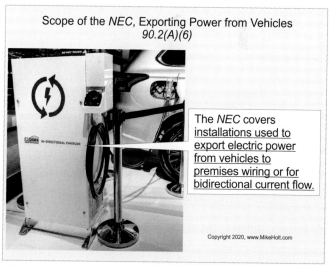

▶Figure 90–8

(5) Installations supplying shore power to watercraft in marinas and boatyards, including monitoring of leakage current. ▶Figure 90–7

Author's Comment:

▸ The battery power supply of an electrical vehicle can be used "bidirectionally" which means it can be used as a backup or alternate power source to supply premises wiring circuits in the event of a power failure. The rules for this application can be found in Article 625.

(B) What is not Covered by the *NEC*. The *Code* does not apply to the installation of electrical or communications systems for:

(1) Transportation Vehicles. The *NEC* does not apply to installations in ships and watercraft <u>other than floating buildings</u>, and automotive vehicles <u>other than mobile homes and recreational vehicles.</u>

(2) Mining Equipment. The *Code* does not apply to installations underground in mines, and in self-propelled mobile surface mining machinery and its attendant electrical trailing cables.

(3) Railways. The *NEC* does not apply to railway power, signaling, energy storage, and communications wiring.

(4) Communications Utilities. The *Code* does not apply to installations under the exclusive control of the communications utility located in building spaces used exclusively for these purposes or located outdoors. ▸Figure 90–9

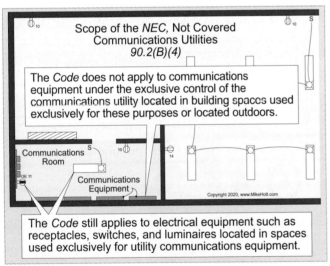

▸Figure 90–9

(5) Electric Utilities. The *NEC* does not apply to electrical installations under the exclusive control of a serving electric utility where such installations: ▸Figure 90–10

a. Consist of service drops or service laterals and associated metering, or ▸Figure 90–11

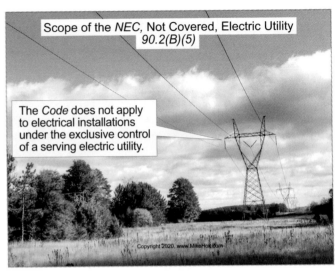

▸Figure 90–10

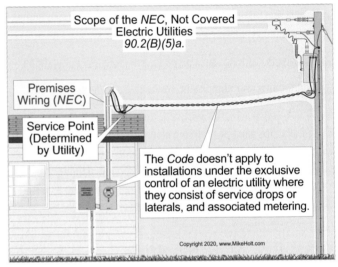

▸Figure 90–11

b. Are on property owned or leased by the utility for the purpose of communications, metering, generation, control, transformation, transmission, energy storage, or distribution of electrical energy, or ▸Figure 90–12

c. Are located in legally established easements or rights-of-way ▸Figure 90–13

90.3 *Code* Arrangement

General Requirements. The *Code* is divided into an introduction and nine chapters followed by informative annexes. Chapters 1, 2, 3, and 4 are general conditions. ▸Figure 90–14

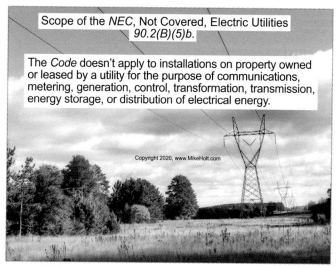

Scope of the *NEC*, Not Covered, Electric Utilities
90.2(B)(5)b.

The *Code* doesn't apply to installations on property owned or leased by a utility for the purpose of communications, metering, generation, control, transformation, transmission, energy storage, or distribution of electrical energy.

Copyright 2020, www.MikeHolt.com

▶Figure 90–12

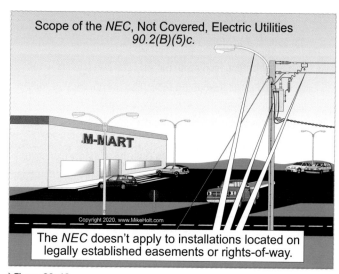

Scope of the *NEC*, Not Covered, Electric Utilities
90.2(B)(5)c.

M-MART

Copyright 2020, www.MikeHolt.com

The *NEC* doesn't apply to installations located on legally established easements or rights-of-way.

▶Figure 90–13

**Code Arrangement
90.3**

General Requirements
• Ch 1 - General
• Ch 2 - Wiring and Protection
• Ch 3 - Wiring Methods & Materials
• Ch 4 - Equipment for General Use
Chapters 1 through 4 generally apply to all applications.

Special Requirements
• Chapter 5 - Special Occupancies
• Chapter 6 - Special Equipment
• Chapter 7 - Special Conditions
Chs 5 through 7 may supplement or modify the requirements in Chapters 1 through 7.

• Ch 8 - Communications Systems
Ch 8 requirements are not subject to requirements in Chapters 1 through 7, unless there is a specific reference in Ch 8 to a rule in Chapters 1 through 7.

• Chapter 9 - Tables
Ch 9 tables are applicable as referenced in the *NEC* and are used for calculating raceway sizes, conductor fill, and voltage drop.

• Annexes A through J
Annexes are for information only and are not enforceable.

Copyright 2020, www.MikeHolt.com

The *NEC* is divided into an introduction and nine chapters, followed by informative annexes.

▶Figure 90–14

The requirements contained in Chapters 5, 6, and 7 apply to special occupancies, special equipment, or other special conditions, which may supplement or modify the requirements contained in Chapters 1 through 7, but not Chapter 8.

Chapter 8 contains the requirements for communications systems (twisted wire, antennas, and coaxial cable) which are not subject to the general requirements of Chapters 1 through 4, or the special requirements of Chapters 5 through 7, unless a specific reference in Chapter 8 is made to a rule in Chapters 1 through 7.

Chapter 9 consists of tables applicable as referenced in the *NEC*. The tables are used to calculate raceway sizing, conductor fill, the radius of raceway bends, and conductor voltage drop.

Annexes are not part of the requirements of the *Code* but are included for informational purposes. There are ten annexes:

▶ Annex A. Product Safety Standards

▶ Annex B. Application Information for Ampacity Calculation

▶ Annex C. Raceway Fill Tables for Conductors and Fixture Wires of the Same Size

▶ Annex D. Examples

▶ Annex E. Types of Construction

▶ Annex F. Critical Operations Power Systems (COPS)

▶ Annex G. Supervisory Control and Data Acquisition (SCADA)

▶ Annex H. Administration and Enforcement

▶ Annex I. Recommended Tightening Torques

▶ Annex J. ADA Standards for Accessible Design

90.4 Enforcement

The *NEC* is intended to be suitable for enforcement by governmental bodies that exercise legal jurisdiction over electrical installations for power, lighting, signaling circuits, and communications systems such as:
▶Figure 90–15

Signaling circuits include:

▶ Article 725. Remote-Control, Signaling, and Power-Limited Circuits

▶ Article 760. Fire Alarm Systems

▶ Article 770. Optical Fiber Cables

Communications systems which include:

▶ Article 810. Radio and Television Equipment (Satellite Antenna)

▶ Article 820. Community Antenna Television and Radio Distribution Systems (Coaxial Cable)

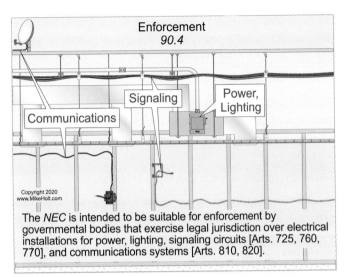

The *NEC* is intended to be suitable for enforcement by governmental bodies that exercise legal jurisdiction over electrical installations for power, lighting, signaling circuits [Arts. 725, 760, 770], and communications systems [Arts. 810, 820].

▶Figure 90–15

Author's Comment:

▶ Once adopted (in part, wholly, or amended), the *National Electrical Code* becomes statutory law for the adopting jurisdiction and is thereby considered a legal document.

Enforcement. The enforcement of the *NEC* is the responsibility of the authority having jurisdiction, who is responsible for interpreting requirements, approving equipment and materials, waiving *Code* requirements, and ensuring equipment is installed in accordance with listing instructions. ▶Figure 90–16

The enforcement of the *NEC* is the responsibility of the authority having jurisdiction, who is responsible for interpreting requirements, approving equipment and materials, waiving *Code* requirements, and ensuring equipment is installed in accordance with listing instructions.

▶Figure 90–16

Author's Comment:

▶ "Authority Having Jurisdiction" is defined in Article 100 as the organization, office, or individual responsible for approving equipment, materials, an installation, or a procedure. See 90.4 and 90.7 for more information.

▶ "Approved" is defined in Article 100 as acceptable to the authority having jurisdiction; usually the electrical inspector.

Interpretation. The authority having jurisdiction is responsible for interpreting the *NEC*.

Author's Comment:

▶ The authority having jurisdiction's decisions must be based on a specific *Code* requirement. If an installation is rejected, the AHJ is legally responsible for informing the installer of the specific *NEC* rule that was violated.

▶ The art of getting along with the AHJ consists of doing good work and knowing what the *Code* says (as opposed to what you think it says). It is also useful to know how to choose your battles when the inevitable disagreement does occur.

Approval of Equipment and Materials. Only the authority having jurisdiction has the authority to approve the installation of equipment and materials. ▶Figure 90–17

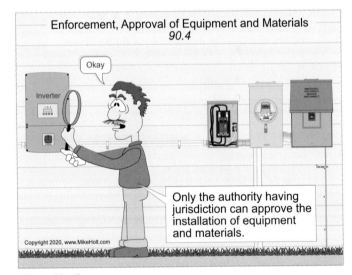

Only the authority having jurisdiction can approve the installation of equipment and materials.

▶Figure 90–17

Author's Comment:

▸ Typically, the AHJ will approve equipment listed by a product testing organization such as Underwriters Laboratories, Inc. (UL). The *NEC* does not require all equipment to be listed, but many state and local authorities having jurisdictions do. See 90.7, 110.2, and 110.3 and the definitions for "Approved," "Identified," "Labeled," and "Listed" in Article 100.

▸ According to the *Code*, the authority having jurisdiction determines the approval of equipment. This means he or she can reject an installation of listed equipment and can approve the use of unlisted equipment. Given our highly litigious society, approval of unlisted equipment is becoming increasingly difficult to obtain.

Approval of Alternate Means. By special permission, the authority having jurisdiction may approve alternate methods where it is assured equivalent safety can be achieved and maintained.

Author's Comment:

▸ "Special Permission" is defined in Article 100 as the written consent of the AHJ.

Waiver of Product Requirements. If the *Code* requires products, constructions, or materials that are not yet available at the time the *NEC* is adopted, the authority having jurisdiction can allow products that were acceptable in the previous *Code* to continue to be used.

Author's Comment:

▸ Sometimes it takes years for testing laboratories to establish product standards for new *NEC* product requirements; then it takes time before manufacturers can design, manufacture, and distribute those products to the marketplace.

90.5 Mandatory Requirements and Explanatory Material

(A) Mandatory Requirements. The words "shall" or "shall not" indicate a mandatory requirement.

Author's Comment:

▸ For greater ease in reading this textbook, we will use the word "must" instead of "shall," and "must not" will be used instead of "shall not."

(B) Permissive Requirements. When the *Code* uses "shall be permitted" it means the action is permitted, but not required. Permissive rules are often contained in exceptions to the general requirement.

Author's Comment:

▸ For greater ease in reading, the phrase "shall be permitted" (as used in the *NEC)* has been replaced in this textbook with "is permitted" or "are permitted."

(C) Explanatory Material. References to other standards or information related to a *Code* rule are included in the form of "Informational Notes." Such notes are for informational purposes only and are not enforceable as an *NEC* requirement.

For example, Informational Note No. 3 in 210.19(A)(1) recommends that the voltage drop of a circuit not exceed 3 percent; this is a recommendation—not a *Code* requirement.

Author's Comment:

▸ For convenience and ease in reading this textbook, "Informational Notes" will simply be identified as "Note."

> ⚡ **Caution**
>
> Informational notes are not enforceable but notes to tables are. Within this textbook, we will call notes contained in a table a "Table Note."

(D) Informative Annexes. Informative annexes contained in the back of the *Code* book are for information only and are not enforceable as requirements of the *NEC*.

90.7 Examination of Equipment for Product Safety

Product evaluation for *Code* compliance, approval, and safety is typically performed by a nationally recognized testing laboratory in accordance with the listing standards.

Except to detect alterations or damage, listed factory-installed internal wiring of equipment that has been processed by a qualified testing laboratory does not need to be inspected for *NEC* compliance at the time of installation. ▸Figure 90–18

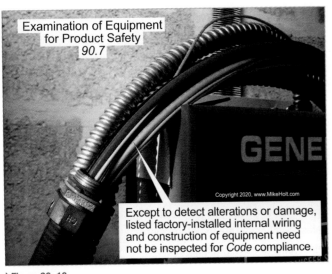

Examination of Equipment for Product Safety
90.7

Copyright 2020, www.MikeHolt.com

Except to detect alterations or damage, listed factory-installed internal wiring and construction of equipment need not be inspected for *Code* compliance.

▶Figure 90–18

Note 1: The requirements contained in Article 300 do not apply to the integral parts of electrical equipment. See 110.3(B).

Note 2: "Listed" is defined in Article 100 as equipment or materials included in a list published by a testing laboratory acceptable to the authority having jurisdiction. The listing organization must periodically inspect the production of listed equipment or material to ensure it meets appropriate designated standards and is suitable for a specified purpose.

ARTICLE 90 PRACTICE QUESTIONS

Please use the 2020 *Code* book to answer the following questions.

Article 90—Introduction to the *National Electrical Code*

1. The *NEC* is _____.

   (a) intended to be a design manual
   (b) meant to be used as an instruction guide for untrained persons
   (c) for the practical safeguarding of persons and property
   (d) published by the Bureau of Standards

2. Compliance with the *Code* and proper maintenance result in an installation that is essentially _____.

   (a) free from hazards
   (b) not necessarily efficient or convenient
   (c) not necessarily adequate for good service or future expansion
   (d) all of these

3. Compliance with the provisions of the *NEC* will result in _____.

   (a) good electrical service
   (b) an efficient electrical system
   (c) an electrical system essentially free from hazard
   (d) all of these

4. The *Code* contains provisions considered necessary for safety, which will not necessarily result in _____.

   (a) efficient use
   (b) convenience
   (c) good service or future expansion of electrical use
   (d) all of these

5. Electrical hazards often occur because the initial _____ did not provide for increases in the use of electricity and therefore wiring systems become overloaded.

   (a) inspection
   (b) owner
   (c) wiring
   (d) builder

6. Hazards often occur because of _____.

   (a) overloading of wiring systems by methods or usage not in conformity with the *NEC*
   (b) initial wiring not providing for increases in the use of electricity
   (c) manufacturing defects
   (d) overloading of wiring systems by methods or usage not in conformity with the *NEC* and initial wiring not providing for increases in the use of electricity

7. Which of the following systems shall be installed and removed in accordance with the *NEC* requirements?

   (a) signaling conductors, equipment, and raceways
   (b) communications conductors, equipment, and raceways
   (c) electrical conductors, equipment, and raceways
   (d) all of these

8. The *NEC* applies to the installation of _____.

   (a) electrical conductors and equipment within or on public and private buildings
   (b) signaling and communication conductors
   (c) optical fiber cables
   (d) all of these

9. This *Code* covers the installation of _____ for public and private premises, including buildings, structures, mobile homes, recreational vehicles, and floating buildings.

    (a) optical fiber cables
    (b) electrical equipment
    (c) raceways
    (d) all of these

10. Installations supplying _____ power to ships and watercraft in marinas and boatyards are covered by the *NEC*.

    (a) shore
    (b) primary
    (c) secondary
    (d) auxiliary

11. Installations used to export electric power from vehicles to premises wiring or for _____ current flow are covered by the *NEC*.

    (a) emergency
    (b) primary
    (c) bidirectional
    (d) secondary

12. The *NEC* does apply to installations in _____.

    (a) floating buildings
    (b) mobile homes
    (c) recreational vehicles
    (d) all of these

13. The *NEC* does not cover electrical installations in ships, watercraft, railway rolling stock, aircraft, or automotive vehicles.

    (a) True
    (b) False

14. The *Code* covers underground mine installations and self-propelled mobile surface mining machinery and its attendant electrical trailing cable.

    (a) True
    (b) False

15. Installations of communications equipment that are under the exclusive control of communications utilities and located outdoors or in building spaces used exclusively for such installations _____ covered by the *NEC*.

    (a) are
    (b) are sometimes
    (c) are not
    (d) may be

16. The *Code* does not cover installations under the exclusive control of an electrical utility such as _____.

    (a) service drops and laterals
    (b) electric utility office buildings
    (c) electric utility warehouses
    (d) electric utility garages

17. Chapters 1 through 4 of the *NEC* apply _____.

    (a) generally to all electrical installations
    (b) only to special occupancies and conditions
    (c) only to special equipment and material
    (d) all of these

18. Chapters 5, 6, and 7 apply to special occupancies, special equipment, or other special conditions and may supplement or modify the requirements in Chapters 1 through 7.

    (a) True
    (b) False

19. Chapters 5, 6, and 7 of the *NEC* apply to _____.

    (a) special occupancies
    (b) special equipment
    (c) special conditions
    (d) all of these

20. Communications wiring such as telephone, antenna, and CATV wiring within a building shall not be required to comply with the installation requirements of Chapters 1 through 7, except where specifically referenced in Chapter 8.

    (a) True
    (b) False

21. Installations shall comply with the material located in the *NEC* Annexes because they are part of the requirements of the *Code*.

    (a) True
    (b) False

22. The _____ has the responsibility for deciding on the approval of equipment and materials.

    (a) manufacturer
    (b) authority having jurisdiction
    (c) testing agency
    (d) the owner of the premises

23. The authority having jurisdiction has the responsibility for _____.

    (a) making interpretations of rules
    (b) deciding upon the approval of equipment and materials
    (c) waiving specific requirements in the *Code* and permitting alternate methods and material if safety is maintained
    (d) all of these

24. If the *NEC* requires new products that are not yet available at the time a new edition is adopted, the _____ may permit the use of the products that comply with the most recent previous edition of the *Code* adopted by that jurisdiction.

    (a) electrical engineer
    (b) master electrician
    (c) authority having jurisdiction
    (d) permit holder

25. In the *NEC*, the word(s) _____ indicate a mandatory requirement.

    (a) shall
    (b) shall not
    (c) shall be permitted
    (d) shall or shall not

ARTICLE
100

DEFINITIONS

Introduction to Article 100—Definitions

Have you ever had a conversation with someone only to discover that what you said and what he or she heard were completely different? This often happens when people have different definitions or interpretations of the words being used, and that is why the definitions of key *NEC* terms are located at the beginning of the *Code* (Article 100), or at the beginning of each article. If we can all agree on important definitions, then we speak the same language and avoid misunderstandings. Words taken out of context have created more than their fair share of problems. Because the *NEC* exists to protect people and property, it is very important for you to be able to convey and comprehend the language used. Review and study Article 100 until you are confident you know the definitions presented.

100 Definitions

Scope. This article contains definitions essential to the application of this *Code*; it does not include general or technical terms from other *code*s and standards. In general, only those used in two or more articles are defined in Article 100.

Definitions are also found in the xxx.2 sections of other articles.

- ▸ Part I of this article contains definitions intended to apply wherever the terms are used throughout the *NEC*.

- ▸ Part III contains definitions applicable to Hazardous (Classified) Locations.

Accessible (as applied to equipment). Capable of being reached for operation, renewal, and inspection. ▸Figure 100–1

Accessible, Readily (Readily Accessible). Capable of being reached quickly for operation, renewal, or inspection without requiring those to whom ready access is necessary to use tools (other than keys), climb over or under obstructions, remove obstacles, resort to using portable ladders, and so forth. ▸Figure 100–2

Note: The use of keys for locks on electrical equipment, and locked doors to electrical equipment rooms and vaults is a common practice and permitted by the *NEC*. ▸Figure 100–3

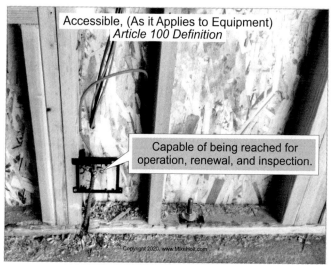

Accessible, (As it Applies to Equipment) Article 100 Definition

Capable of being reached for operation, renewal, and inspection.

Copyright 2020, www.MikeHolt.com

▸Figure 100–1

Adjustable-Speed Drive System. A combination of an adjustable speed drive, its associated motor(s), and any other equipment associated with the two.

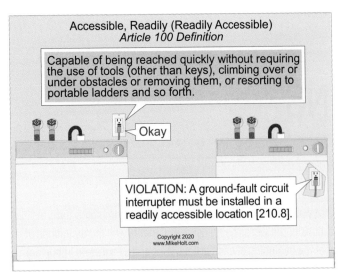

▶Figure 100–2

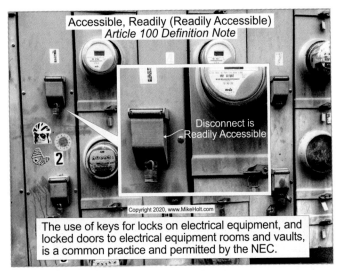

▶Figure 100–3

Author's Comment

▸ An adjustable-speed drive is a piece of equipment that provides a way to adjust the speed of an electric motor. Adjustable-speed drives are often referred to as "variable-speed drives" or "variable-frequency drives (VFDs)."

▸ A variable-frequency drive is a type of electronic adjustable-speed drive that controls the speed of an alternating-current motor by changing the frequency and voltage of the motor's power supply.

Ampacity. The current, in amperes, a conductor can carry continuously under its conditions of use without exceeding its temperature rating. ▶Figure 100–4

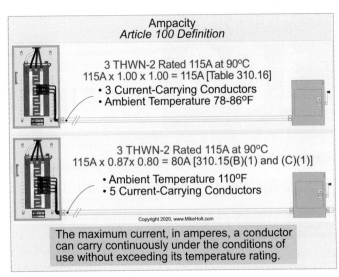

▶Figure 100–4

Author's Comment

▸ See 310.10 and 310.15 for details and examples.

Appliance [Article 422]. Electrical equipment, other than industrial equipment, built in standardized sizes. Examples of appliances are ranges, ovens, cooktops, refrigerators, drinking water coolers, and beverage dispensers.

Approved. Acceptable to the authority having jurisdiction; usually the electrical inspector. ▶Figure 100–5

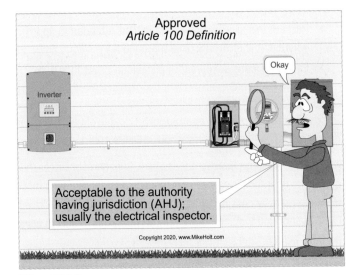

▶Figure 100–5

Author's Comment:

▶ Product listing does not mean the product is approved, but it can be a basis for approval. See 90.4, 90.7, and 110.2 and the definitions in this article for "Authority Having Jurisdiction," "Identified," "Labeled," and "Listed."

Arc-Fault Circuit Interrupter (AFCI). A device intended to de-energize the circuit when it detects the current waveform characteristics unique to an arcing fault. ▶Figure 100–6 and ▶Figure 100–7

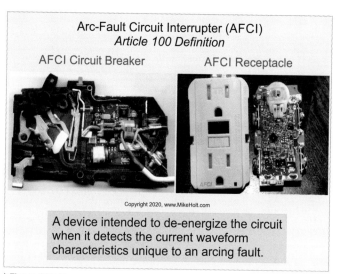

▶Figure 100–6

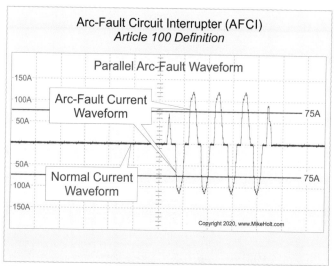

▶Figure 100–7

Attachment Fitting. A device that, by insertion into a locking support and mounting receptacle, establishes a connection between the conductors of the attached utilization equipment and the branch-circuit conductors connected to the locking support and mounting receptacle.

Note: An attachment fitting is different than an attachment plug, because no cord is associated with the fitting. An attachment fitting in combination with a locking support and mounting receptacle secures the associated utilization equipment in place and supports its weight.

Attachment Plug (Plug Cap), (Plug). A wiring device at the end of a flexible cord intended to be inserted into a receptacle in order to make an electrical connection. ▶Figure 100–8

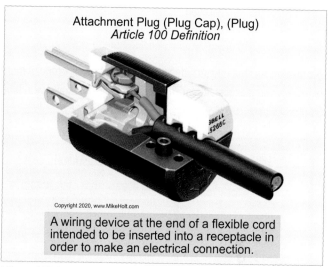

▶Figure 100–8

Authority Having Jurisdiction (AHJ). The organization, office, or individual responsible for approving equipment, materials, an installation, or a procedure. See 90.4 and 90.7 for more information.

Note: The authority having jurisdiction may be a federal, state, or local government department or individual such as a fire chief, fire marshal, chief of a fire prevention bureau, labor or health department, a building official, electrical inspector, or others having statutory authority. In some circumstances, the property owner or his or her agent assumes the role, and at government installations, the commanding officer or departmental official may be the authority having jurisdiction.

Author's Comment:

▶ The authority having jurisdiction is typically the electrical inspector who has legal statutory authority. In the absence of federal, state, or local regulations, the operator of the facility or his or her agent (such as an architect or engineer of the facility) can assume the role.

▸ Most expect the "authority having jurisdiction" to have at least some prior experience in the electrical field, such as having studied electrical engineering or having obtained an electrical contractor's license. In a few states this is a legal requirement. Memberships, certifications, and active participation in electrical organizations such as the International Association of Electrical Inspectors (IAEI) speak to an individual's qualifications. Visit www.IAEl.org for more information about that organization.

Automatic. Functioning without needing human intervention.

Bathroom. An area that includes a <u>sink (basin)</u> as well as one or more of the following: a toilet, urinal, tub, shower, bidet, or similar plumbing fixture. ▸Figure 100–9

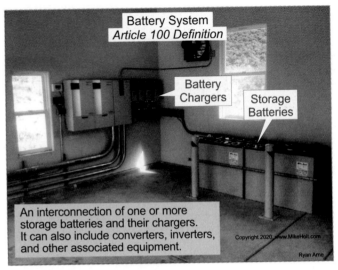

An interconnection of one or more storage batteries and their chargers. It can also include converters, inverters, and other associated equipment.

▸Figure 100–10

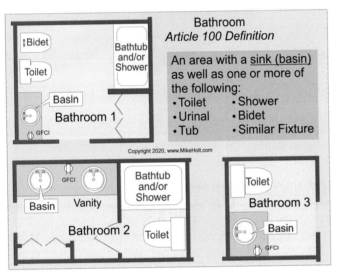

▸Figure 100–9

Battery System. An interconnection of one or more storage batteries and their chargers. It can also include converters, inverters, and other associated equipment. ▸Figure 100–10

Bonded (Bonding). Connected to establish electrical continuity and conductivity. ▸Figure 100–11 and ▸Figure 100–12

Bonding Conductor or Jumper. A conductor that ensures electrical conductivity between metal parts of the electrical installation. ▸Figure 100–13

Author's Comment:

▸ Either the term "Bonding Conductor" or "Bonding Jumper" can be used. They can be short or several feet long and are typically used to ensure electrical conductivity between two metallic objects.

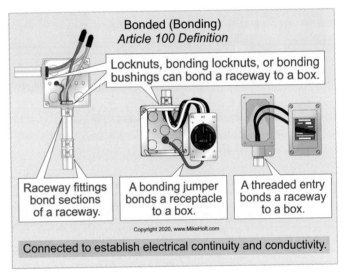

▸Figure 100–11

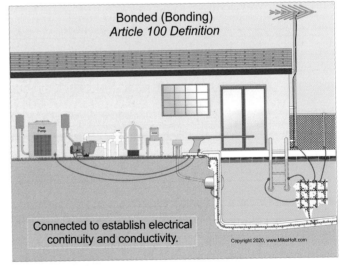

▸Figure 100–12

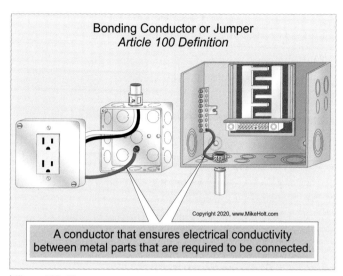

Bonding Conductor or Jumper
Article 100 Definition

A conductor that ensures electrical conductivity between metal parts that are required to be connected.

▶Figure 100–13

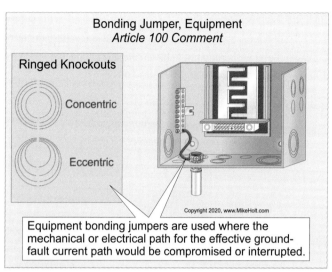

Bonding Jumper, Equipment
Article 100 Comment

Ringed Knockouts

Concentric

Eccentric

Equipment bonding jumpers are used where the mechanical or electrical path for the effective ground-fault current path would be compromised or interrupted.

▶Figure 100–15

Bonding Jumper, Equipment. A connection between two or more portions of the equipment grounding conductor. ▶Figure 100–14

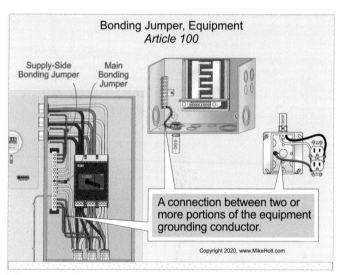

Bonding Jumper, Equipment
Article 100

Supply-Side Bonding Jumper

Main Bonding Jumper

A connection between two or more portions of the equipment grounding conductor.

▶Figure 100–14

Author's Comment:

▶ Equipment bonding jumpers are used where the mechanical or electrical path for the effective ground-fault current path would be compromised or interrupted. ▶**Figure 100–15**

Bonding Jumper, Main. A conductor, screw, or strap used to connect the circuit equipment grounding conductor to the neutral conductor or to the supply-side bonding jumper at the service equipment in accordance with 250.24(B). ▶Figure 100–16 and ▶Figure 100–17

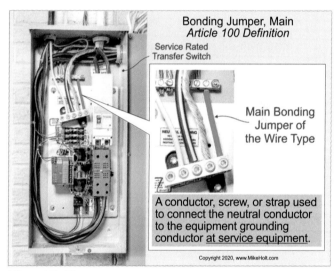

Bonding Jumper, Main
Article 100 Definition

Service Rated Transfer Switch

Main Bonding Jumper of the Wire Type

A conductor, screw, or strap used to connect the neutral conductor to the equipment grounding conductor at service equipment.

▶Figure 100–16

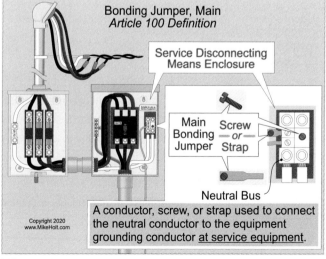

Bonding Jumper, Main
Article 100 Definition

Service Disconnecting Means Enclosure

Main Bonding Jumper — *or* — Screw Strap

Neutral Bus

A conductor, screw, or strap used to connect the neutral conductor to the equipment grounding conductor at service equipment.

▶Figure 100–17

Bonding Jumper, Supply-Side. The conductor installed on the supply side of a service or separately derived system that ensures conductivity between metal parts required to be electrically connected. ▸Figure 100–18, ▸Figure 100–19, and ▸Figure 100–20

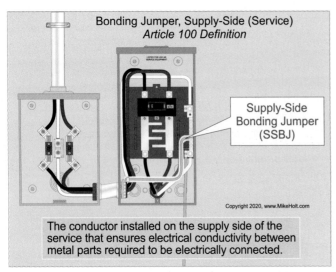

Bonding Jumper, Supply-Side (Service)
Article 100 Definition

The conductor installed on the supply side of the service that ensures electrical conductivity between metal parts required to be electrically connected.

▸Figure 100–18

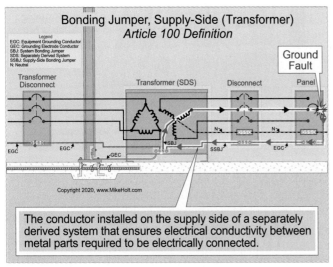

Bonding Jumper, Supply-Side (Transformer)
Article 100 Definition

The conductor installed on the supply side of a separately derived system that ensures electrical conductivity between metal parts required to be electrically connected.

▸Figure 100–19

Bonding Jumper, System. The connection between the neutral conductor or grounded-phase conductor and the supply-side bonding jumper or equipment grounding conductor, or both, at a separately derived system transformer. ▸Figure 100–21

Branch Circuit. The conductors between the final overcurrent device and the receptacle outlets, lighting outlets, or other outlets as defined in this article. ▸Figure 100–22

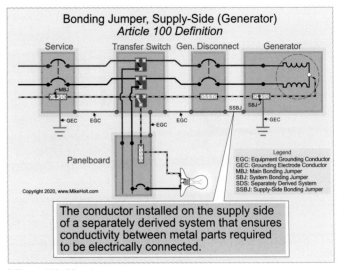

Bonding Jumper, Supply-Side (Generator)
Article 100 Definition

Legend
EGC: Equipment Grounding Conductor
GEC: Grounding Electrode Conductor
MBJ: Main Bonding Jumper
SBJ: System Bonding Jumper
SDS: Separately Derived System
SSBJ: Supply-Side Bonding Jumper

The conductor installed on the supply side of a separately derived system that ensures conductivity between metal parts required to be electrically connected.

▸Figure 100–20

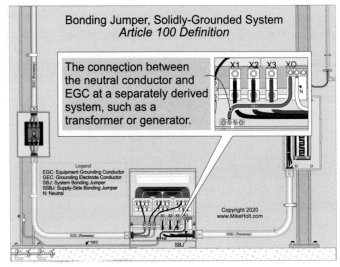

Bonding Jumper, Solidly-Grounded System
Article 100 Definition

The connection between the neutral conductor and EGC at a separately derived system, such as a transformer or generator.

Legend
EGC: Equipment Grounding Conductor
GEC: Grounding Electrode Conductor
SBJ: System Bonding Jumper
SSBJ: Supply-Side Bonding Jumper
N: Neutral

▸Figure 100–21

Branch Circuit, Individual (Individual Branch Circuit). A branch circuit that only supplies one load.

Branch Circuit, Multiwire (Multiwire Branch Circuit). A branch circuit consisting of two or more circuit phase conductors with a common neutral conductor. There must be a voltage between the phase conductors and an equal difference of voltage from each phase conductor to the common neutral conductor. ▸Figure 100–23

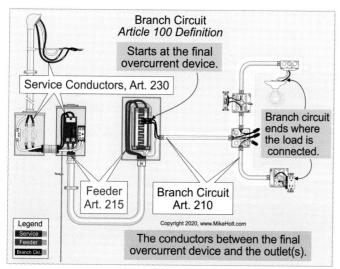

▶Figure 100-22

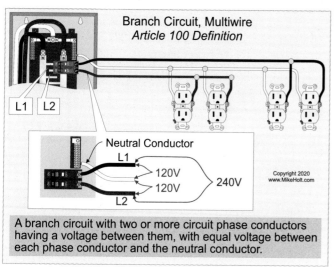

▶Figure 100-23

Author's Comment:

▶ Multiwire branch circuits offer the advantage of fewer conductors within a raceway which can result in smaller raceways, and reduced material and labor costs. In addition, multiwire branch circuits can reduce circuit voltage drop by as much as 50 percent. Because of the dangers associated with the use of multiwire branch circuits and the need for extra care, the *NEC* contains additional requirements to ensure a safe installation. See 210.4, 300.13(B), and 408.41 in this textbook for details.

▶ Hazard of an Open Neutral

Example: *A 3-wire, single-phase, 120/240V multiwire circuit supplies a 1,200W, 120V hair dryer and a 600W, 120V television.* ▶Figure 100-24

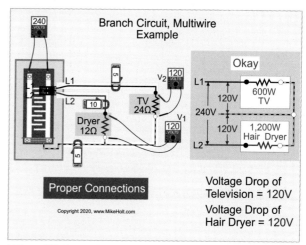

▶Figure 100-24

If the neutral conductor of the multiwire circuit is interrupted, it will cause the 120V television to operate at 160V and consume 1,067W of power (instead of 600W) for only a few seconds before it burns up.
▶Figure 100-25

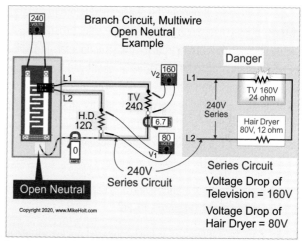

▶Figure 100-25

Solution:

Step 1: *Determine the resistance of each appliance.*

$$R = E^2/P$$

R of the hair dryer = 120V²/1,200W
R of the hair dryer = 12 ohms

● ● ●

R of the television = 120V²/600W

R of the television = 24 ohms

Step 2: *Determine the current of the circuit.*

I = Volts/Resistance

Volts = 240V

R = 36 ohms (12 ohms + 24 ohms)

I = 240V/36 ohms

I = 6.70A

Step 3: *Determine the operating voltage for each appliance.*

Volts = I × R

I = 6.70A

R = 12 ohms for hair dryer and 24 ohms for TV

Voltage of hair dryer = 6.70A × 12 ohms

Voltage of hair dryer = 80V

Voltage of television = 6.70A × 24 ohms

Voltage of television = 160V

Answer: *160V*

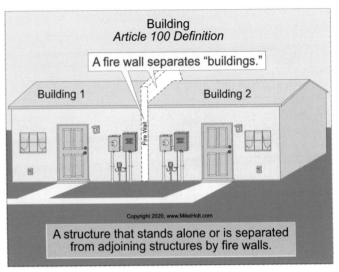

Building
Article 100 Definition

A fire wall separates "buildings."

Building 1 — Fire Wall — Building 2

Copyright 2020, www.MikeHolt.com

A structure that stands alone or is separated from adjoining structures by fire walls.

▶Figure 100–26

> **Warning**
>
> ⚠ Failure to terminate the phase conductors to separate phases can cause the neutral conductor to become overloaded because the current from the phase conductors is additive and the insulation can be damaged or destroyed by excessive heat. Conductor overheating is known to decrease the service life of insulation, which creates the potential for arcing faults and can ultimately lead to fires. It is not known just how long conductor insulation lasts, but heat does decrease its life span.

Building. A structure that stands alone or is separated from adjoining structures by fire walls. ▶Figure 100–26

Cabinet. A surface-mounted or flush-mounted enclosure provided with a frame in which a door can be hung. ▶Figure 100–27

> **Author's Comment:**
>
> ▸ Cabinets are used to enclose panelboards. See the definition of "Panelboard" in this article.

Cable, Coaxial. A cylindrical assembly containing a conductor centered inside a metallic shield, separated by a dielectric material, and covered by an insulating jacket. ▶Figure 100–28

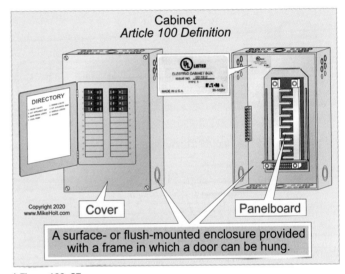

Cabinet
Article 100 Definition

DIRECTORY

UL LISTED

Cover — Panelboard

A surface- or flush-mounted enclosure provided with a frame in which a door can be hung.

Copyright 2020 www.MikeHolt.com

▶Figure 100–27

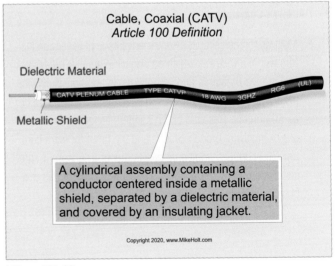

Cable, Coaxial (CATV)
Article 100 Definition

Dielectric Material

CATV PLENUM CABLE   TYPE CATVP   18 AWG   3GHZ   RG6   (UL)

Metallic Shield

A cylindrical assembly containing a conductor centered inside a metallic shield, separated by a dielectric material, and covered by an insulating jacket.

Copyright 2020, www.MikeHolt.com

▶Figure 100–28

Cable, Optical Fiber. An assembly of optical fibers. ▶Figure 100–29

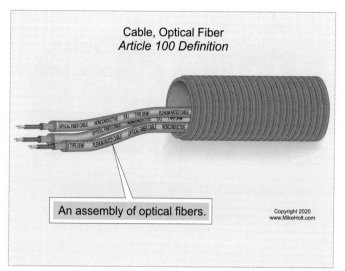

▶Figure 100–29

Note: A field-assembled optical fiber cable is an assembly of one or more optical fibers within a jacket. The jacket is installed like a raceway into which the optical fibers are inserted.

Cable, Optical Fiber, Composite. A cable containing optical fibers and current-carrying electrical conductors. ▶Figure 100–30

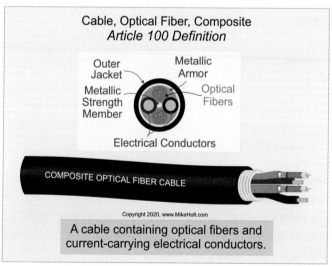

▶Figure 100–30

Author's Comment:

▸ Article 770 permits the use of composite optical fiber cables only where the optical fibers and current-carrying electrical conductors are functionally associated [770.133(A)].

Cable, Optical Fiber, Conductive. An optical fiber cable containing conductive members such as metallic strength members, metallic vapor barriers, or metallic armor or sheath. ▶Figure 100–31

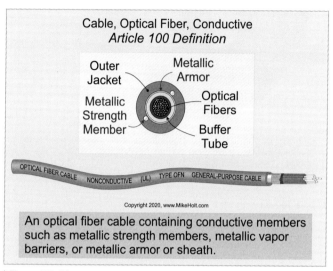

▶Figure 100–31

Cable, Optical Fiber, Nonconductive. An optical fiber cable without any electrically conductive materials. ▶Figure 100–32

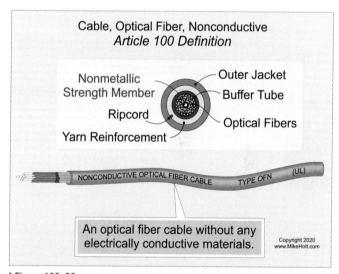

▶Figure 100–32

Cable Routing Assembly. A channel or channels (with their fittings) that support and route communications wires and cables, and optical fiber, data, Class 2, Type PLTC, and power-limited fire alarm cables in plenum, riser, and general-purpose applications. ▶Figure 100–33

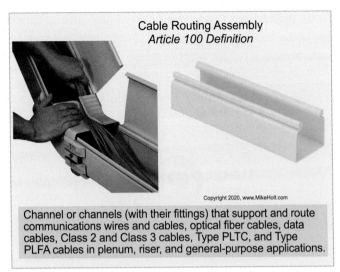

Cable Routing Assembly
Article 100 Definition

Channel or channels (with their fittings) that support and route communications wires and cables, optical fiber cables, data cables, Class 2 and Class 3 cables, Type PLTC, and Type PLFA cables in plenum, riser, and general-purpose applications.

▶Figure 100–33

Author's Comment:

▶ A cable routing assembly is typically a U-shaped trough (with or without covers) designed to hold cables. It is not a raceway.

Charge Controller. Equipment that controls dc voltage or dc current, or both. It is used to charge a battery or other energy storage device.
▶Figure 100–34

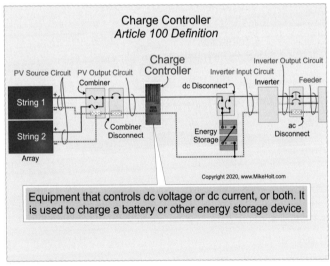

Charge Controller
Article 100 Definition

Equipment that controls dc voltage or dc current, or both. It is used to charge a battery or other energy storage device.

▶Figure 100–34

Circuit Breaker. A device designed to be opened and closed manually and opens automatically at a preset overcurrent without damage to itself. Circuit breakers are available in different configurations such as adjustable trip (electronically controlled), instantaneous trip/motor-circuit protectors, and inverse time. ▶Figure 100–35

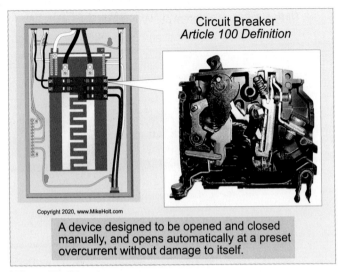

Circuit Breaker
Article 100 Definition

A device designed to be opened and closed manually, and opens automatically at a preset overcurrent without damage to itself.

▶Figure 100–35

Circuit Breaker, Adjustable. Adjustable circuit breakers permit the circuit breaker to be set to trip at various values of current, time (or both), within a predetermined range.

Circuit Breaker, Instantaneous Trip. Instantaneous trip breakers only operate on the principle of electromagnetism and are used for motors. These devices are sometimes called "motor-circuit protectors." This type of overcurrent protective device does not provide overload protection. It only provides short-circuit and ground-fault protection; overload protection must be provided separately.

Author's Comment:

▶ Instantaneous trip circuit breakers have no intentional time delay and are sensitive to current inrush, vibration, and shock. Consequently, they should not be used where these factors are known to exist.

Circuit Breaker, Inverse Time. This type of circuit breaker is purposely designed to delay its tripping action during an overcurrent condition. The intent is to compensate for the inrush of current during the normal start-up of equipment such as vacuum cleaners or air conditioners and helps avoid "nuisance tripping."

Author's Comment:

▶ Inverse time breakers operate on the principle that as the current increases, the time it takes for the devices to open decreases. They provide ordinary overcurrent protection during overload, short-circuit, or ground-fault conditions. This is the most common type of circuit breaker purchased over the counter.

Class 1 Circuit. The wiring system between the load side of a Class 1 circuit overcurrent protective device and the connected equipment.
▶Figure 100–36

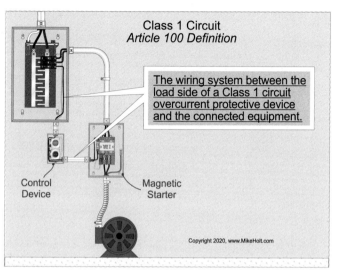

Class 1 Circuit
Article 100 Definition

The wiring system between the load side of a Class 1 circuit overcurrent protective device and the connected equipment.

Control Device

Magnetic Starter

Copyright 2020, www.MikeHolt.com

▶Figure 100–36

Note: See 725.41 for the voltage and power limitations of Class 1 circuits.

Class 2 Circuit. The portion of the wiring system between the load side of a Class 2 power supply and the connected Class 2 equipment.
▶Figure 100–37

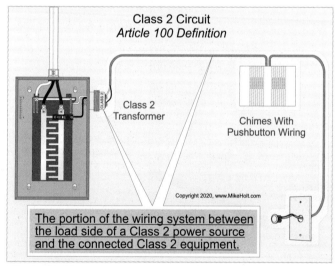

Class 2 Circuit
Article 100 Definition

Class 2 Transformer

Chimes With Pushbutton Wiring

The portion of the wiring system between the load side of a Class 2 power source and the connected Class 2 equipment.

Copyright 2020, www.MikeHolt.com

▶Figure 100–37

Due to power the limitations of its power supply, a Class 2 circuit is considered safe from a fire initiation standpoint and provides acceptable electric shock protection.

Author's Comment:

▶ Class 2 circuits are rendered safe by limiting the power supply to 100 VA for circuits operating at 30V or less, and the current to 5 mA for circuits over 30V [715.121(A) and Chapter 9, Table 11(A)].

▶ Class 2 circuits typically include wiring for low-energy, low-voltage loads such as thermostats, programmable controllers, burglar alarms, and security systems. This type of circuit also includes twisted-pair or coaxial cable that interconnects computers for local area networks (LANs), power over ethernet applications (POE), and programmable controller I/O circuits [725.121(A)(3) and 725.121(A)(4)].

Class 3 Circuit. The portion of the wiring system between the load side of a Class 3 power supply and the connected Class 3 equipment.
▶Figure 100–38

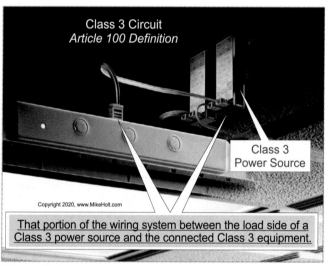

Class 3 Circuit
Article 100 Definition

Class 3 Power Source

Copyright 2020, www.MikeHolt.com

That portion of the wiring system between the load side of a Class 3 power source and the connected Class 3 equipment.

▶Figure 100–38

Author's Comment:

▶ Class 3 circuits are used when the power demand exceeds 30 VA but is not more than 100 VA [Chapter 9, Table 11(A)].

Clothes Closet. A nonhabitable room or space intended primarily for the storage of garments and apparel. ▶Figure 100–39

Author's Comment:

▶ The definition of a "Clothes Closet" provides clarification in the application of overcurrent protective devices [240.24(D)] and luminaires [410.16] in clothes closets.

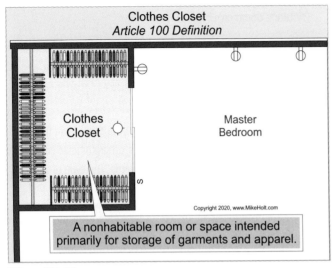

▶Figure 100–39

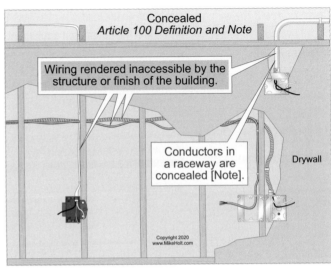

▶Figure 100–41

Communications Equipment. Electronic telecommunications equipment used for the transmission of audio, video, and data including support equipment (such as computers) and the conductors used solely for the operation of the equipment.

Note: Communications equipment includes the computers, routers, and servers essential to the transmission of audio, video, and data. ▶Figure 100–40

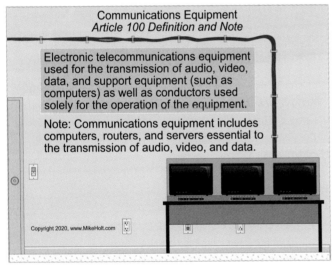

▶Figure 100–40

Concealed. Rendered inaccessible by the structure or finish of the building. ▶Figure 100–41

Note: Conductors in a concealed raceway are considered concealed even though they may be made accessible by withdrawing them from the raceway.

Author's Comment:

▶ Wiring behind panels designed to allow access, such as removable ceiling tile and wiring in accessible attics, is not considered concealed; it is considered exposed. See the definition of "Exposed (as applied to wiring methods)."

▶ Boxes are not permitted to be concealed by the finish of the building. ▶Figure 100–42

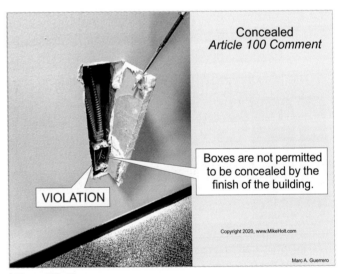

▶Figure 100–42

Conduit Body. A fitting installed in a conduit or tubing system that provides access to conductors through a removable cover. ▶Figure 100–43

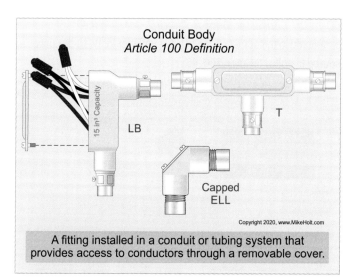

A fitting installed in a conduit or tubing system that provides access to conductors through a removable cover.

▶Figure 100–43

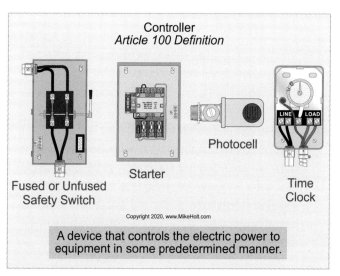

A device that controls the electric power to equipment in some predetermined manner.

▶Figure 100–45

Continuous Load. A load where the maximum current is expected to exist for 3 hours or more continuously such as in schools, office buildings, stores, or parking lot lighting.

Control Circuit. The circuit of a control apparatus or system that carries the electric signals directing the performance of a controller but does not carry the main power current. ▶Figure 100–44

Coordination, Selective (Selective Coordination). Localization of an overcurrent condition to restrict outages to the circuit or equipment affected, accomplished by the choice of overcurrent protective devices. Selective coordination includes all currents from overloads, short circuits, or ground faults. ▶Figure 100–46

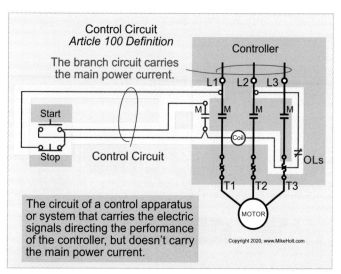

The circuit of a control apparatus or system that carries the electric signals directing the performance of the controller, but doesn't carry the main power current.

▶Figure 100–44

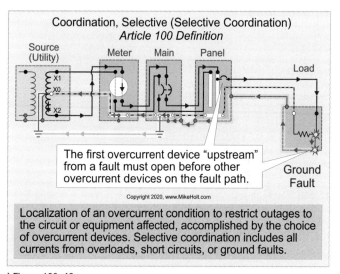

Localization of an overcurrent condition to restrict outages to the circuit or equipment affected, accomplished by the choice of overcurrent devices. Selective coordination includes all currents from overloads, short circuits, or ground faults.

▶Figure 100–46

Controller. A device that controls the electric power delivered to electrical equipment in some predetermined manner. This includes time clocks, lighting contactors, photocells, and equipment with similar functions. ▶Figure 100–45

▸ Selective coordination means the overcurrent protection scheme confines the interruption to a specific circuit rather than to the entire electrical system. For example, if someone plugs in a space heater and raises the total demand on a 20A circuit to 25A, or if a short circuit or ground fault occurs with selective coordination, the only breaker or fuse that will open is the one protecting just that branch circuit. Coordinating overcurrent protection for an electrical system is especially important in healthcare facilities and data centers where the loss of power ahead of the troubled circuit can have dire consequences—including loss of life.

DC-to-DC Converter. A device that can provide an output dc voltage and current at a higher or lower value than the input dc voltage and current. ▸Figure 100–47

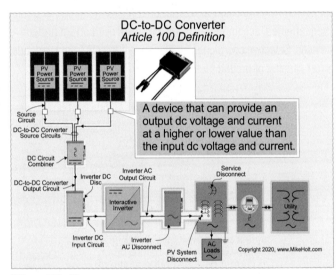

▸Figure 100–47

▸ DC-to-DC converters are intended to maximize the output of independent PV modules and reduce losses due to variances between modules' outputs. They are directly wired to each module and are bolted to the module frame or the PV rack.

▸ A dc-to-dc converter enables a PV inverter to automatically maintain a fixed circuit voltage, at the optimal point for dc/ac conversion by the inverter, regardless of circuit length and individual module performance.

DC-to-DC Converter Output Circuit. The dc circuit conductors connected to the output circuit of a dc combiner for dc-to-dc converter source circuits. ▸Figure 100–48

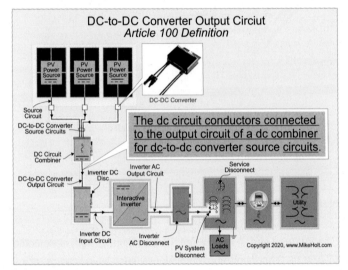

▸Figure 100–48

Demand Factor. The ratio of the maximum load demand to the total connected load.

Device. A component of an electrical installation, other than a conductor, intended to carry or control electric energy as its principal function. ▸Figure 100–49

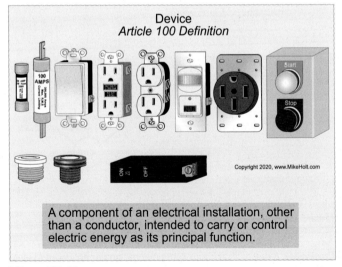

▸Figure 100–49

Author's Comment:

▶ Devices generally do not consume electric energy and include receptacles, switches, illuminated switches, circuit breakers, fuses, time clocks, controllers, attachment plugs, and so forth. Some (such as illuminated switches, contactors, or relays) consume very small amounts of energy and are still classified as a device based on their primary function.

Disconnecting Means (Disconnect). A device that disconnects the circuit conductors from their power source. Examples include switches, attachment plugs, and circuit breakers. ▶Figure 100–50

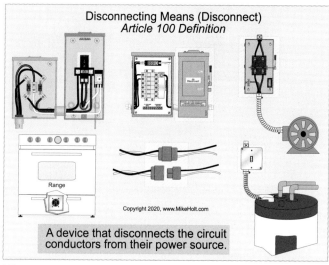

Disconnecting Means (Disconnect)
Article 100 Definition

A device that disconnects the circuit conductors from their power source.

▶Figure 100–50

Dormitory Unit. A building or a space in a building in which group sleeping accommodations are provided in one room for more than 16 persons who are not members of the same family; or a series of closely associated rooms, under joint occupancy and single management, with or without meals, but without individual cooking facilities. ▶Figure 100–51

Duty, Continuous (Continuous Duty). Operation at a substantially constant load for an indefinite amount of time.

Duty, Varying (Varying Duty). Operation at loads, and for intervals of time, which may both be subject to wide variation.

Dwelling, One-Family (One-Family Dwelling). A building that consists solely of one dwelling unit.

Dwelling, Two-Family (Two-Family Dwelling). A building that consists solely of two dwelling units. ▶Figure 100–52

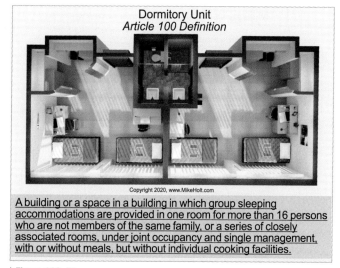

Dormitory Unit
Article 100 Definition

A building or a space in a building in which group sleeping accommodations are provided in one room for more than 16 persons who are not members of the same family, or a series of closely associated rooms, under joint occupancy and single management, with or without meals, but without individual cooking facilities.

▶Figure 100–51

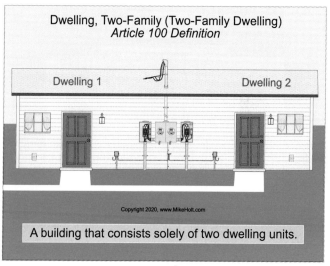

Dwelling, Two-Family (Two-Family Dwelling)
Article 100 Definition

Dwelling 1   Dwelling 2

A building that consists solely of two dwelling units.

▶Figure 100–52

Dwelling, Multifamily (Multifamily Dwelling). A building that contains three or more dwelling units. ▶Figure 100–53

Dwelling Unit. A space that provides independent living facilities with space for eating, living, sleeping, and permanent provisions for cooking and sanitation. ▶Figure 100–54

Effective Ground-Fault Current Path. An intentionally constructed low-impedance conductive path designed to carry ground-fault current from the point of a ground fault to the source for the purpose of opening the circuit overcurrent protective device. ▶Figure 100–55

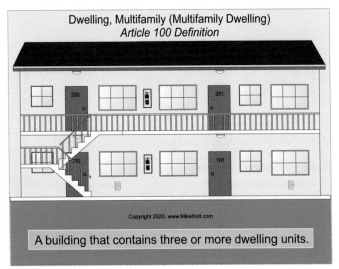

Dwelling, Multifamily (Multifamily Dwelling)
Article 100 Definition

A building that contains three or more dwelling units.

▶Figure 100–53

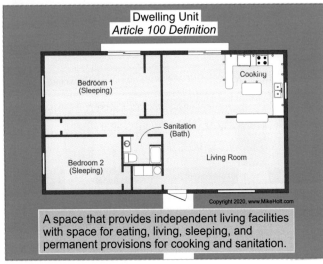

Dwelling Unit
Article 100 Definition

A space that provides independent living facilities with space for eating, living, sleeping, and permanent provisions for cooking and sanitation.

▶Figure 100–54

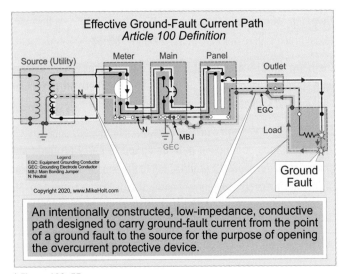

Effective Ground-Fault Current Path
Article 100 Definition

An intentionally constructed, low-impedance, conductive path designed to carry ground-fault current from the point of a ground fault to the source for the purpose of opening the overcurrent protective device.

▶Figure 100–55

Author's Comment:

▶ The effective ground-fault current path is intended to help remove dangerous voltage from a ground fault by opening the circuit overcurrent protective device.

Electric Power Production and Distribution Network. A serving electric utility that is connected to premises wiring and is not controlled by an interactive system. ▶Figure 100–56

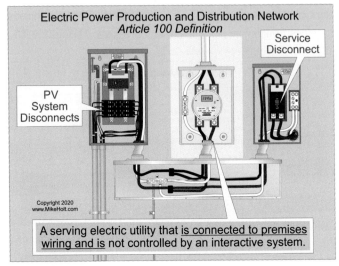

Electric Power Production and Distribution Network
Article 100 Definition

A serving electric utility that is connected to premises wiring and is not controlled by an interactive system.

▶Figure 100–56

Author's Comment:

▶ An interactive system is an electric power production system that operates in parallel with, and may deliver power to, the serving electric utility. An example is a PV system interactively connected in parallel to the utility by an interactive inverter.

Electric Sign [Article 600]. A fixed, stationary, or portable self-contained, electrically operated and/or electrically illuminated piece of equipment with words or symbols designed to convey information or attract attention. ▶Figure 100–57

Electric-Discharge Lighting. Systems of illumination utilizing fluorescent lamps, high-intensity discharge (HID) lamps, or neon tubing. ▶Figure 100–58

Electric Vehicle. An on-road use automobile, bus, truck, van, neighborhood electric vehicle, or motorcycle primarily powered by an electric motor. ▶Figure 100–59

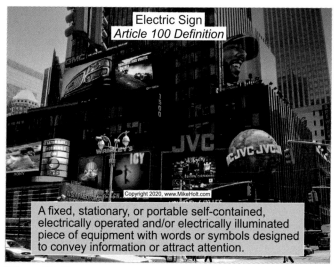

A fixed, stationary, or portable self-contained, electrically operated and/or electrically illuminated piece of equipment with words or symbols designed to convey information or attract attention.

▶Figure 100-57

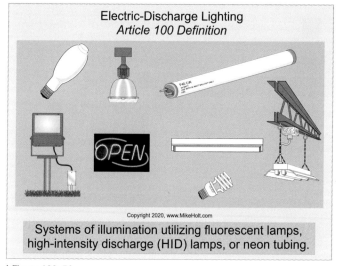

Systems of illumination utilizing fluorescent lamps, high-intensity discharge (HID) lamps, or neon tubing.

▶Figure 100-58

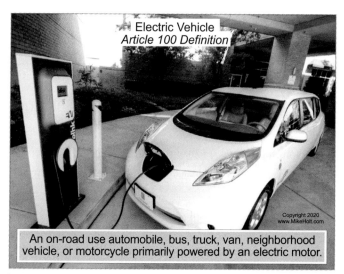

An on-road use automobile, bus, truck, van, neighborhood vehicle, or motorcycle primarily powered by an electric motor.

▶Figure 100-59

Off-road, self-propelled electric industrial trucks, hoists, lifts, transports, golf carts, airline ground support equipment, tractors, and boats are not electric vehicles.

Author's Comment:

▸ The portion of plug-in hybrid type vehicles containing both an electric motor and a combustion engine that pertains to re-charging the electric motor is covered by Article 625.

Electrical Datum Plane. A specified distance above a water level above which electrical equipment can be installed and electrical connections can be made.

Author's Comment:

▸ This definition previously included the specific elevations of the electrical datum plane which acted as requirements. The detailed requirements in 682.5 appear as though they only apply within that article, and not to the others that also use the term.

Enclosed. Surrounded by a case, housing, fence, or wall(s) that prevents accidental contact with energized parts.

Energized. Electrically connected to a source of voltage.

Equipment. A general term including fittings, devices, appliances, luminaires, machinery, and the like as part of (or in connection with) an electrical installation. ▶Figure 100-60

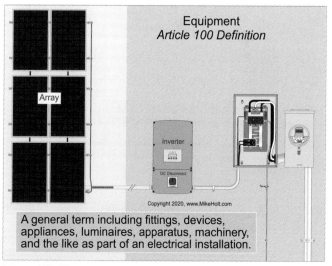

A general term including fittings, devices, appliances, luminaires, apparatus, machinery, and the like as part of an electrical installation.

▶Figure 100-60

Exposed (as applied to live parts). Capable of being accidentally touched or approached nearer than a safe distance. ▶Figure 100-61

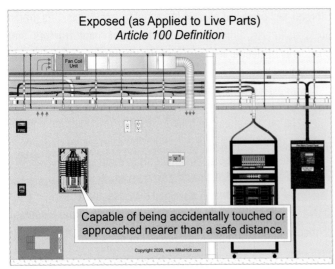

▶Figure 100-61

Note: This term applies to parts that are not suitably guarded, isolated, or insulated for the condition such as line-side lugs in a meter socket or panelboard.

Exposed (as applied to wiring methods). On or attached to the surface of a building, or behind panels designed to allow access. ▶Figure 100-62

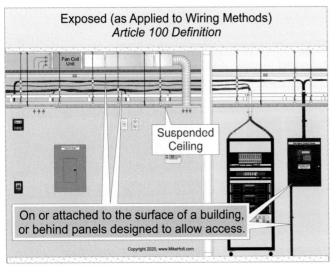

▶Figure 100-62

Fault Current. The current delivered at a point on the system during a short-circuit condition. ▶Figure 100-63

Note: A short circuit can occur during abnormal conditions such as a fault between circuit conductors or a ground fault.

Feeder. The conductors between the service disconnect, a separately derived system (typically a transformer), or other power-supply source and the final branch-circuit overcurrent device. ▶Figure 100-64

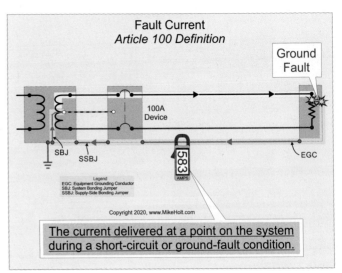

▶Figure 100-63

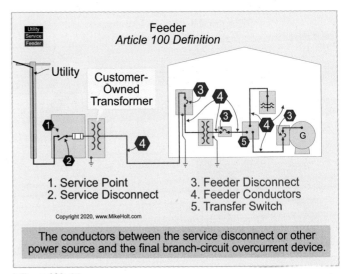

▶Figure 100-64

Author's Comment:

▶ An "other power-supply source" includes solar PV systems or conductors from generators. ▶Figure 100-65

Festoon Lighting. A string of outdoor lights suspended between two points. ▶Figure 100-66

Field Evaluation Body (FEB). An organization or part of an organization that performs field evaluations of electrical equipment and materials.

Field Labeled (as applied to evaluated products). Equipment or materials which have a label, symbol, or other identifying mark of a field evaluation body (FEB) indicating the equipment or materials were evaluated and found to comply with the requirements described in the accompanying field evaluation report.

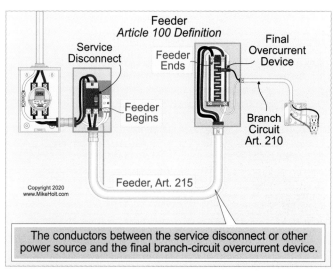

The conductors between the service disconnect or other power source and the final branch-circuit overcurrent device.

▶Figure 100–65

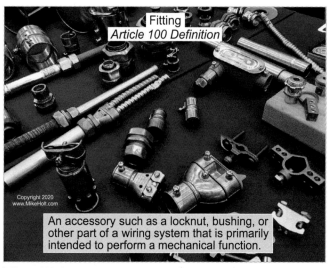

An accessory such as a locknut, bushing, or other part of a wiring system that is primarily intended to perform a mechanical function.

▶Figure 100–67

A string of outdoor lights suspended between two points.

▶Figure 100–66

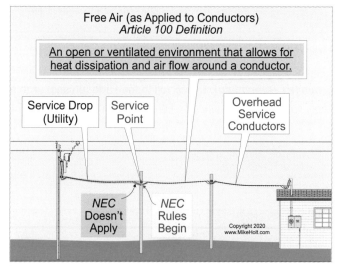

▶Figure 100–68

Fitting. An accessory such as a locknut, bushing, or other part of a wiring system that is primarily intended to perform a mechanical rather than an electrical function. ▶Figure 100–67

Free Air (as applied to conductors). An open or ventilated environment that allows for heat dissipation and air flow around a conductor. ▶Figure 100–68

Garage. A building or portion of a building where self-propelled vehicles can be kept.

Generating Capacity, Inverter. The sum of parallel-connected inverters' maximum continuous output power at 40°C in watts or kilowatts.

Ground. The Earth. ▶Figure 100–69

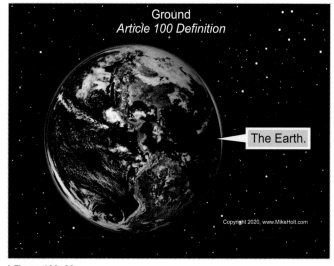

The Earth.

▶Figure 100–69

Ground Fault. An unintentional electrical connection between a phase conductor and normally noncurrent-carrying conductors, metal parts of enclosures, raceways, or equipment. ▶Figure 100–70

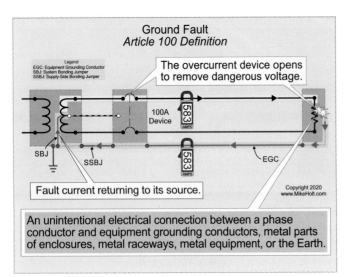

▶Figure 100–70

Grounded (Grounding). Connected to the Earth (ground) or to a conductive body that extends the Earth connection. ▶Figure 100–71

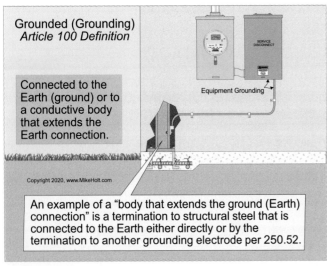

▶Figure 100–71

Author's Comment:

▸ An example of a "body that extends the ground (earth) connection" is a termination to structural steel that is connected to the Earth either directly or by the termination to another grounding electrode in accordance with 250.52.

Grounded Conductor. The system or circuit conductor that is intentionally connected to the Earth (ground). ▶Figure 100–72

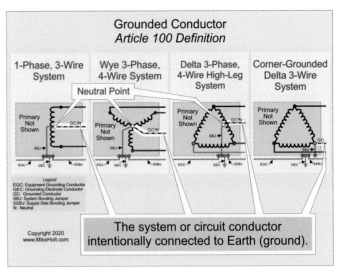

▶Figure 100–72

Note: Although an equipment grounding conductor is grounded, it is not considered a grounded conductor.

Author's Comment:

▸ There are two types of grounded conductors; neutral conductors and grounded-phase conductors. A system where the transformer secondary is wye connected with the neutral point grounded will have a neutral. ▶Figure 100–73

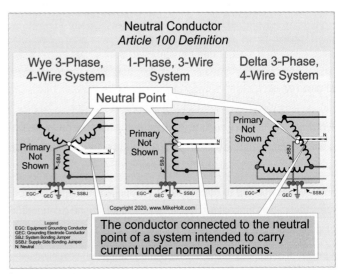

▶Figure 100–73

Author's Comment:

▸ A system where the transformer secondary is delta connected with one corner winding grounded will have a grounded-phase conductor. ▶Figure 100–74

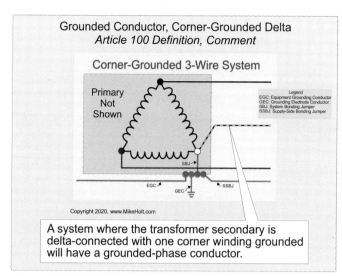

Figure 100–74

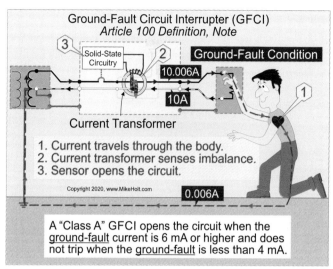

Figure 100–76

Grounded, Solidly (Solidly Grounded). Connected to ground (earth) without inserting any resistor or impedance device. ▶Figure 100–75

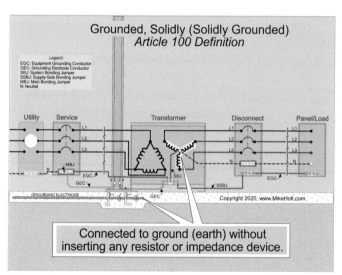

▶Figure 100–75

Ground-Fault Circuit Interrupter (GFCI). A device intended to protect people by de-energizing a circuit when ground-fault current exceeds the value established for a "Class A" device.

Note: A Class A ground-fault circuit interrupter opens the circuit when the ground-fault current is 6 mA or higher and does not trip when the ground-fault current is less than 4 mA. ▶Figure 100–76

Author's Comment:

▶ A GFCI-protective device operates on the principle of monitoring the unbalanced current between the current-carrying circuit conductors. On a 120V circuit, the GFCI will monitor the unbalanced current between the phase and neutral conductors; on 240V circuits, monitoring is between all circuit conductors. Receptacles, circuit breakers, cord sets, and other types of devices that incorporate GFCI protection are commercially available. ▶Figure 100–77

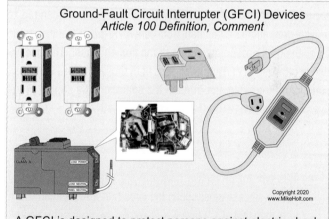

▶Figure 100–77

Ground-Fault Current Path. An electrically conductive path from the point of a ground fault on a wiring system through normally noncurrent-carrying conductors, <u>neutral conductors,</u> equipment, or the Earth to the electrical supply source. ▶Figure 100–78

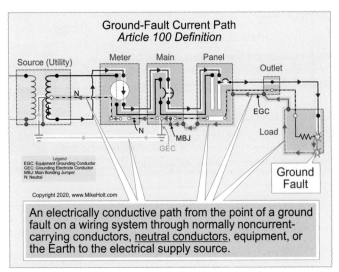

Ground-Fault Current Path
Article 100 Definition

An electrically conductive path from the point of a ground fault on a wiring system through normally noncurrent-carrying conductors, <u>neutral conductors</u>, equipment, or the Earth to the electrical supply source.

▶Figure 100–78

Note: Examples of ground-fault current paths are any combination of equipment grounding conductors, metallic raceways, metal cable sheaths, electrical equipment, and any other electrically conductive material such as metal, water, and gas piping; steel framing members; stucco mesh; metal ducting; reinforcing steel; shields of communications cables; <u>neutral</u> conductors; and the Earth itself.

Ground-Fault Protection of Equipment. A system intended to provide protection of equipment from damaging ground-fault currents by opening all phase conductors of the faulted circuit. This protection is provided at current levels less than those required to protect conductors from damage through the operation of a supply circuit overcurrent device [215.10, 230.95, and 240.13].

Author's Comment:

▶ This type of protective device is not intended to protect people since it trips (opens the circuit) at a higher current level than that of a "Class A" GFCI-protective device. It is typically referred to as ground-fault protection for equipment, or GFPE; but should never be called a GFCI.

Grounding Conductor, Equipment (Equipment Grounding Conductor). The conductive path(s) that <u>is part of an effective</u> ground-fault current path and connects metal parts of equipment to the system neutral conductor or grounded-phase conductor [250.110 through 250.126]. ▶Figure 100–79

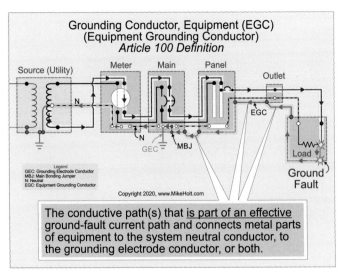

**Grounding Conductor, Equipment (EGC)
(Equipment Grounding Conductor)**
Article 100 Definition

The conductive path(s) that <u>is part of an effective</u> ground-fault current path and connects metal parts of equipment to the system neutral conductor, to the grounding electrode conductor, or both.

▶Figure 100–79

Note 1: The circuit equipment grounding conductor also performs bonding.

Author's Comment:

▶ To quickly remove dangerous touch voltage on metal parts from a ground fault, the equipment grounding conductor (EGC) must be connected to the system neutral conductor at the source and have low enough impedance so fault current will quickly rise to a level that will open the circuit's overcurrent protective device [250.4(A)(3)]. ▶Figure 100–80

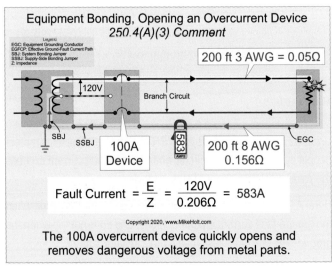

Equipment Bonding, Opening an Overcurrent Device
250.4(A)(3) Comment

$$\text{Fault Current} = \frac{E}{Z} = \frac{120V}{0.206\Omega} = 583A$$

The 100A overcurrent device quickly opens and removes dangerous voltage from metal parts.

▶Figure 100–80

Note 2: An equipment grounding conductor can be any one or a combination of the types listed in 250.118. ▶Figure 100–81

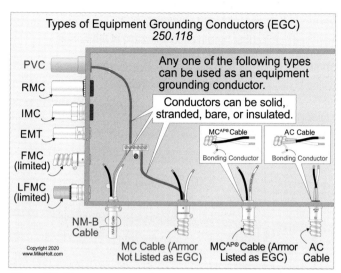

▶Figure 100–81

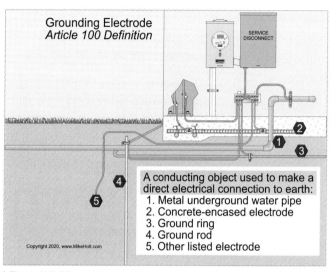

▶Figure 100–82

Author's Comment:

▸ Equipment grounding conductors include:

  ▸ A bare or insulated conductor

  ▸ Rigid metal conduit

  ▸ Intermediate metal conduit

  ▸ Electrical metallic tubing

  ▸ Listed flexible metal conduit as limited by 250.118(5)

  ▸ Listed liquidtight flexible metal conduit as limited by 250.118(6)

  ▸ Armored cable

  ▸ The copper metal sheath of mineral-insulated cable

  ▸ Metal-clad cable as limited by 250.118(10)

  ▸ Metal cable trays as limited by 250.118(11) and 392.60

  ▸ Electrically continuous metal raceways listed for grounding

  ▸ Surface metal raceways listed for grounding

  ▸ Metal enclosures

Grounding Electrode. A conducting object used to make a direct electrical connection to the Earth [250.50 through 250.70]. ▶Figure 100–82

Grounding Electrode Conductor. The conductor used to connect the system neutral conductor or grounded-phase conductor, or the equipment to the grounding electrode system. ▶Figure 100–83

Guest Room. An accommodation combining living, sleeping, sanitary, and storage facilities. ▶Figure 100–84

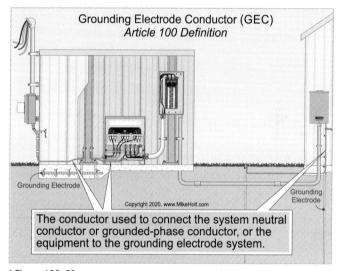

▶Figure 100–83

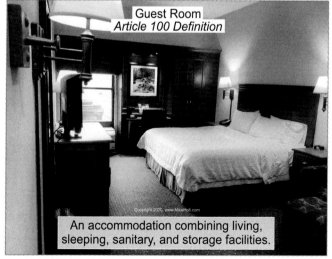

▶Figure 100–84

Guest Suite. An accommodation with two or more contiguous rooms comprising a compartment (with or without doors between such rooms) that provides living, sleeping, sanitary, and storage facilities.

Habitable Room. A room in a building for living, sleeping, eating, or cooking. Bathrooms, toilet rooms, closets, hallways, storage or utility spaces, and similar areas are excluded. ▶Figure 100–85

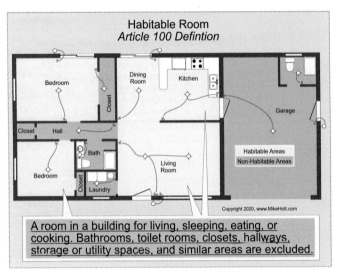

▶Figure 100–85

Handhole Enclosure. An underground enclosure with an open or closed bottom that is sized to allow personnel to reach into but not enter the enclosure. ▶Figure 100–86

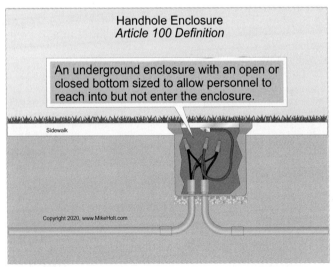

▶Figure 100–86

Author's Comment:

▶ See 314.30 for the installation requirements for handhole enclosures.

Hermetic Refrigerant Motor-Compressor. A compressor and motor enclosed in the same housing and operating in refrigerant.

Hoistway. A vertical opening or space in which an elevator or dumbwaiter is designed to operate. ▶Figure 100–87

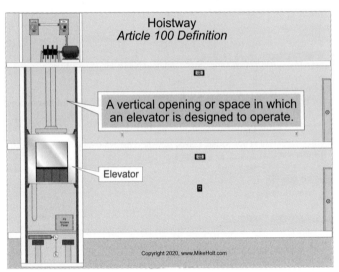

▶Figure 100–87

Hybrid System. A system comprised of multiple electric power sources such as photovoltaic, wind, micro-hydro generators, engine-driven generators, and others; but not the serving electric utility power system. ▶Figure 100–88

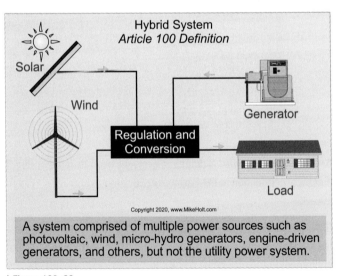

▶Figure 100–88

Identified (as applied to equipment). Recognized as suitable for a specific purpose, function, use, environment, or application where described in a *Code* requirement. ▶Figure 100–89

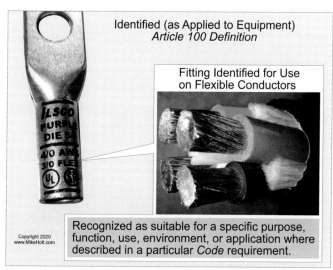

▶Figure 100–89

Author's Comment:

▶ See 90.4, 90.7, and 110.3(A)(1) and the definitions for "Approved," "Labeled," and "Listed" in this article.

Information Technology Equipment (ITE). Equipment used for the creation and manipulation of data, voice, and video. It does not include communications equipment. ▶Figure 100–90

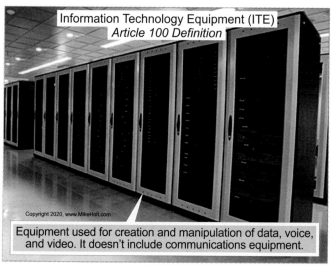

▶Figure 100–90

Innerduct. A nonmetallic raceway placed within a larger raceway. ▶Figure 100–91

In Sight From (Within Sight From). Visible and not more than 50 ft away from the equipment. ▶Figure 100–92

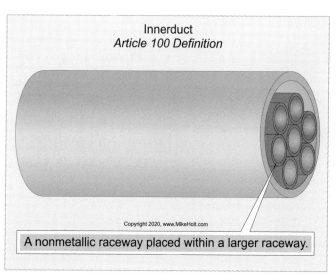

▶Figure 100–91

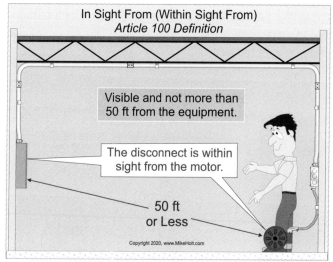

▶Figure 100–92

Interactive Inverter. An inverter intended to be used in parallel with a power source(s), such as the serving electric utility, to supply common loads and is capable of delivering power to the serving electric utility. ▶Figure 100–93

Author's Comment:

▶ A listed interactive inverter automatically stops exporting power upon loss of utility voltage and cannot be reconnected until the voltage has been restored. Interactive inverters can automatically or manually resume exporting power to the utility once the utility source is restored.

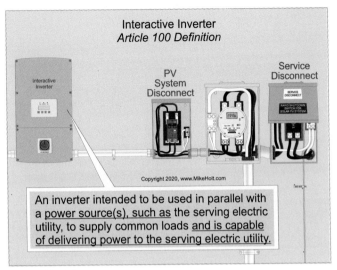

▶Figure 100–93

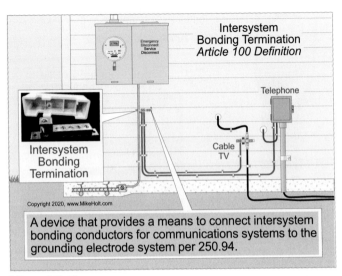

▶Figure 100–95

Interactive System. An electric power production system that operates in parallel with, and may deliver power to, the serving electric utility. ▶Figure 100–94

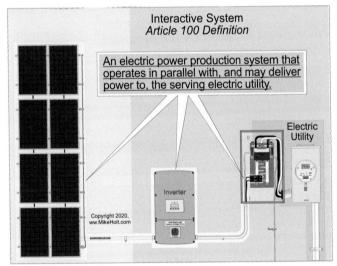

▶Figure 100–94

Interrupting Rating. The highest short-circuit current at rated voltage the device is identified to safely interrupt under standard test conditions.

Intersystem Bonding Termination. A device that provides a means to connect intersystem bonding conductors for communications systems (twisted wire, antennas, and coaxial cable) to the grounding electrode system, in accordance with 250.94. ▶Figure 100–95

Author's Comment:

▸ Overcurrent protective devices have two current ratings, "rated current" and "fault current." Rated current protects circuits under normal conditions and the rating is labeled on the handle of the circuit breaker. The fault current rating or "ampere interrupting capacity" (AIC) is the amount of current the device can safely handle during a ground fault or short circuit. Fault current ratings range up to the tens, or even hundreds, of thousands of amperes!

▸ For more information, see 110.9 in this textbook.

Inverter. Equipment that changes direct current to alternating current. ▶Figure 100–96

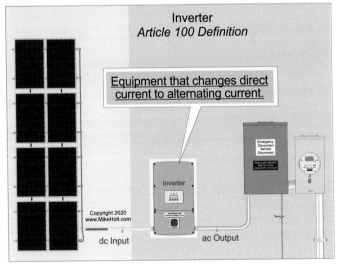

▶Figure 100–96

Inverter Input Circuit. Conductors connected to the direct-current input of an inverter. ▶Figure 100–97

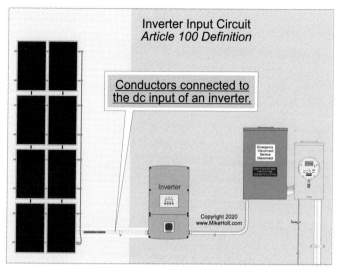

▶Figure 100–97

Inverter Output Circuit. The circuit conductors connected to the alternating-current output of an inverter. ▶Figure 100–98

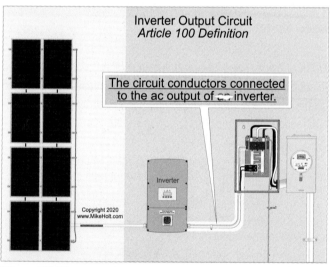

▶Figure 100–98

Inverter, Multimode. Equipment having the capabilities of both interactive and stand-alone inverters. ▶Figure 100–99

Island Mode. The operational mode for stand-alone power production equipment or an isolated microgrid (or for a multimode inverter or an interconnected microgrid) that is disconnected from an electric power production and distribution network or other primary power source.

Isolated. Not readily accessible to persons unless special means for access are used.

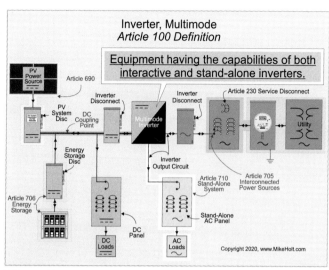

▶Figure 100–99

Kitchen. An area with a sink and permanent provisions for food preparation and cooking. ▶Figure 100–100

▶Figure 100–100

Author's Comment:

▶ An area like an employee break room with a sink and cord-and-plug-connected cooking appliance such as a microwave oven is not considered a kitchen.

Labeled. Equipment or materials that have a label, symbol, or other identifying mark in the form of a sticker, decal, printed label, or with the identifying mark molded or stamped into the product by a recognized testing laboratory acceptable to the authority having jurisdiction. ▶Figure 100–101

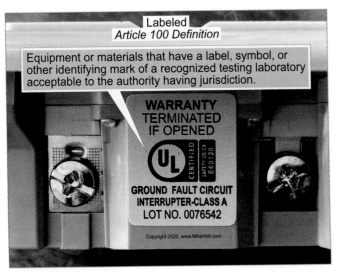

▶Figure 100–101

Author's Comment:

▸ Labeling and listing of equipment typically provides the basis for equipment approval by the authority having jurisdiction [90.4, 90.7, 110.2, and 110.3].

Note: When a listed product is of such a size, shape, material, or surface texture that it is not possible to legibly apply the complete label to the product, it may appear on the smallest unit container in which the product is packaged.

Laundry Area. An area containing (or designed to contain) a laundry tray, clothes washer, or clothes dryer. ▶Figure 100–102

▶Figure 100–102

Author's Comment:

▸ A "laundry tray" is a fixed laundry or utility sink with necessary plumbing connections most commonly installed near the washer and dryer. A "laundry area" is such by design regardless if the laundry equipment is in place or not.

Lighting Outlet. An outlet for connecting a luminaire. ▶Figure 100–103

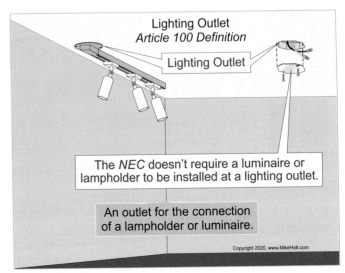

▶Figure 100–103

Lighting Track (Track Lighting). A manufactured assembly designed to support and energize luminaires that can be readily repositioned on the track, and whose length may be altered by the addition or subtraction of sections of track. ▶Figure 100–104

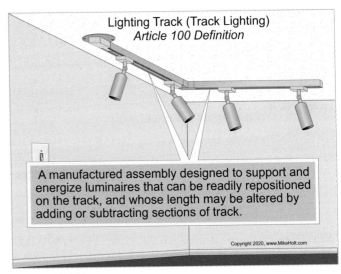

▶Figure 100–104

Listed. Equipment or materials included in a list published by a recognized testing laboratory acceptable to the authority having jurisdiction. The listing organization must periodically inspect the production of listed equipment or material to ensure they meet appropriate designated standards and are suitable for a specified purpose.

Note: Examples of nationally recognized testing laboratories (NRTLs) are Underwriters Laboratory (UL) and Canadian Standards Association (CSA). Both are accepted in either the United States or Canada and most electrical equipment is marked by both agencies. Always look for at least one of these seals and accept no imitations or counterfeits.

Author's Comment:

▶ The *NEC* does not require all electrical equipment to be listed, but some *Code* requirements do specifically call for product listing. Organizations such as OSHA are increasingly requiring listed equipment to be used when such equipment is available [90.7, 110.2, and 110.3].

Location, Damp (Damp Location). Locations protected from weather and not subject to saturation with water or other liquids. ▶Figure 100–105

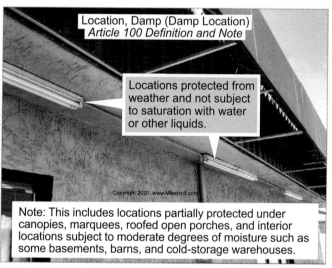
▶Figure 100–105

Note: This includes locations partially protected under canopies, marquees, roofed open porches, and interior locations subject to moderate degrees of moisture such as some basements, barns, and cold-storage warehouses.

Location, Dry (Dry Location). An area not normally subjected to dampness or wetness, but which may temporarily be subjected to dampness or wetness, such as a building under construction.

Location, Wet (Wet Location). An installation underground, in concrete slabs in direct contact with the Earth, areas subject to saturation with water, and unprotected locations exposed to weather. ▶Figure 100–106 and ▶Figure 100–107

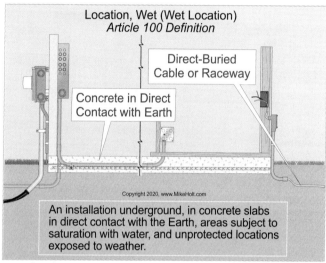
▶Figure 100–106

▶Figure 100–107

Luminaire. A complete lighting unit consisting of a light source with parts designed to position the light source and connect it to the power supply. It may also include parts to protect and distribute the light. ▶Figure 100–108

Messenger or Messenger Wire. A wire that is run along with, or integral to, a cable or conductor to provide mechanical support for the cable or conductor. ▶Figure 100–109

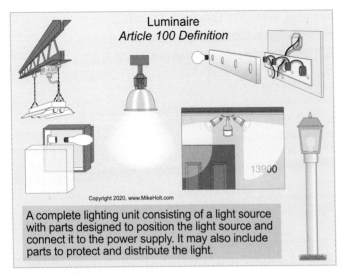

Luminaire
Article 100 Definition

A complete lighting unit consisting of a light source with parts designed to position the light source and connect it to the power supply. It may also include parts to protect and distribute the light.

▶Figure 100–108

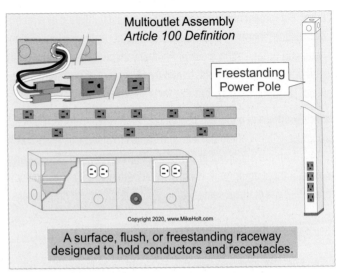

Multioutlet Assembly
Article 100 Definition

Freestanding Power Pole

A surface, flush, or freestanding raceway designed to hold conductors and receptacles.

▶Figure 100–110

Messenger or Messenger Wire
Article 100 Definition

Festoon Lighting

A wire that is run along with, or integral to, a cable or conductor to provide mechanical support for the cable or conductor.

▶Figure 100–109

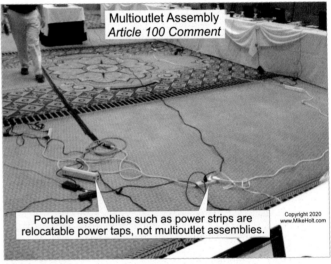

Multioutlet Assembly
Article 100 Comment

Portable assemblies such as power strips are relocatable power taps, not multioutlet assemblies.

▶Figure 100–111

Multioutlet Assembly. A surface, flush, or freestanding raceway designed to hold conductors and receptacles. ▶Figure 100–110

Author's Comment:

▶ Portable assemblies such as power strips are relocatable power taps, not multioutlet assemblies. ▶Figure 100–111

Neutral Conductor. The conductor connected to the neutral point of a system that is intended to carry current under normal conditions. ▶Figure 100–112

Neutral Point. The common point of a 4-wire, three-phase, wye-connected system; the midpoint of a 3-wire, single-phase system; or the midpoint of the single-phase portion of a three-phase, delta-connected system. ▶Figure 100–113

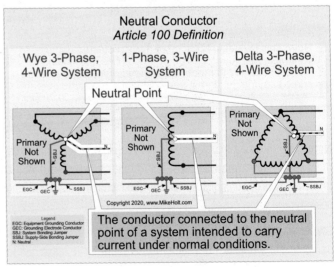

Neutral Conductor
Article 100 Definition

| Wye 3-Phase, 4-Wire System | 1-Phase, 3-Wire System | Delta 3-Phase, 4-Wire System |

Neutral Point

Legend
EGC: Equipment Grounding Conductor
GEC: Grounding Electrode Conductor
SBJ: System Bonding Jumper
SSBJ: Supply-Side Bonding Jumper
N: Neutral

The conductor connected to the neutral point of a system intended to carry current under normal conditions.

▶Figure 100–112

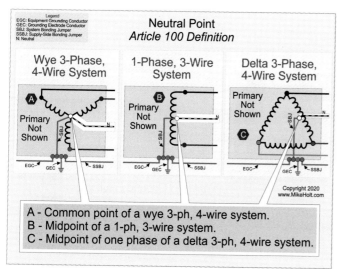

A - Common point of a wye 3-ph, 4-wire system.
B - Midpoint of a 1-ph, 3-wire system.
C - Midpoint of one phase of a delta 3-ph, 4-wire system.

▶Figure 100–113

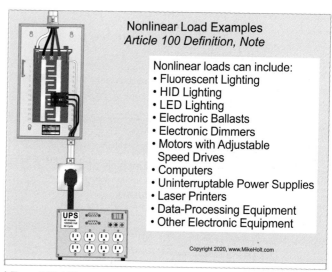

▶Figure 100–115

Nonautomatic. Requiring human intervention to perform a function.

Nonlinear Load. A load where the shape of the current waveform does not follow the shape of the applied sinusoidal voltage waveform. ▶Figure 100–114

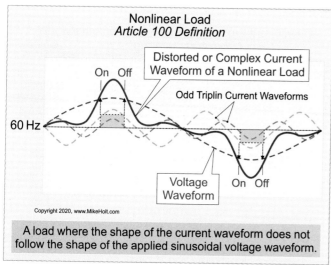

A load where the shape of the current waveform does not follow the shape of the applied sinusoidal voltage waveform.

▶Figure 100–114

Note: Single-phase nonlinear loads include electronic equipment such as copy machines, laser printers, and electric-discharge lighting. Three-phase nonlinear loads include uninterruptible power supplies, induction motors, and electronic switching devices such as adjustable-speed drive systems. ▶Figure 100–115

Author's Comment:

▶ The subject of nonlinear loads is beyond the scope of this textbook. For more information on this topic, visit www.MikeHolt.com, click on the "Technical" link, then on the "Power Quality" link.

Outlet. A point in the wiring system where electricity is made available to supply utilization equipment. ▶Figure 100–116

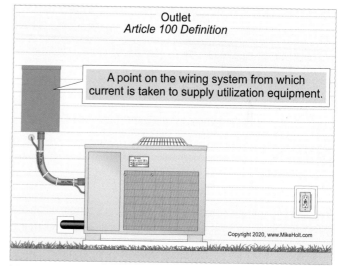

▶Figure 100–116

Author's Comment:

▶ This includes receptacle and lighting outlets, as well as those for ceiling paddle fans and smoke alarms. ▶Figure 100–117

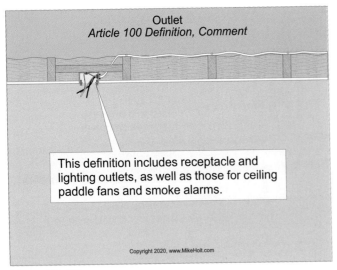

▶Figure 100–117

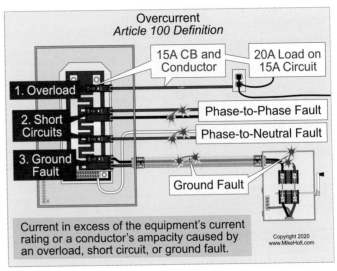

▶Figure 100–119

Outline Lighting. An arrangement of an electrically powered light source used to outline or call attention to building features such as the shape of a building or the decoration of a window. ▶Figure 100–118

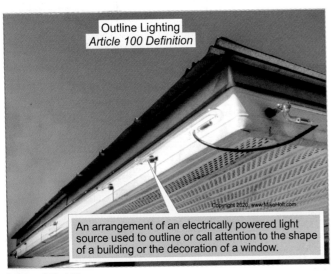

▶Figure 100–118

Overcurrent. Current in excess of the equipment's current rating or a conductor's ampacity caused by an overload, short circuit, or ground fault. ▶Figure 100–119

Overcurrent Protective Device, Branch Circuit. A device capable of providing protection from an overload, short circuit, or ground fault for service, feeder, and branch circuits.

Overcurrent Protective Device, Supplementary. A device intended to provide limited overcurrent protection for specific applications and utilization equipment, such as luminaires and appliances. This limited protection is In addition to the protection required and provided by the branch-circuit overcurrent protective device. ▶Figure 100–120

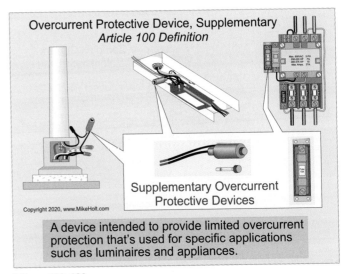

▶Figure 100–120

Overload. The operation of equipment above its current rating, or current in excess of a conductor's ampacity. If an overload condition persists long enough, the result can be equipment failure or a fire from damaging or dangerous overheating. A fault, such as a short circuit or ground fault, is not an overload. ▶Figure 100–121

Panelboard. An assembly designed for the distribution of light, heat, or power circuits with overcurrent devices and typically placed in a cabinet. ▶Figure 100–122

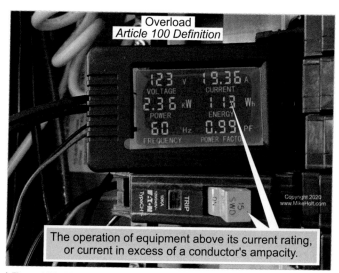

The operation of equipment above its current rating, or current in excess of a conductor's ampacity.

▶Figure 100–121

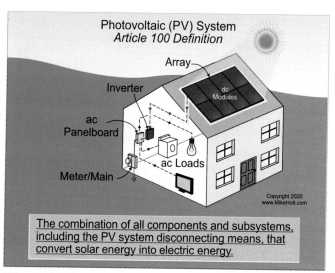

The combination of all components and subsystems, including the PV system disconnecting means, that convert solar energy into electric energy.

▶Figure 100–123

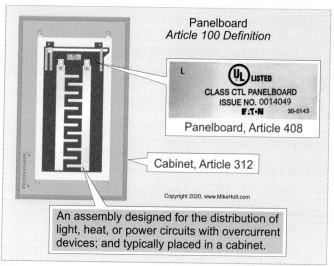

Panelboard, Article 408

Cabinet, Article 312

An assembly designed for the distribution of light, heat, or power circuits with overcurrent devices; and typically placed in a cabinet.

▶Figure 100–122

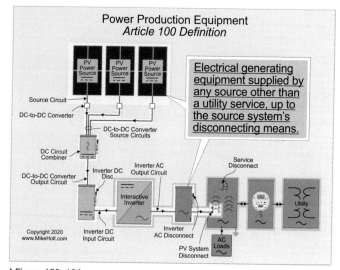

Electrical generating equipment supplied by any source other than a utility service, up to the source system's disconnecting means.

▶Figure 100–124

Author's Comment:

▸ See the definition of "Cabinet" in this article.

▸ The slang term in the electrical field for a panelboard is "the guts." This is the interior of the panelboard assembly and is covered by Article 408, while the cabinet is covered by Article 312.

Photovoltaic (PV) System. The combination of all components and subsystems, including the PV system disconnecting means, that convert solar energy into electric energy for utilization loads. ▶Figure 100–123

Power Production Equipment. Electrical generating equipment supplied by any source other than a utility service, up to the source system's disconnecting means. ▶Figure 100–124

Note: Examples of power production equipment include such items as generators, solar photovoltaic systems, and fuel cell systems.

Premises Wiring. The interior and exterior wiring including power, lighting, control, and signaling circuits, and all associated hardware, fittings, and wiring devices. This includes permanently and temporarily installed wiring from the service point to the outlets. Where there is no service point, it is the wiring from and including the electric power source (such as a generator, transformer, or PV system) to the outlets. ▶Figure 100–125

Premises wiring does not include the internal wiring of electrical equipment and appliances such as luminaires, dishwashers, water heaters, motors, controllers, motor control centers, air-conditioning equipment, and so on [90.7 and 300.1(B)]. ▶Figure 100–126

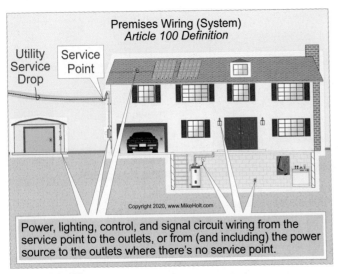

Premises Wiring (System)
Article 100 Definition

Utility Service Drop

Service Point

Power, lighting, control, and signal circuit wiring from the service point to the outlets, or from (and including) the power source to the outlets where there's no service point.

▶Figure 100–125

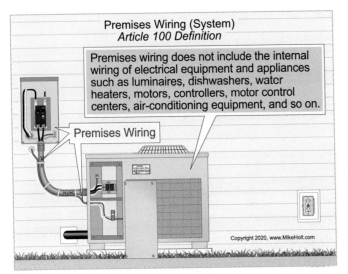

Premises Wiring (System)
Article 100 Definition

Premises wiring does not include the internal wiring of electrical equipment and appliances such as luminaires, dishwashers, water heaters, motors, controllers, motor control centers, air-conditioning equipment, and so on.

Premises Wiring

▶Figure 100–126

Note: Electric power sources include (but not limited to) interconnected or stand-alone batteries, PV systems, other distributed generation systems, and generators.

Prime Mover. The machine that supplies mechanical horsepower to a generator.

Qualified Person. A person who has the skill and knowledge related to the construction and operation of electrical equipment and its installation. This person must have received safety training to recognize and avoid the hazards involved with electrical systems. ▶Figure 100–127

Note: NFPA 70E, *Standard for Electrical Safety in the Workplace,* provides information on the safety training requirements expected of a "qualified person."

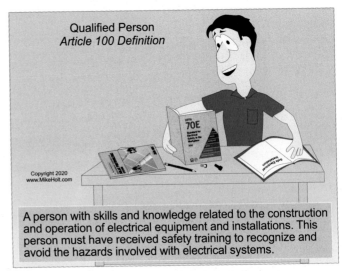

Qualified Person
Article 100 Definition

A person with skills and knowledge related to the construction and operation of electrical equipment and installations. This person must have received safety training to recognize and avoid the hazards involved with electrical systems.

▶Figure 100–127

Author's Comment:

▶ Examples of this safety training include, but are not limited to, training in the use of special precautionary techniques, personal protective equipment (PPE), insulating and shielding materials, and the use of insulated tools and test equipment when working on or near exposed conductors or circuit parts that can become energized.

▶ In many parts of the United States, electricians, electrical contractors, electrical inspectors, and electrical engineers must complete from 6 to 24 hours of *NEC* review each year as a requirement to maintain licensing. This, in and of itself, does not make one qualified to deal with the specific hazards involved with electrical systems.

Raceway. A channel designed for the installation of conductors, cables, or busbars.

Author's Comment:

▶ A cable tray system is not a raceway; it is a support system for cables and raceways [392.2].

Raceway, Communications. An enclosed nonmetallic channel designed for holding communications wires and cables; optical fiber cables; data cables associated with information technology and communications equipment; Class 2, Type PLTC, and power-limited fire alarm cables in plenum spaces, risers, and general-purpose applications. ▶Figure 100–128

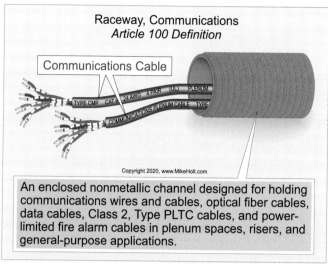

Raceway, Communications
Article 100 Definition

Communications Cable

Copyright 2020, www.MikeHolt.com

An enclosed nonmetallic channel designed for holding communications wires and cables, optical fiber cables, data cables, Class 2, Type PLTC cables, and power-limited fire alarm cables in plenum spaces, risers, and general-purpose applications.

▶Figure 100–128

Rainproof. Constructed, protected, or treated to prevent rain from interfering with the successful operation of the apparatus under specified test conditions.

Raintight. Constructed or protected so exposure to a beating rain will not result in the entrance of water under specified test conditions.

Receptacle. A contact device installed at an outlet for the connection of an attachment plug, or for the direct connection of equipment designed to mate with the contact device (SQL receptacle). ▶Figure 100–129

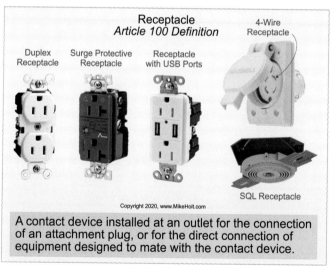

Receptacle
Article 100 Definition

Duplex Receptacle

Surge Protective Receptacle

Receptacle with USB Ports

4-Wire Receptacle

SQL Receptacle

Copyright 2020, www.MikeHolt.com

A contact device installed at an outlet for the connection of an attachment plug, or for the direct connection of equipment designed to mate with the contact device.

▶Figure 100–129

Author's Comment:

▶ For additional information about listed locking support and mounting receptacles, visit www.safetyquicklight.com.

A single receptacle contains one contact device on a yoke or strap; a multiple receptacle has more than one contact device on the same yoke or strap. ▶Figure 100–130

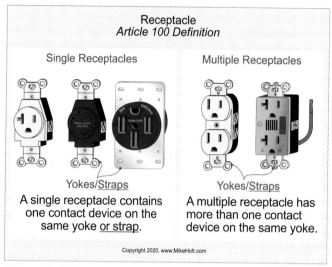

Receptacle
Article 100 Definition

Single Receptacles

Multiple Receptacles

Yokes/Straps

A single receptacle contains one contact device on the same yoke or strap.

Yokes/Straps

A multiple receptacle has more than one contact device on the same yoke.

Copyright 2020, www.MikeHolt.com

▶Figure 100–130

Author's Comment:

▶ A yoke (also called a "strap") is the metal mounting structure for such items as receptacles, switches, switches with pilot lights, and switch/receptacles to name a few. ▶Figure 100–131 and ▶Figure 100–132

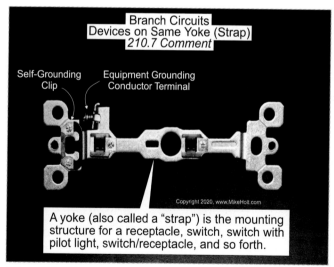

Branch Circuits
Devices on Same Yoke (Strap)
210.7 Comment

Self-Grounding Clip

Equipment Grounding Conductor Terminal

Copyright 2020, www.MikeHolt.com

A yoke (also called a "strap") is the mounting structure for a receptacle, switch, switch with pilot light, switch/receptacle, and so forth.

▶Figure 100–131

Note: A duplex receptacle is an example of a multiple receptacle with two receptacles on the same yoke or strap.

Receptacle Outlet. An opening in an outlet box where receptacles have been installed.

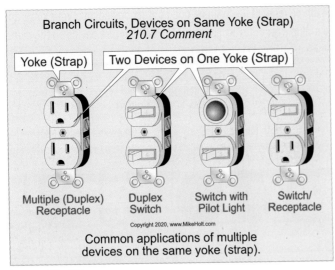

Branch Circuits, Devices on Same Yoke (Strap)
210.7 Comment

Yoke (Strap) | Two Devices on One Yoke (Strap)

Multiple (Duplex) Receptacle | Duplex Switch | Switch with Pilot Light | Switch/Receptacle

Copyright 2020, www.MikeHolt.com

Common applications of multiple devices on the same yoke (strap).

▶Figure 100–132

Reconditioned. Electromechanical systems, equipment, apparatus, or components that are restored to operating conditions. This process differs from normal servicing of equipment that remains within a facility, or replacement of listed equipment on a one-to-one basis.

Note: The term reconditioned is frequently referred to as rebuild, refurbished, or remanufactured.

Remote-Control Circuit. An electric circuit that controls another circuit by a relay or equivalent device installed in accordance with Article 725. ▶Figure 100–133

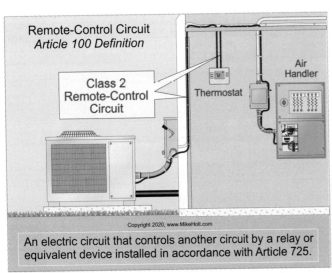

Remote-Control Circuit
Article 100 Definition

Class 2 Remote-Control Circuit

Thermostat

Air Handler

Copyright 2020, www.MikeHolt.com

An electric circuit that controls another circuit by a relay or equivalent device installed in accordance with Article 725.

▶Figure 100–133

Retrofit Kit. An assembly of parts for the field conversion of utilization equipment.

Sealable Equipment. Equipment enclosed with a means of sealing or locking so live parts cannot be made accessible without opening the enclosure.

Note: The equipment may or may not be operable without opening the enclosure.

Separately Derived System. An electrical source, other than a service, having no direct connection(s) to the circuit conductors of any other electrical source other than those established by grounding and bonding connections. ▶Figure 100–134, ▶Figure 100–135, and ▶Figure 100–136

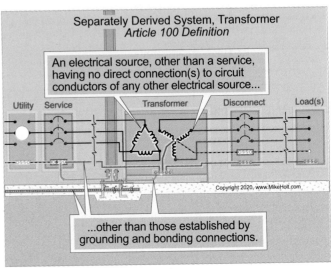

Separately Derived System, Transformer
Article 100 Definition

An electrical source, other than a service, having no direct connection(s) to circuit conductors of any other electrical source...

Utility | Service | Transformer | Disconnect | Load(s)

Copyright 2020, www.MikeHolt.com

...other than those established by grounding and bonding connections.

▶Figure 100–134

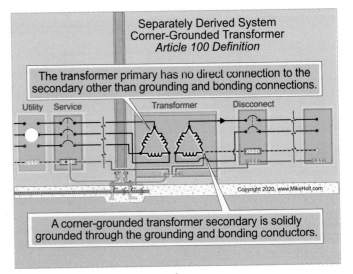

Separately Derived System
Corner-Grounded Transformer
Article 100 Definition

The transformer primary has no direct connection to the secondary other than grounding and bonding connections.

Utility | Service | Transformer | Disconnect

Copyright 2020, www.MikeHolt.com

A corner-grounded transformer secondary is solidly grounded through the grounding and bonding conductors.

▶Figure 100–135

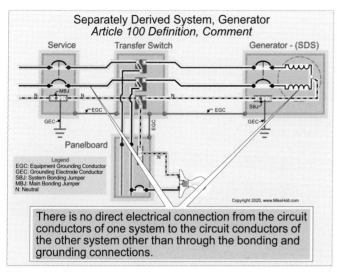

▶Figure 100-136

Author's Comment:

▸ A generator is not a separately derived system if the neutral conductor is solidly interconnected to a service-supplied system neutral conductor. An example is a generator provided with a transfer switch that includes a neutral conductor that is not switched. ▶Figure 100-137

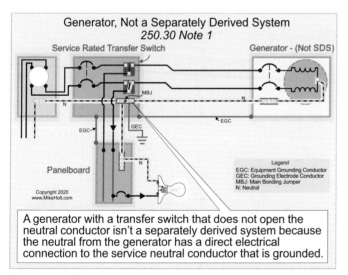

▶Figure 100-137

Author's Comment:

▸ Separately derived systems are much more complicated than the *Code*'s definition suggests and understanding them requires additional study. For more information, see 250.30.

Service [Article 230]. The conductors and equipment <u>connecting</u> the serving electric utility to the wiring system of the premises served. ▶Figure 100-138

▶Figure 100-138

Author's Comment:

▸ A service can only be supplied by the serving electric utility and is not covered by the *NEC*. If power is supplied by other than the serving electric utility, the conductors and equipment are part of a feeder and covered by the *Code*.

▸ Conductors from UPS systems, solar PV systems, generators, or transformers are not service conductors. See the definitions of "Feeder" and "Service Conductors" in this article.

Service Conductors. The conductors from the serving electric utility service point to the service disconnect. ▶Figure 100-139

Author's Comment:

▸ Service conductors can include overhead service conductors, overhead service-entrance conductors, and underground service conductors. These conductors are not under the exclusive control of the serving electric utility, which means they are owned by the customer and are covered by the requirements in Article 230.

Service Conductors, Overhead (Overhead Service Conductors). Overhead conductors between the serving electric utility service point and the first point of connection to the service-entrance conductors at the building. ▶Figure 100-140

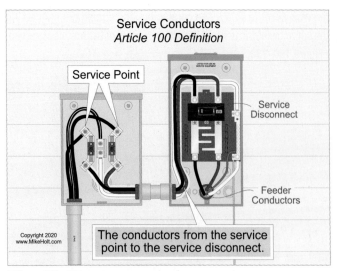

Service Conductors
Article 100 Definition

Service Point

Service Disconnect

Feeder Conductors

The conductors from the service point to the service disconnect.

▶Figure 100–139

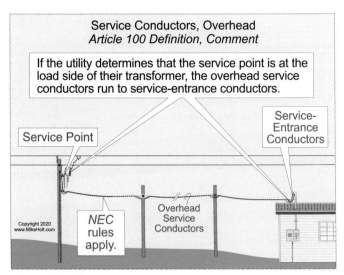

Service Conductors, Overhead
Article 100 Definition, Comment

If the utility determines that the service point is at the load side of their transformer, the overhead service conductors run to service-entrance conductors.

Service Point

Service-Entrance Conductors

NEC rules apply.

Overhead Service Conductors

▶Figure 100–141

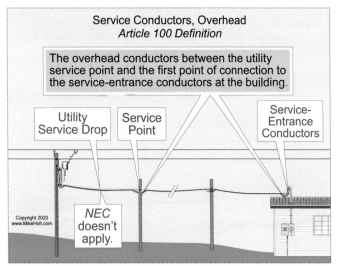

Service Conductors, Overhead
Article 100 Definition

The overhead conductors between the utility service point and the first point of connection to the service-entrance conductors at the building.

Utility Service Drop

Service Point

Service-Entrance Conductors

NEC doesn't apply.

▶Figure 100–140

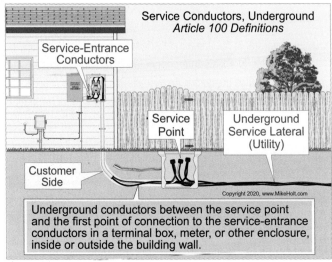

Service Conductors, Underground
Article 100 Definitions

Service-Entrance Conductors

Service Point

Underground Service Lateral (Utility)

Customer Side

Underground conductors between the service point and the first point of connection to the service-entrance conductors in a terminal box, meter, or other enclosure, inside or outside the building wall.

▶Figure 100–142

Author's Comment:

▸ The service point is typically determined by the serving electric utility. If the utility determines the service point is at the load side of their transformer, the overhead service conductors run to the service-entrance conductors. ▶Figure 100–141

Service Conductors, Underground (Underground Service Conductors). Underground conductors between the service point and the first point of connection to the service-entrance conductors in a terminal box, meter, or other enclosure; inside or outside the building wall. ▶Figure 100–142

Author's Comment:

▸ Service conductors fall within the requirements of Article 230 since they are not under the exclusive control of the serving electric utility.

Note: Where there is no terminal box, meter, or other enclosure the point of connection is the point of entrance of the service conductors into the building.

Service Drop. Utility-owned overhead conductors between the serving electric utility and the service point. ▶Figure 100–143

Author's Comment:

▸ The *NEC* does not apply to service drops.

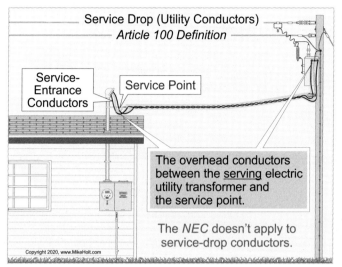

▶Figure 100–143

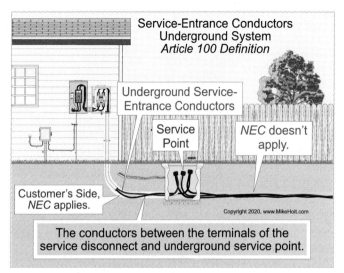

▶Figure 100–145

Service-Entrance Conductors, Overhead (Overhead Service-Entrance Conductors). The conductors between the terminals of the service disconnect and service drop or overhead service conductors. ▶Figure 100–144

Author's Comment:

▶ Underground service-entrance conductors fall within the requirements of Article 230 since they are not under the exclusive control of the serving electric utility.

Service Equipment (Service Disconnect). Disconnects such as circuit breakers or switches connected to the serving electric utility, intended to control and disconnect the power from the serving electric utility. ▶Figure 100–146

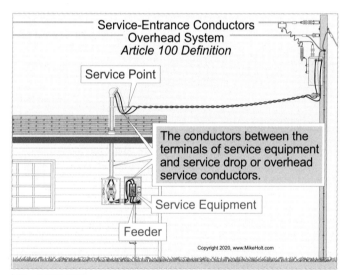

▶Figure 100–144

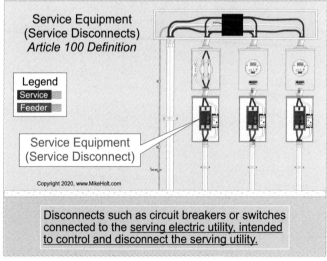

▶Figure 100–146

Author's Comment:

▶ Overhead service-entrance conductors are covered by the requirements of Article 230, since they are not under the exclusive control of the serving electric utility.

Service-Entrance Conductors, Underground (Underground Service-Entrance Conductors). The conductors between the terminals of the service disconnect and underground service point. ▶Figure 100–145

Author's Comment:

▶ It's important to know where a service begins and where it ends in order to properly apply the *Code* requirements. Sometimes the service ends before the metering equipment. ▶Figure 100–147 and ▶Figure 100–148

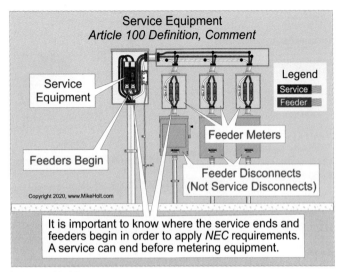

▶Figure 100–147

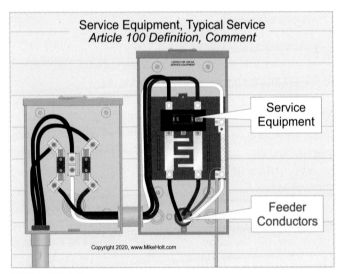

▶Figure 100–148

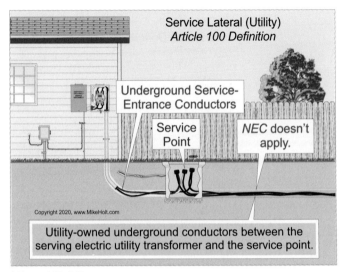

▶Figure 100–149

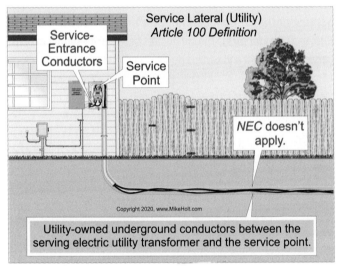

▶Figure 100–150

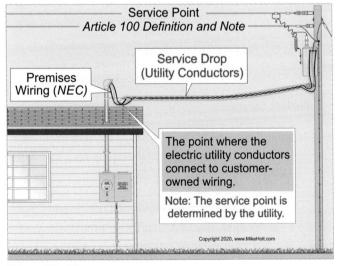

▶Figure 100–151

Author's Comment:

▸ Service equipment is often referred to as the "service disconnect" or "service main."

▸ Meter socket enclosures are not considered service equipment [230.66].

Service Lateral. Utility-owned underground conductors between the serving electric utility transformer and the service point. ▶Figure 100–149 and ▶Figure 100–150

Service Point. The point where the serving electric utility conductors connect to customer-owned wiring. ▶Figure 100–151

Author's Comment:

▶ The service point is typically determined by the serving electric utility and may vary with different utilities and different types of occupancies.

▶ For utility-owned transformers, the service point will be at the serving electric utility's transformer secondary terminals, at the service drop, or at the meter socket enclosure depending on where their conductors terminate. ▶Figure 100–152

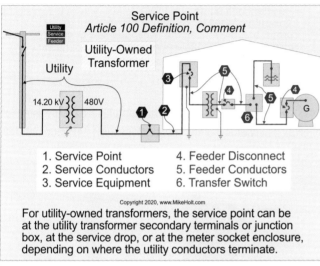

1. Service Point 4. Feeder Disconnect
2. Service Conductors 5. Feeder Conductors
3. Service Equipment 6. Transfer Switch

Copyright 2020, www.MikeHolt.com

For utility-owned transformers, the service point can be at the utility transformer secondary terminals or junction box, at the service drop, or at the meter socket enclosure, depending on where the utility conductors terminate.

▶Figure 100–152

▶ For customer-owned transformers, the service point will be at the termination of the serving electric utility's conductors; often at the utility's pole. ▶Figure 100–153

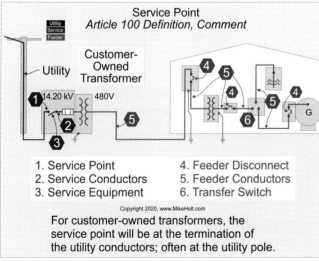

1. Service Point 4. Feeder Disconnect
2. Service Conductors 5. Feeder Conductors
3. Service Equipment 6. Transfer Switch

Copyright 2020, www.MikeHolt.com

For customer-owned transformers, the service point will be at the termination of the utility conductors; often at the utility pole.

▶Figure 100–153

Short-Circuit Current Rating. The prospective symmetrical fault current at a nominal voltage to which electrical equipment can be connected without sustaining damage exceeding defined acceptance criteria.

Signaling Circuit [Article 725]. A circuit that energizes signaling equipment. ▶Figure 100–154

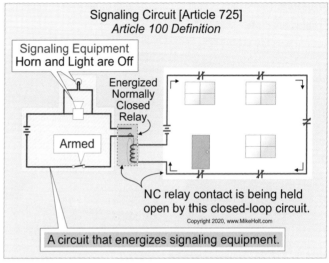

▶Figure 100–154

Special Permission. Written consent from the authority having jurisdiction.

Author's Comment:

▶ See the definition of "Authority Having Jurisdiction."

Stand-Alone System. A system capable of supplying power independently of a serving electric utility. ▶Figure 100–155

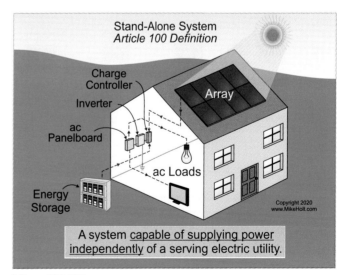

▶Figure 100–155

▶ Although stand-alone systems can operate independently of the serving electric utility, they may include a connection to the serving electric utility for use when not operating in stand-alone mode ("island mode").

Structure. That which is built or constructed, other than equipment. ▶Figure 100–156

Structure
Article 100 Definition

That which is built or constructed, other than equipment.

▶Figure 100–156

Surge-Protective Device. A protective device intended to limit transient voltages by diverting or limiting surge current and preventing its continued flow while remaining capable of repeating these functions. ▶Figure 100–157 and ▶Figure 100–158

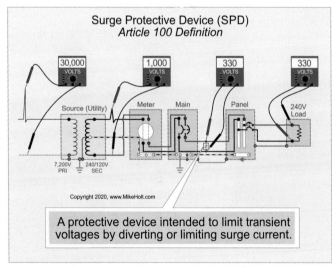

Surge Protective Device (SPD)
Article 100 Definition

A protective device intended to limit transient voltages by diverting or limiting surge current.

▶Figure 100–157

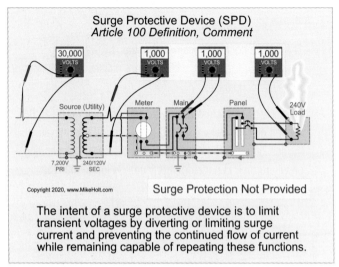

Surge Protective Device (SPD)
Article 100 Definition, Comment

Surge Protection Not Provided

The intent of a surge protective device is to limit transient voltages by diverting or limiting surge current and preventing the continued flow of current while remaining capable of repeating these functions.

▶Figure 100–158

Type 1. A permanently connected surge protective device listed for installation at or ahead of the service disconnect. ▶Figure 100–159

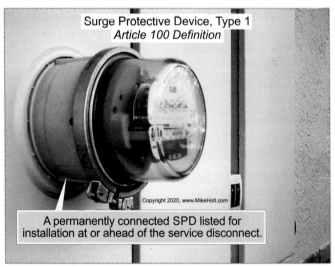

Surge Protective Device, Type 1
Article 100 Definition

A permanently connected SPD listed for installation at or ahead of the service disconnect.

▶Figure 100–159

Type 2. A permanently connected surge protective device listed for installation on the load side of the service disconnect. ▶Figure 100–160

Type 3. A surge protective device listed for installation on branch circuits. ▶Figure 100–161

▶ Type 3 surge protective devices can be installed anywhere on the load side of branch-circuit overcurrent protection up to the equipment served, provided there is a conductor at least 30 ft long between the connection and the service or transformer [242.16].

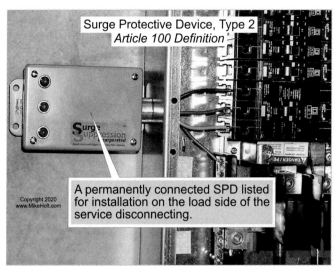

▶Figure 100–160

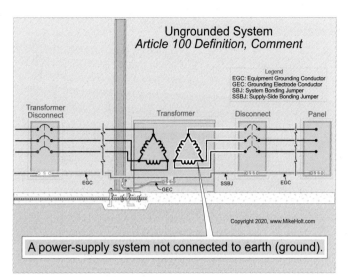

▶Figure 100–162

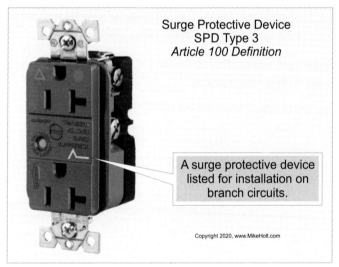

▶Figure 100–161

Type 4. A component surge protective device which includes those installed in receptacles and relocatable power taps (power strips).

Note: For further information, see UL 1449, *Standard for Surge Protective Devices.*

Switch, General-Use Snap (General-Use Snap Switch). A switch constructed to be installed in a device box or a box cover.

Ungrounded System. A power-supply system not connected to earth (ground). ▶Figure 100–162

Author's Comment:

▶ An electrical system can be ungrounded, but the enclosure must still be connected to the Earth [250.4(B)].

Utilization Equipment. Equipment that utilizes electricity for electronic, electromechanical, chemical, heating, lighting, or similar purposes.

Voltage of a Circuit. The greatest effective root-mean-square (RMS) difference of voltage between any two conductors of the circuit. ▶Figure 100–163

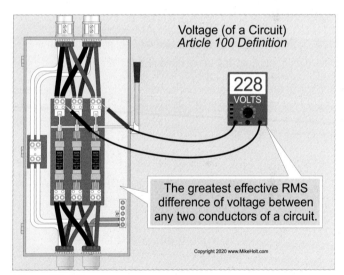

▶Figure 100–163

Voltage, Nominal (Nominal Voltage). A value assigned for conveniently designating voltage classes. Examples are 120/240V, 120/208V, or 277/480V [220.5(A)]. ▶Figure 100–164

Note 1: The actual voltage at which a circuit operates can vary from the nominal within a range that permits satisfactory operation of equipment.

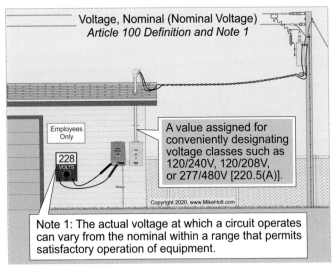

Voltage, Nominal (Nominal Voltage)
Article 100 Definition and Note 1

A value assigned for conveniently designating voltage classes such as 120/240V, 120/208V, or 277/480V [220.5(A)].

Note 1: The actual voltage at which a circuit operates can vary from the nominal within a range that permits satisfactory operation of equipment.

▶Figure 100–164

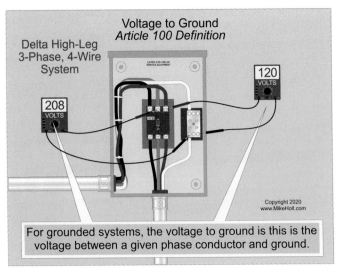

Voltage to Ground
Article 100 Definition

Delta High-Leg 3-Phase, 4-Wire System

For grounded systems, the voltage to ground is this is the voltage between a given phase conductor and ground.

▶Figure 100–165

Author's Comment:

▶ Common voltage ratings of electrical equipment are 115V, 200V, 208V, 230V, and 460V. The electrical power supplied might be at the 240V, nominal, voltage but will be less at the equipment. Therefore, electrical equipment is rated at a value less than the nominal system voltage.

Note 3: Some battery units are rated 48V dc, nominal, even if they have a charging float voltage of up to 58V dc.

Voltage to Ground. For grounded systems, this is the voltage between a phase conductor and ground; typically, the neutral. ▶Figure 100–165

For ungrounded systems, the voltage to ground is the greatest difference of voltage (RMS) between any two phase conductors.

Watertight. Constructed so moisture will not enter the enclosure under specific test conditions.

Weatherproof. Constructed or protected so exposure to the weather will not interfere with successful operation.

Author's Comment:

▶ Article 100 now includes a "Part III" which contains definitions specific to Hazardous (Classified) Locations. While a few of the definitions are new to the *Code*, most were moved from Chapter 5 to this new part.

ARTICLE 100

PRACTICE QUESTIONS

Please use the 2020 *Code* book to answer the following questions.

Article 100—Definitions

1. Article 100 contains definitions essential to the application of the *Code*. Definitions are also found in _____.

   (a) the index
   (b) the annex
   (c) xxx.2 of other articles
   (d) article scope(s)

2. Equipment that is capable of being reached for operation, renewal, and inspection defines _____.

   (a) accessible (as applied to equipment)
   (b) accessible (as applied to wiring methods)
   (c) accessible, readily
   (d) all of these

3. An arc-fault circuit interrupter is a device intended to de-energize the circuit when a(an) _____ is detected.

   (a) overcurrent condition
   (b) arc fault
   (c) ground fault
   (d) harmonic fundamental

4. A _____ is an area that includes a sink (basin) with a toilet, urinal, tub, shower, bidet or similar plumbing fixtures.

   (a) bath area
   (b) bathroom
   (c) rest area
   (d) master suite

5. A conductor installed on the supply side of a service or within a service equipment enclosure, or for a separately derived system, to ensure the required electrical conductivity between metal parts required to be electrically connected is known as the _____.

   (a) supply-side bonding jumper
   (b) ungrounded conductor
   (c) electrical supply source
   (d) grounding electrode conductor

6. The *NEC* defines a(an) _____ as a structure that stands alone or that is separated from adjoining structures by fire walls.

   (a) unit
   (b) apartment
   (c) building
   (d) utility

7. Conductive optical fiber cables contain noncurrent-carrying conductive members such as metallic _____.

   (a) strength members
   (b) vapor barriers
   (c) armor or sheath
   (d) any of these

8. _____ is a term indicating that there is purposely introduced delay in the tripping action of the circuit breaker which decreases as the magnitude of the current increases.

   (a) Adverse time
   (b) Inverse time
   (c) Time delay
   (d) Timed unit

9. "Communications equipment" is the electronic equipment that performs the telecommunications operations for the transmission of _____, and includes power equipment, technical support equipment, and conductors dedicated solely to the operation of the equipment.

    (a) audio
    (b) video
    (c) data
    (d) all of these

10. The selection and installation of overcurrent protective devices so that an overcurrent condition will be localized to restrict outages to the circuit or equipment affected, is called _____.

    (a) overcurrent protection
    (b) interrupting capacity
    (c) selective coordination
    (d) overload protection

11. A dormitory unit is a building or a space in a building in which group sleeping accommodations are provided for more than _____ persons who are not members of the same family in one room, or a series of closely associated rooms, under joint occupancy and single management, with or without meals, but without individual cooking facilities.

    (a) six
    (b) ten
    (c) twelve
    (d) sixteen

12. An effective ground-fault current path is an intentionally constructed, low-impedance electrically conductive path designed and intended to carry current during a ground-fault condition from the point of a ground fault on a wiring system to _____.

    (a) ground
    (b) earth
    (c) the electrical supply source
    (d) the grounding electrode

13. Off-road, self-propelled electric vehicles, such as _____ are not considered electric vehicles.

    (a) industrial trucks, hoists, and lifts
    (b) golf carts and airline ground support equipment
    (c) tractors and boats
    (d) all of these

14. As applied to wiring methods, on or attached to the surface or behind access panels designed to allow access is known as _____.

    (a) open
    (b) uncovered
    (c) exposed
    (d) bare

15. An accessory, such as a locknut, intended primarily to perform a mechanical function rather than an electrical function best describes _____.

    (a) a part
    (b) equipment
    (c) a device
    (d) a fitting

16. The word "Earth" best describes what *NEC* term?

    (a) bonded
    (b) ground
    (c) effective ground-fault current path
    (d) guarded

17. Connected to ground without the insertion of any resistor or impedance device is referred to as _____.

    (a) grounded
    (b) solidly grounded
    (c) effectively grounded
    (d) a grounding conductor

18. The installed conductive path(s) that is part of a ground-fault current path and connects normally noncurrent-carrying metal parts of equipment together and to the system grounded conductor or to the grounding electrode conductor, or both, is known as a(an) _____ conductor.

    (a) grounding electrode
    (b) grounding
    (c) equipment grounding
    (d) neutral

19. A _____ is an accommodation with two or more contiguous rooms comprising a compartment that provides living sleeping sanitary and storage facilities.

    (a) guest room
    (b) guest suite
    (c) dwelling unit
    (d) single-family dwelling

20. Information and technology equipment and systems are used for creation and manipulation of _____.

    (a) data
    (b) voice
    (c) video
    (d) all of these

21. A device that provides a means to connect intersystem bonding conductors for _____ systems to the grounding electrode system is an intersystem bonding termination.

    (a) limited-energy
    (b) low-voltage
    (c) communications
    (d) power and lighting

22. When defining different levels of accessibility, _____ means not readily accessible to persons unless special means for access are used.

    (a) readily accessible
    (b) not readily accessible
    (c) isolated
    (d) accessible to qualified persons only

23. Lighting track is a manufactured assembly designed to support and _____ luminaires that are capable of being readily repositioned on the track.

    (a) connect
    (b) protect
    (c) energize
    (d) all of these

24. The term "Luminaire" means a single individual lampholder by itself.

    (a) True
    (b) False

25. A(An) _____ is a point on the wiring system at which current is taken to supply utilization equipment.

    (a) box
    (b) receptacle
    (c) outlet
    (d) device

26. A panel, including buses and automatic overcurrent devices, designed to be placed in a cabinet or cutout box and accessible only from the front is known as a _____.

    (a) switchboard
    (b) disconnect
    (c) panelboard
    (d) switch

27. According to Article 100, a _____ is the machine that supplies the mechanical horsepower to a generator.

    (a) prime mover
    (b) motor
    (c) capacitor
    (d) starter

28. Constructed, protected, or treated so as to prevent rain from interfering with the successful operation of the apparatus under specified test conditions defines the term _____.

    (a) raintight
    (b) waterproof
    (c) weathertight
    (d) rainproof

29. An outlet where one or more receptacles are installed is called _____.

    (a) a device
    (b) equipment
    (c) a receptacle
    (d) a receptacle outlet

30. A(An) _____ system is an electrical source other than a service having no direct connection(s) to circuit conductors of any other electrical source other than those established by grounding and bonding connections.

    (a) separately derived
    (b) classified
    (c) direct
    (d) emergency

31. A service drop is defined as the overhead conductors between the utility electric supply system and the _____.

    (a) service equipment
    (b) service point
    (c) grounding electrode
    (d) equipment grounding conductor

32. The underground conductors between the utility electric supply system and the service point are known as the _____.

    (a) utility service
    (b) service lateral
    (c) service drop
    (d) main service conductors

33. A stand-alone system supplies power independently of an electrical production and distribution network.

    (a) True
    (b) False

34. The voltage of a circuit is defined by the *Code* as the _____ root-mean-square (effective) difference of potential between any two conductors of the circuit concerned.

    (a) lowest
    (b) greatest
    (c) average
    (d) nominal

ARTICLE 110

REQUIREMENTS FOR ELECTRICAL INSTALLATIONS

Introduction to Article 110—Requirements for Electrical Installations

Article 110 sets the stage for how the rest of the *NEC* is implemented. It is critical for you to completely understand all aspects of this article since it is the foundation for much of the *Code*. As you read and master Article 110, you are building your foundation for correctly applying the *NEC*. While the purpose of the *National Electrical Code* is to provide a safe installation, this article is perhaps focused a little more on providing an installation that is safe for the installer and maintenance electrician, so time spent here is a good investment.

Part I. General Requirements

110.1 Scope

Article 110 covers the general requirements for the examination and approval, installation and use, and access to spaces about electrical equipment. ▶Figure 110–1

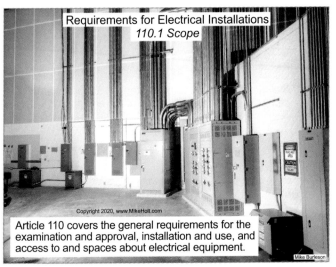

▶Figure 110–1

Note: See Annex J for information regarding ADA accessibility design.

Author's Comment:

▶ Requirements for people with disabilities include things like mounting heights for switches and receptacles, and requirements for the distance that objects (such as wall sconces) protrude from a wall.

110.2 Approval of Conductors and Equipment

The authority having jurisdiction must approve all electrical conductors and equipment. ▶Figure 110–2

▶Figure 110–2

Author's Comment:

▶ For a better understanding of product approval, review 90.4, 90.7, and 110.3 and the definitions for "Approved," "Identified," "Labeled," and "Listed" in Article 100.

110.3 Use and Product Listing (Certification) of Equipment

(A) Guidelines for Approval. The authority having jurisdiction must approve equipment. In doing so, consideration must be given to the following:

(1) Suitability for installation and use in accordance with the *NEC*

Note 1: Equipment may be new, reconditioned, refurbished, or remanufactured.

Note 2: Suitability of equipment use may be identified by a description marked on, or provided with, a product to identify the suitability of the product for a specific purpose, environment, or application. Special conditions of use or other limitations may be marked on the equipment, in the product instructions, or included in the appropriate listing and labeling information. Suitability of equipment may be evidenced by listing or labeling.

(2) Mechanical strength and durability

(3) Wire-bending and connection space

(4) Electrical insulation

(5) Heating effects under all conditions of use

(6) Arcing effects

(7) Classification by type, size, voltage, current capacity, and specific use

(8) Other factors contributing to the practical safeguarding of persons using or in contact with the equipment

(B) Installation and Use. Equipment <u>that is listed, labeled, or both</u> must be installed and used in accordance with any instructions included in the listing or labeling. ▶Figure 110–3

(C) Product Listing. Product testing, evaluation, and listing must be performed by a recognized qualified testing laboratory in accordance with standards that achieve effective safety to comply with the *NEC*.

Note: OSHA recognizes qualified electrical testing laboratories that provide product certification that meets their electrical standards.

110.4 Voltage Rating of Electrical Equipment

The circuit nominal system voltage is not permitted to be greater than the rating of the equipment. ▶Figure 110–4

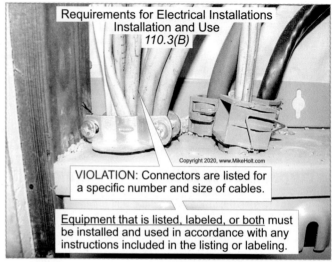

Requirements for Electrical Installations
Installation and Use
110.3(B)

VIOLATION: Connectors are listed for a specific number and size of cables.

<u>Equipment that is listed, labeled, or both</u> must be installed and used in accordance with any instructions included in the listing or labeling.

▶Figure 110–3

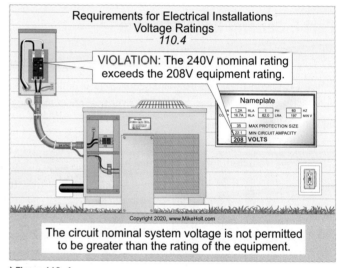

Requirements for Electrical Installations
Voltage Ratings
110.4

VIOLATION: The 240V nominal rating exceeds the 208V equipment rating.

The circuit nominal system voltage is not permitted to be greater than the rating of the equipment.

▶Figure 110–4

110.5 Conductor Material

Conductors must be copper, aluminum, or <u>copper-clad aluminum</u> unless otherwise provided in this *Code*; and when the conductor material is not specified in a rule, the sizes given in the *NEC* are based on a copper conductor. ▶Figure 110–5

110.6 Conductor Sizes

Conductor sizes are expressed in American Wire Gage (AWG) or circular mils (cmil). ▶Figure 110–6

Requirements for Electrical Installations, Conductor Material
110.5

COPPER

ALUMINUM

COPPER-CLAD ALUMINUM

Copyright 2020, www.MikeHolt.com

Conductors must be copper, aluminum, or copper-clad aluminum unless stated otherwise in the *NEC*. When conductor material is not specified, the *Code* rule is based on copper.

▶Figure 110–5

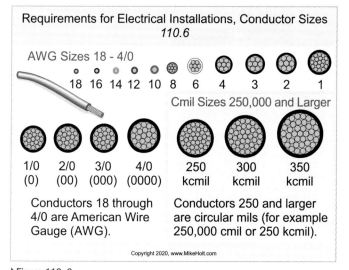

Requirements for Electrical Installations, Conductor Sizes
110.6

AWG Sizes 18 - 4/0

18 16 14 12 10 8 6 4 3 2 1

Cmil Sizes 250,000 and Larger

| 1/0 (0) | 2/0 (00) | 3/0 (000) | 4/0 (0000) | 250 kcmil | 300 kcmil | 350 kcmil |

Conductors 18 through 4/0 are American Wire Gauge (AWG).

Conductors 250 and larger are circular mils (for example 250,000 cmil or 250 kcmil).

Copyright 2020, www.MikeHolt.com

▶Figure 110–6

110.7 Wiring Integrity

Electrical installations must be free from short circuits, ground faults, or any connections to conductive metal parts unless required or permitted by the *Code*. ▶Figure 110–7

110.11 Deteriorating Agents

Electrical equipment and conductors must be suitable for the environment and the conditions for which they will be used. Consideration must also be given to the presence of corrosive gases, fumes, vapors, liquids, or other substances that can have a deteriorating effect on conductors and equipment. ▶Figure 110–15

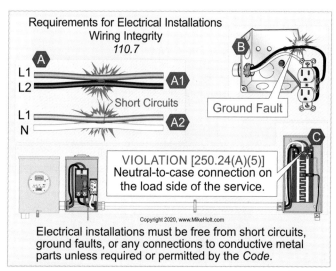

Requirements for Electrical Installations
Wiring Integrity
110.7

Short Circuits

Ground Fault

VIOLATION [250.24(A)(5)]
Neutral-to-case connection on the load side of the service.

Copyright 2020, www.MikeHolt.com

Electrical installations must be free from short circuits, ground faults, or any connections to conductive metal parts unless required or permitted by the *Code*.

▶Figure 110–7

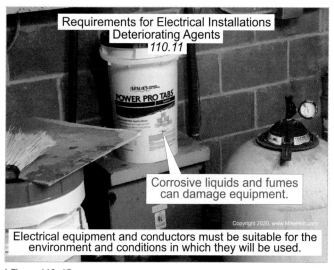

Requirements for Electrical Installations
Deteriorating Agents
110.11

Corrosive liquids and fumes can damage equipment.

Copyright 2020, www.MikeHolt.com

Electrical equipment and conductors must be suitable for the environment and conditions in which they will be used.

▶Figure 110–15

Note 1: Raceways, cable trays, cablebus, cable armor, boxes, cable sheathing, cabinets, elbows, couplings, fittings, supports, and support hardware must be suitable for the environment; see 300.6. ▶Figure 110–16

Note 2: Some cleaning and lubricating compounds contain chemicals that can cause plastic to deteriorate.

Equipment identified for indoor use must be protected against damage from the weather during construction.

Note 3: See Table 110.28 for NEMA enclosure-type designations.

Note 4: For minimum flood provisions, see the *International Building Code (IBC)* and the *International Residential Code* (IRC).

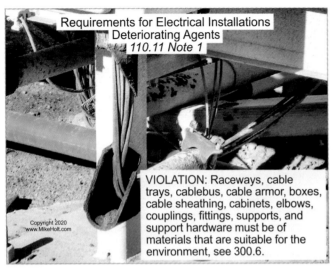

Requirements for Electrical Installations
Deteriorating Agents
110.11 Note 1

VIOLATION: Raceways, cable trays, cablebus, cable armor, boxes, cable sheathing, cabinets, elbows, couplings, fittings, supports, and support hardware must be of materials that are suitable for the environment, see 300.6.

▶Figure 110–16

110.12 Mechanical Execution of Work

Electrical equipment must be installed in a neat and workmanlike manner. ▶Figure 110–17

Requirements for Electrical Installations
Mechanical Execution of Work
110.12

Electrical equipment must be installed in a neat and workmanlike manner.

▶Figure 110–17

Author's Comment:

▶ This rule is perhaps one of the most subjective of the entire *Code* and its application is still ultimately a judgment call made by the authority having jurisdiction.

▶ The National Electrical Contractors Association (*NEC*A) created a series of *National Electrical Installation Standards* (NEIS)® that established the industry's first quality guidelines for electrical installations. These standards define a benchmark

(baseline) of quality and workmanship for installing electrical products and systems. They explain what installing electrical products and systems in a "neat and workmanlike manner" means. For more information about these standards, visit www.NECA-NEIS.org.

(A) Unused Openings. Unused openings must be closed by fittings that provide protection substantially equivalent to the wall of the equipment. ▶Figure 110–18

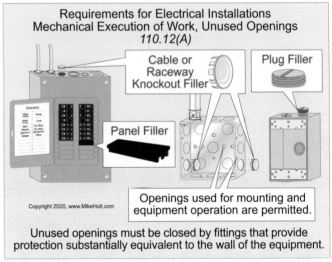

Requirements for Electrical Installations
Mechanical Execution of Work, Unused Openings
110.12(A)

Cable or Raceway Knockout Filler

Plug Filler

Panel Filler

Openings used for mounting and equipment operation are permitted.

Unused openings must be closed by fittings that provide protection substantially equivalent to the wall of the equipment.

▶Figure 110–18

(B) Integrity of Electrical Equipment. Internal parts of electrical equipment must not be damaged or contaminated by foreign material, such as paint, plaster, cleaners, and so forth. ▶Figure 110–19

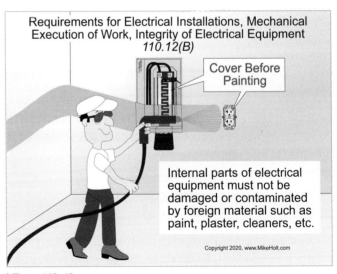

Requirements for Electrical Installations, Mechanical Execution of Work, Integrity of Electrical Equipment
110.12(B)

Cover Before Painting

Internal parts of electrical equipment must not be damaged or contaminated by foreign material such as paint, plaster, cleaners, etc.

▶Figure 110–19

▸ Precautions must be taken to provide protection from contamination of the internal parts of panelboards and receptacles during building construction. Be sure the electrical equipment is properly masked and protected before sheetrock, painting, or other phases of the project that can contaminate or cause damage begins. ▸Figure 110-20

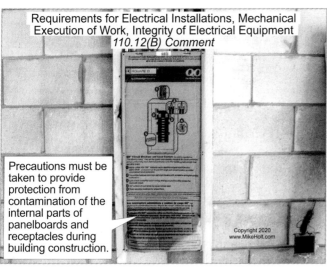

▸Figure 110-20

Electrical equipment containing damaged (such as items broken, bent, or cut) parts, or those that have been deteriorated by corrosion, chemical action, or overheating are not permitted to be installed. ▸Figure 110-21

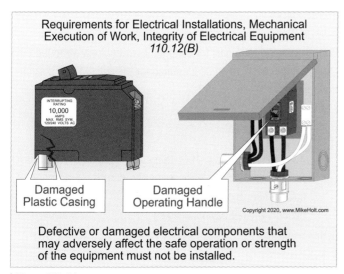

▸Figure 110-21

▸ Damaged parts include cracked insulators, arc shields not in place, overheated fuse clips, and damaged or missing switch handles or circuit-breaker handles.

(C) Cables and Conductors. Cables and conductors must be installed in a neat and workmanlike manner. ▸Figure 110-22

▸Figure 110-22

Exposed cables must be supported by the structural components of the building so they will not be damaged by normal building use. Support must be by straps, staples, hangers, cable ties, or similar fittings designed and installed in a manner that will not damage the cable. ▸Figure 110-23

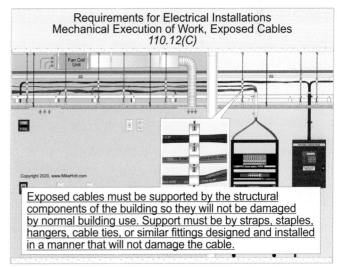

▸Figure 110-23

Note 1: Industry practices are described in ANSI/*NECA*/FOA 301, *Standard for Installing and Testing Fiber Optic Cables*, and other ANSI-approved installation standards.

Note 3: Paint, plaster, cleaners, abrasives, corrosive residues, or other contaminants can result in an undetermined alteration of optical fiber cable properties.

110.13 Mounting and Cooling of Equipment

(A) Mounting. Electrical equipment must be firmly secured to the surface on which it is mounted. ▶Figure 110–24

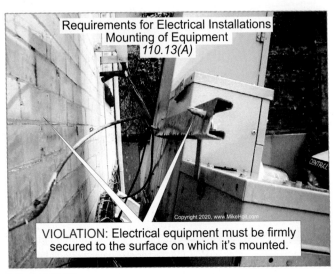

VIOLATION: Electrical equipment must be firmly secured to the surface on which it's mounted.

▶Figure 110–24

110.14 Conductor Termination and Splicing

Conductor terminal and splicing devices must be identified for the conductor material and must be properly installed and used in accordance with the manufacturer's instructions [110.3(B)]. ▶Figure 110–25

Author's Comment:

▶ Conductor terminals suitable for aluminum wire only will be marked "AL." Those acceptable for copper wire only will be marked "CU." Terminals suitable for both copper and aluminum will be marked "CU-AL" or "AL-CU." For 6 AWG and smaller, the markings can be printed on the container or on an information sheet inside the container. A "7" or "75" indicates a 75°C rated terminal, and a "9" or "90" indicates a 90°C rated terminal. If a terminal bears no marking, it can be used only with copper conductors. ▶Figure 110–26

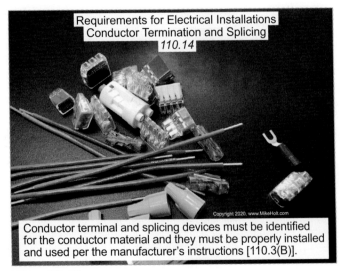

Requirements for Electrical Installations
Conductor Termination and Splicing
110.14

Conductor terminal and splicing devices must be identified for the conductor material and they must be properly installed and used per the manufacturer's instructions [110.3(B)].

▶Figure 110–25

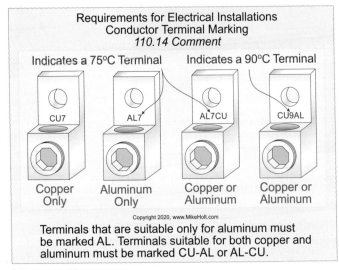

Requirements for Electrical Installations
Conductor Terminal Marking
110.14 Comment

Indicates a 75°C Terminal   Indicates a 90°C Terminal

CU7 — Copper Only
AL7 — Aluminum Only
AL7CU — Copper or Aluminum
CU9AL — Copper or Aluminum

Terminals that are suitable only for aluminum must be marked AL. Terminals suitable for both copper and aluminum must be marked CU-AL or AL-CU.

▶Figure 110–26

Connectors and terminals for conductors more finely stranded than Class B and Class C must be identified for the use of finely stranded conductors. ▶Figure 110–27

Author's Comment:

▶ According to Article 100, "Identified" means the item is recognized as suitable for a specific purpose, function, or environment by listing, labeling, or other means approved by the authority having jurisdiction.

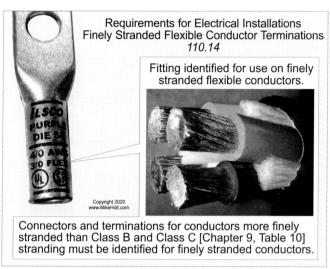

Requirements for Electrical Installations
Finely Stranded Flexible Conductor Terminations
110.14

Fitting identified for use on finely stranded flexible conductors.

Connectors and terminations for conductors more finely stranded than Class B and Class C [Chapter 9, Table 10] stranding must be identified for finely stranded conductors.

▶Figure 110–27

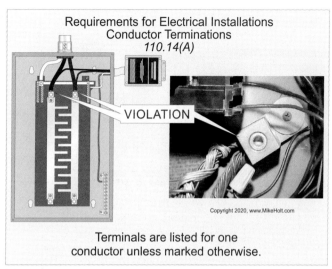

Requirements for Electrical Installations
Conductor Terminations
110.14(A)

VIOLATION

Terminals are listed for one conductor unless marked otherwise.

▶Figure 110–28

▶ Conductor terminations must comply with the manufacturer's instructions as required by 110.3(B). For example, if the instructions for the device say, "Suitable for 18-12 AWG Stranded," then only stranded conductors can be used with the terminating device. If they say, "Suitable for 18-12 AWG Solid," then only solid conductors are permitted, and if the instructions say, "Suitable for 18-12 AWG," then either solid or stranded conductors can be used with the terminating device.

Copper and Aluminum Mixed. Copper and aluminum conductors (dissimilar metals) are not permitted to contact each other in a device unless the device is listed and identified for this purpose.

Author's Comment:

▶ Few terminations are listed for mixing aluminum and copper conductors, but if they are, that will be marked on the product package or terminal device. The reason copper and aluminum should not be in contact with each other is because corrosion develops between the two different metals due to galvanic action, resulting in increased contact resistance at the splicing device. This increased resistance can cause the splice to overheat and result in a fire.

(A) Conductor Terminations. Conductor terminals must ensure a good connection without damaging the conductors.

Terminals are listed for one conductor unless marked otherwise. Terminals for more than one conductor must be identified for this purpose, either within the equipment instructions or on the terminal itself.
▶Figure 110–28

Author's Comment:

▶ Split-bolt connectors are commonly listed for only two conductors, although some are listed for three. However, it is a common industry practice to terminate as many conductors as possible within a split-bolt connector, even though this violates the *NEC*. ▶Figure 110–29

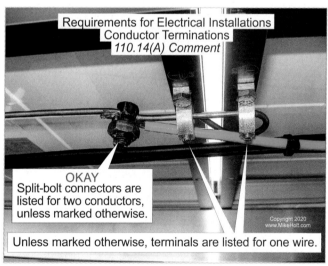

Requirements for Electrical Installations
Conductor Terminations
110.14(A) Comment

OKAY
Split-bolt connectors are listed for two conductors, unless marked otherwise.

Unless marked otherwise, terminals are listed for one wire.

▶Figure 110–29

(B) Conductor Splices. Conductors must be spliced by a splicing device that is identified for the purpose. ▶Figure 110–30

Unused circuit conductors are not required to be removed. However, to prevent an electrical hazard, the free ends of the conductors must be insulated to prevent the exposed end(s) from touching energized parts. This requirement can be met by using an insulated twist-on or push-on wire connector. ▶Figure 110–31

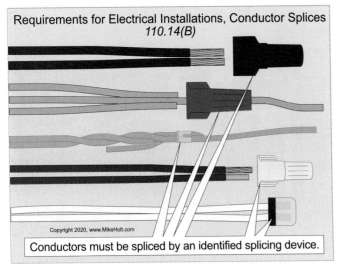

Conductors must be spliced by an identified splicing device.

▶Figure 110–30

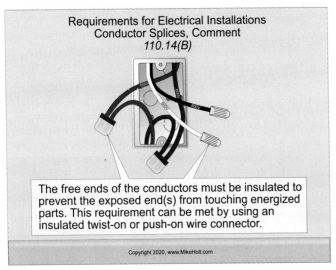

Requirements for Electrical Installations
Conductor Splices, Comment
110.14(B)

The free ends of the conductors must be insulated to prevent the exposed end(s) from touching energized parts. This requirement can be met by using an insulated twist-on or push-on wire connector.

Copyright 2020, www.MikeHolt.com

▶Figure 110–31

Author's Comment:

▸ According to Article 100, "Energized" means electrically connected to a source of voltage.

▸ Pre-twisting conductors before applying twist-on wire connectors has been a very common practice in the field for years. The question (and subsequent debate) has always been, "Is pre-twisting required?" The *NEC* does not require that practice and, in fact, Ideal® made a statement about their Wing-Nut® twist-on connectors which said, "Pre-twisting is acceptable, but not required." Always follow the manufacturer's instructions and there will be no question [110.3(B)].

▸ Reusing twist-on connectors seems to be another point of contention in the field. Should they be reused? Some say

that they just never seem quite the same once they have been used, while others say they reuse them all the time. Defer to the manufacturer's instructions; Ideal® and 3M® both indicate in their information that it is perfectly fine to reuse their twist-on connectors. ▶Figure 110–32

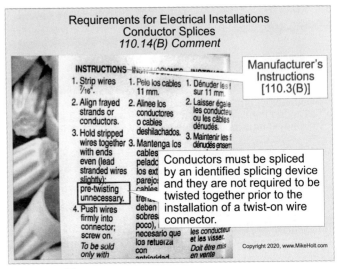

Requirements for Electrical Installations
Conductor Splices
110.14(B) Comment

Manufacturer's Instructions [110.3(B)]

Conductors must be spliced by an identified splicing device and they are not required to be twisted together prior to the installation of a twist-on wire connector.

▶Figure 110–32

Underground Splices, Single Conductors. Single direct burial types UF or USE conductors can be spliced underground with a device listed for direct burial [300.5(E) and 300.15(G)]. ▶Figure 110–33

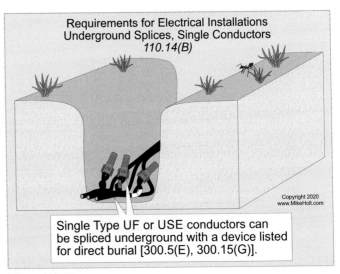

Requirements for Electrical Installations
Underground Splices, Single Conductors
110.14(B)

Single Type UF or USE conductors can be spliced underground with a device listed for direct burial [300.5(E), 300.15(G)].

▶Figure 110–33

Underground Splices, Multiconductor Cable. The individual conductors of multiconductor UF or USE cable can be spliced underground with a listed splice kit that encapsulates the conductors and cable jacket.

Author's Comment:

▶ Electrical connection failures are the cause of many equipment and building fires. Improper terminations, poor workmanship, not following the manufacturer's instructions, and improper torqueing can all cause poor electrical connections. Improper electrical terminations can damage and melt conductor insulation resulting in short circuits and ground faults.

(C) Conductor Size to Terminal Temperature Rating. Conductors are sized in accordance with 110.14(C)(1) and (2).

(1) Equipment Terminals. Unless equipment is listed and marked otherwise, conductors are sized in accordance with (a) or (b) as follows:

(a) Equipment Rated 100A or Less

(2) Conductors with an insulation temperature rating greater than 60°C are permitted, but the conductor must be sized in accordance with the ampacities in the 60°C temperature column of Table 310.16. ▶Figure 110–34

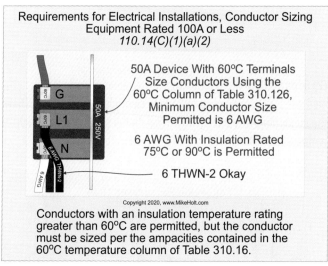

Requirements for Electrical Installations, Conductor Sizing
Equipment Rated 100A or Less
110.14(C)(1)(a)(2)

50A Device With 60°C Terminals Size Conductors Using the 60°C Column of Table 310.126, Minimum Conductor Size Permitted is 6 AWG

6 AWG With Insulation Rated 75°C or 90°C is Permitted

6 THWN-2 Okay

Copyright 2020, www.MikeHolt.com

Conductors with an insulation temperature rating greater than 60°C are permitted, but the conductor must be sized per the ampacities contained in the 60°C temperature column of Table 310.16.

▶Figure 110–34

▶ **Example**

Question: *According to Table 310.16, what size THWN-2 conductor is required for a circuit rated 50A?*

(a) 10 AWG   (b) 8 AWG   (c) 6 AWG   (d) 4 AWG

Answer: *(c) 6 AWG rated 55A at 60°C [110.14(C)(1)(a)(2) and Table 310.16]*

(3) Conductors terminating on terminals rated 75°C can be sized in accordance with the ampacities in the 75°C temperature column of Table 310.16. ▶Figure 110–35

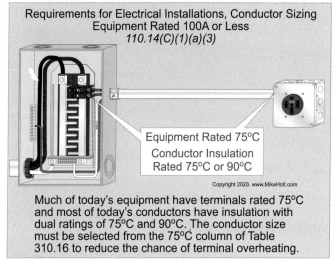

Requirements for Electrical Installations, Conductor Sizing
Equipment Rated 100A or Less
110.14(C)(1)(a)(3)

Equipment Rated 75°C
Conductor Insulation Rated 75°C or 90°C

Copyright 2020, www.MikeHolt.com

Much of today's equipment have terminals rated 75°C and most of today's conductors have insulation with dual ratings of 75°C and 90°C. The conductor size must be selected from the 75°C column of Table 310.16 to reduce the chance of terminal overheating.

▶Figure 110–35

▶ **Example**

Question: *According to Table 310.16, what size THHN conductor is required for a 50A circuit where the equipment is listed for use at 75°C?* ▶Figure 110–36

(a) 10 AWG   (b) 8 AWG   (c) 6 AWG   (d) 4 AWG

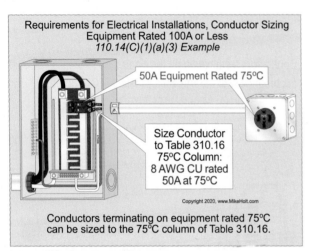

Requirements for Electrical Installations, Conductor Sizing
Equipment Rated 100A or Less
110.14(C)(1)(a)(3) Example

50A Equipment Rated 75°C

Size Conductor to Table 310.16 75°C Column: 8 AWG CU rated 50A at 75°C

Copyright 2020, www.MikeHolt.com

Conductors terminating on equipment rated 75°C can be sized to the 75°C column of Table 310.16.

▶Figure 110–36

Answer: *(b) 8 AWG rated 50A at 75°C [110.14(C)(1)(a)(3) and Table 310.16]*

(b) Equipment Rated Over 100A

(2) Conductors with an insulation temperature rating greater than 75°C are permitted, but the conductor must be sized in accordance with the ampacities in the 75°C temperature column of Table 310.16. ▶Figure 110–37

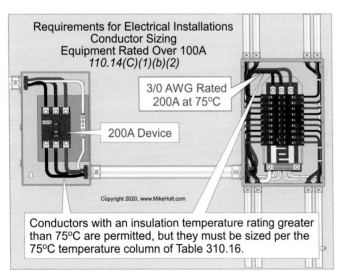

Requirements for Electrical Installations
Conductor Sizing
Equipment Rated Over 100A
110.14(C)(1)(b)(2)

3/0 AWG Rated 200A at 75°C

200A Device

Copyright 2020, www.MikeHolt.com

Conductors with an insulation temperature rating greater than 75°C are permitted, but they must be sized per the 75°C temperature column of Table 310.16.

▶Figure 110–37

▶ **Example**

Question: *According to Table 310.16, what size THHN conductor is required to supply a 150A feeder?* ▶Figure 110–38

(a) 1/0 AWG   (b) 2/0 AWG   (c) 3/0 AWG   (d) 4/0 AWG

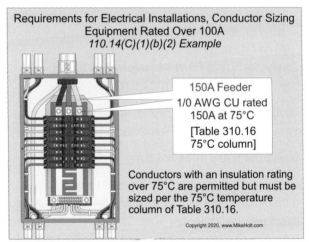

Requirements for Electrical Installations, Conductor Sizing
Equipment Rated Over 100A
110.14(C)(1)(b)(2) Example

150A Feeder
1/0 AWG CU rated 150A at 75°C
[Table 310.16 75°C column]

Conductors with an insulation rating over 75°C are permitted but must be sized per the 75°C temperature column of Table 310.16.

Copyright 2020, www.MikeHolt.com

▶Figure 110–38

Answer: *(a) 1/0 AWG rated 150A at 75°C [110.14(C)(1)(b)(2) and Table 310.16]*

(2) Separate Connector. Splicing and terminating devices with terminals rated 90°C and not connected to electrical equipment can have the conductors sized in accordance with the ampacities in the 90°C temperature column of Table 310.16. ▶Figure 110–39

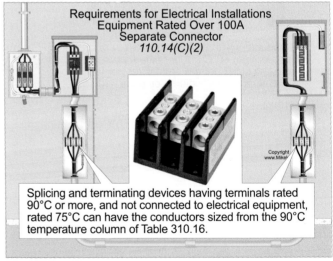

Requirements for Electrical Installations
Equipment Rated Over 100A
Separate Connector
110.14(C)(2)

Copyright www.MikeHolt...

Splicing and terminating devices having terminals rated 90°C or more, and not connected to electrical equipment, rated 75°C can have the conductors sized from the 90°C temperature column of Table 310.16.

▶Figure 110–39

▶ **Example 1**

Question: *According to Table 310.16, what size aluminum conductor can be used to interconnect busbars protected by a 200A overcurrent protective device if all terminals are rated 90°C?*

(a) 1/0 AWG   (b) 2/0 AWG   (c) 3/0 AWG   (d) 4/0 AWG

Answer: *(d) 4/0 AWG aluminum rated 205A at 90°C [Table 310.16]*

▶ **Example 2**

Question: *What size XHHW copper conductor can be used to interconnect 90°C rated power distribution blocks protected by a 400A overcurrent protective device serving a 320A continuous load?* ▶Figure 110–40

(a) 250 kcmil   (b) 300 kcmil   (c) 350 kcmil   (d) 400 kcmil

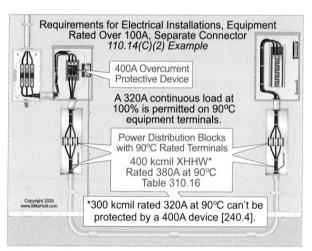

▶Figure 110–40

Note: *350 kcmil is rated 350A at 90°C; however, 350 kcmil cannot be used because it cannot be protected by a 400A overcurrent protective device [240.4].*

Answer: *(d) 400 kcmil rated 380A at 90°C [Table 310.16]*

▶ **Example 3**

Question: *What size XHHW copper conductor can be used to interconnect 90°C rated power distribution blocks protected by a 400A overcurrent protective device serving a 375A continuous load?* ▶Figure 110–41

(a) 250 kcmil   (b) 300 kcmil   (c) 350 kcmil   (d) 400 kcmil

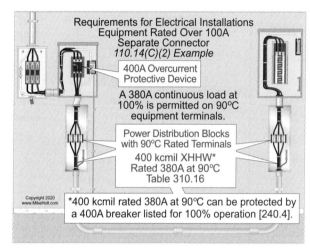

▶Figure 110–41

Answer: *(d) 400 kcmil rated 380A at 90°C [Table 310.16]*

	Size							Size
	60°C (140°F)	**75°C (167°F)**	**90°C (194°F)**	**60°C (140°F)**	**75°C (167°F)**	**90°C (194°F)**		
	TW UF	RHW THHW THW THWN XHHW USE	RHH RHW-2 THHN THHW THW-2 THWN-2 USE-2 XHHW XHHW-2	TW UF	THW THWN XHHW	THHN THW-2 THWN-2 THHW XHHW XHHW-2		
AWG kcmil		Copper			Aluminum/Copper–Clad Aluminum			**AWG kcmil**
14	15	20	25					14
12	20	25	30	15	20	25		12
10	30	35	40	25	30	35		10
8	40	50	55	35	40	45		8
6	55	65	75	40	50	55		6
4	70	85	95	55	65	75		4
3	85	100	115	65	75	85		3
2	95	115	130	75	90	100		2
1	110	130	145	85	100	115		1
1/0	125	150	170	100	120	135		1/0
2/0	145	175	195	115	135	150		2/0
3/0	165	200	225	130	155	175		3/0
4/0	195	230	260	150	180	205		4/0
250	215	255	290	170	205	230		250
300	240	285	320	195	230	260		300
350	260	310	350	210	250	280		350
400	280	335	380	225	270	305		400
500	320	380	430	260	310	350		500

Table 310.16 Ampacities of Insulated Conductors Based on Not More Than Three Current-Carrying Conductors and Ambient Temperature of 30°C (86°F)

(D) Terminal Connection Torque. Tightening torque values for terminal connections must be as indicated on equipment or installation instructions. An approved means (a torque tool) must be used to achieve the indicated torque value. ▶Figure 110–42 and ▶Figure 110–43

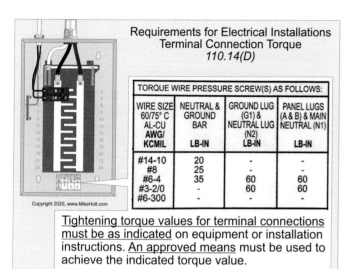

Requirements for Electrical Installations
Terminal Connection Torque
110.14(D)

TORQUE WIRE PRESSURE SCREW(S) AS FOLLOWS:

WIRE SIZE 60/75° C AL-CU AWG/ KCMIL	NEUTRAL & GROUND BAR LB-IN	GROUND LUG (G1) & NEUTRAL LUG (N2) LB-IN	PANEL LUGS (A & B) & MAIN NEUTRAL (N1) LB-IN
#14-10	20	-	-
#8	25	-	-
#6-4	35	60	60
#3-2/0	-	60	60
#6-300	-	-	-

Copyright 2020, www.MikeHolt.com

Tightening torque values for terminal connections must be as indicated on equipment or installation instructions. An approved means must be used to achieve the indicated torque value.

▶Figure 110–42

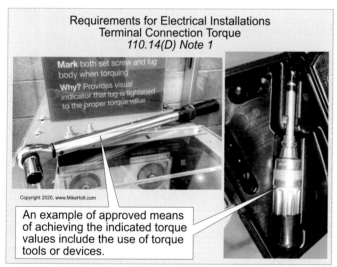

Requirements for Electrical Installations
Terminal Connection Torque
110.14(D) Note 1

Mark both set screw and lug body when torquing
Why? Provides visual indicator that lug is tightened to the proper torque value

Copyright 2020, www.MikeHolt.com

An example of approved means of achieving the indicated torque values include the use of torque tools or devices.

▶Figure 110–43

Author's Comment:

▶ Conductors must terminate in devices that have been properly tightened in accordance with the manufacturer's torque specifications included with equipment instructions. Failure to torque terminals properly can result in excessive heating of terminals or splicing devices due to a loose connection. A loose connection can also lead to arcing which increases the heating effect and may also lead to a short circuit or

ground fault. Any of these can result in a fire or other failure, including an arc flash event. Improper torqueing is also a violation of 110.3(B), which requires all equipment to be installed in accordance with listing or labeling instructions.

Note 1: Examples of approved means of achieving the indicated torque values include the use of torque tools or devices such as shear bolts or breakaway-style devices with visual indicators that demonstrate the proper torque has been applied.

Note 2: The equipment manufacturer can be contacted if numeric torque values are not indicated on the equipment, or if the installation instructions are not available. Annex I of UL Standard 486A-486B, *Standard for Safety-Wire Connectors,* provides torque values in the absence of manufacturer's recommendations.

Note 3: Additional information for torqueing threaded connections and terminations can be found in Section 8.11 of NFPA 70B, *Recommended Practice for Electrical Equipment Maintenance.*

110.15 High-Leg Conductor Identification

On a 4-wire, delta-connected, three-phase system (where the midpoint of one phase winding of the secondary is grounded) the conductor with the resulting 208V to ground (high-leg) must be durably and permanently marked by an outer finish (insulation) that is orange in color or other effective means. Such identification must be placed at each point where a connection is made if the neutral conductor is present [230.56]. ▶Figure 110–44

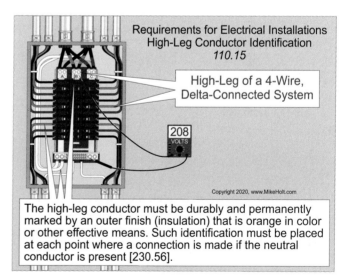

Requirements for Electrical Installations
High-Leg Conductor Identification
110.15

High-Leg of a 4-Wire, Delta-Connected System

208 VOLTS

Copyright 2020, www.MikeHolt.com

The high-leg conductor must be durably and permanently marked by an outer finish (insulation) that is orange in color or other effective means. Such identification must be placed at each point where a connection is made if the neutral conductor is present [230.56].

▶Figure 110–44

110.16 Arc Flash Hazard Warning

(A) Arc Flash Hazard Warning Label. In other than dwelling units, switchboards, switchgear, panelboards, industrial control panels, meter socket enclosures, and motor control centers must be marked to warn qualified persons of the danger associated with an arc flash resulting from a short circuit or ground fault. The arc flash hazard warning label must be permanently affixed, have sufficient durability to withstand the environment involved [110.21(B)], and be clearly visible to qualified persons before they examine, adjust, service, or perform maintenance on the equipment. ▸Figure 110–45

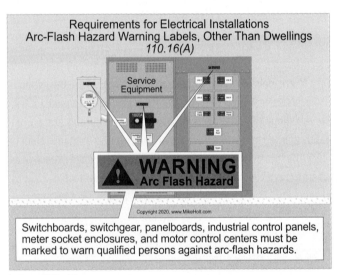

Requirements for Electrical Installations
Arc-Flash Hazard Warning Labels, Other Than Dwellings
110.16(A)

Service Equipment

⚠ WARNING
Arc Flash Hazard

Copyright 2020, www.MikeHolt.com

Switchboards, switchgear, panelboards, industrial control panels, meter socket enclosures, and motor control centers must be marked to warn qualified persons against arc-flash hazards.

▸Figure 110–45

▸ Examples of this safety training include (but are not limited to) training in the use of special precautionary techniques, personal protective equipment (PPE), insulating and shielding materials, and in the use of insulated tools and test equipment when working on or near exposed conductors or circuit parts that can become energized.

▸ In many parts of the United States, electricians, electrical contractors, electrical inspectors, and electrical engineers must complete from 6 to 24 hours of *NEC* review each year as a requirement to maintain licensing. This does not necessarily make one qualified to deal with the specific hazards involved with electrical systems.

▸ This rule is intended to warn qualified persons who work on energized electrical systems that an arc flash hazard exists and to the level of danger present. They will then be able to select the necessary personal protective equipment (PPE) in accordance with industry accepted safe work practice standards. ▸Figure 110–46

Requirements for Electrical Installations
Arc-Flash Hazard Warning
110.16(A) Comment

Copyright 2020
www.MikeHolt.com

This rule is intended to warn qualified persons that an arc flash warning exists so they'll select proper personal protective equipment (PPE) in accordance with industry accepted safe work practice standards.

▸Figure 110–46

(B) Service Disconnect. In addition to the requirements in 110.16(A), a service disconnect rated 1,200A or more must have a field or factory installed label containing the following details and have sufficient durability to withstand the environment: ▸Figure 110–47

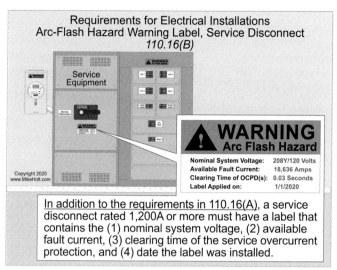

▶Figure 110–47

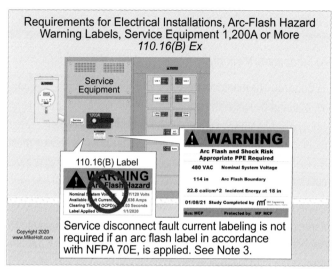

▶Figure 110–48

(1) Nominal system voltage

(2) Available fault current at the line-side of the service overcurrent protective device

(3) Clearing time of the service overcurrent protective device

(4) Date the label was installed

Author's Comment:

▶ Determining the available fault current on the line side of equipment terminals requires you to know the available fault current (provided by the electric utility), the conductor material, the length of the conductors, and the wiring method used to install the conductors. With this information, you can use an app or computer software to determine the available fault current at the line terminals.

Ex: Service disconnect fault current labeling is not required if an arc flash label in accordance with NFPA 70E, Standard for Electrical Safety in the Workplace, is applied. See Note 3. ▶Figure 110–48

Note 1: NFPA 70E, *Standard for Electrical Safety in the Workplace,* provides guidance in determining the severity of potential exposure, planning safe work practices, arc flash labeling, and selecting personal protective equipment. ▶Figure 110–49

▶Figure 110–49

Note 3: NFPA 70E, *Standard for Electrical Safety in the Workplace* provides specific criteria for developing arc flash labels such as nominal system voltage, incident energy levels, arc flash boundaries, and selecting personal protective equipment.

Author's Comment:

▶ The information required by 110.16(B)(1), (2), and (3) is necessary in order to determine the incident energy and arc flash boundary distance by using of an app or computer software to ensure the label complies with NFPA 70E to increase safety during future work on service equipment.

110.21 Markings

(A) Equipment Markings

(1) General. The manufacturer's name, trademark, or other descriptive marking by which the organization responsible for the product can be identified must be placed on all electrical equipment. Other markings indicating voltage, current, wattage, or other ratings must be provided as specified elsewhere in this *Code*. The marking or label must be of sufficient durability to withstand the environment involved.

(2) Reconditioned Equipment. Reconditioned equipment must be marked with the name, trademark, or other descriptive marking by which the organization responsible for its reconditioning can be identified, along with the date of the reconditioning.

Reconditioned equipment must be identified as "reconditioned" and the original listing mark removed. Approval of the reconditioned equipment must not be based solely on the equipment's original listing.

Ex: In industrial occupancies, where conditions of maintenance and supervision ensure that only qualified persons service the equipment, the markings indicated in 110.21(A)(2) are not required for equipment that is reconditioned by the owner or operator as part of a regular equipment maintenance program.

Note 1: Industry standards are available for the application of reconditioned and refurbished equipment.

Note 2: The term "reconditioned" may be interchangeable with terms such as "rebuilt," "refurbished," or "remanufactured."

Note 3: The original listing mark may include the mark of the certifying body and not the entire equipment label.

(B) Field-Applied Hazard Markings. Where caution, warning, or danger labels are required, the labels must meet the following requirements:

(1) The markings must warn of the hazards using effective words, colors, symbols, or a combination of the three. ▶Figure 110–50

Note: ANSI Z535.4, *Product Safety Signs and Labels,* provides guidelines for the design and durability of signs and labels.

(2) The label cannot be handwritten and must be permanently affixed to the equipment. ▶Figure 110–51

Ex: Labels containing information that is likely to change can be handwritten, if it is legible.

(3) The marking must be of sufficient durability to withstand the environment involved.

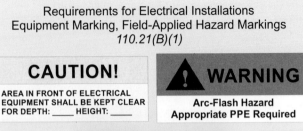

Requirements for Electrical Installations
Equipment Marking, Field-Applied Hazard Markings
110.21(B)(1)

CAUTION!
AREA IN FRONT OF ELECTRICAL EQUIPMENT SHALL BE KEPT CLEAR FOR DEPTH: _____ HEIGHT: _____

⚠ **WARNING**
Arc-Flash Hazard
Appropriate PPE Required

⚡ **DANGER**
Electrical Hazard
Authorized Personel Only

Copyright 2020
www.MikeHolt.com

The markings must warn of the hazards using effective words, colors, symbols, or a combination of the three.

▶Figure 110–50

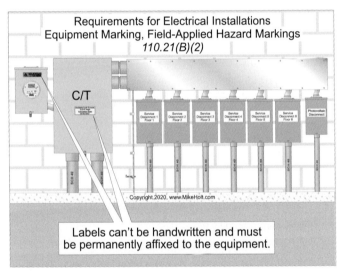

Requirements for Electrical Installations
Equipment Marking, Field-Applied Hazard Markings
110.21(B)(2)

C/T

Copyright 2020, www.MikeHolt.com

Labels can't be handwritten and must be permanently affixed to the equipment.

▶Figure 110–51

110.22 Identification of Disconnecting Means

(A) General. Each disconnect must be legibly marked to indicate its purpose unless located and arranged so the purpose is evident. In other than one- or two-family dwellings, the marking must include the identification of the circuit source that supplies the disconnecting means. The marking must be of sufficient durability to withstand the environment involved. ▶Figure 110–52

Author's Comment:

▶ See 408.4 for additional requirements for identification markings on circuit directories for switchboards and panelboards.

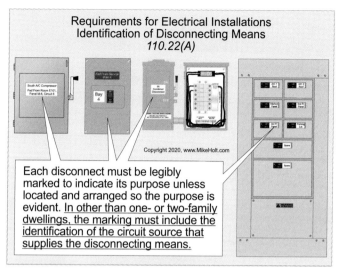

▶Figure 110–52

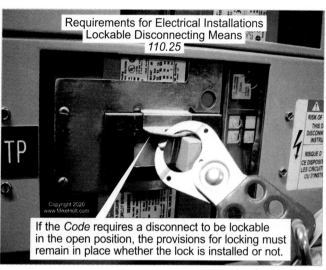

▶Figure 110–54

(C) Tested Series Combination Systems. Tested series-rated installations must be legibly field marked to indicate the equipment has been applied with a series combination rating in accordance with 240.86(B), be permanently affixed, and have sufficient durability to withstand the environment involved in accordance with 110.21(B) and state:

> **CAUTION—SERIES COMBINATION SYSTEM**
> **RATED _____ AMPERES. IDENTIFIED**
> **REPLACEMENT COMPONENTS REQUIRED**

110.25 Lockable Disconnecting Means

If the *Code* requires a disconnect to be lockable in the open position, the provisions for locking must remain in place whether the lock is installed or not. ▶Figure 110–54

Part II. 1,000V, Nominal, or Less

110.26 Spaces About Electrical Equipment

For the purposes of safe operation and maintenance of equipment, access and working space must be provided around all electrical equipment. ▶Figure 110–55

▶Figure 110–55

Author's Comment:

▶ Spaces around electrical equipment (width, depth, and height) consist of working space for worker protection [110.26(A)] and dedicated space to provide access to, and protection of, equipment [110.26(E)].

(A) Working Space. Equipment that may need examination, adjustment, servicing, or maintenance while energized must have working space provided in accordance with 110.26(A)(1), (2), (3), and (4):

Author's Comment:

▶ The phrase "while energized" is the root of many debates. As always, check with the authority having jurisdiction to see what equipment he or she believes needs a clear working space.

Note: NFPA 70E, *Standard for Electrical Safety in the Workplace*, provides guidance in determining the severity of potential exposure, planning safe work practices including establishing an electrically safe work condition, arc flash labeling, and selecting personal protective equipment.

(1) Depth of Working Space. The depth of working space, which is measured from the enclosure front, cannot be less than the distances contained in Table 110.26(A)(1), which are dependent on voltage and three different conditions. ▶Figure 110–56

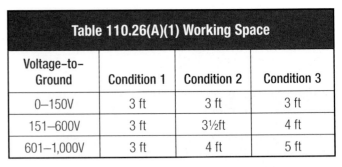

Table 110.26(A)(1) Working Space			
Voltage-to-Ground	Condition 1	Condition 2	Condition 3
0–150V	3 ft	3 ft	3 ft
151–600V	3 ft	3½ft	4 ft
601–1,000V	3 ft	4 ft	5 ft

▶Figure 110–58, ▶Figure 110–59, and ▶Figure 110–60

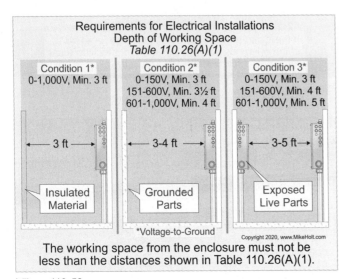

▶Figure 110–56

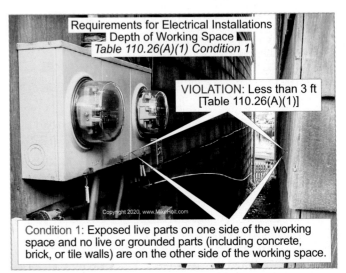

▶Figure 110–58

Author's Comment:

▶ Depth of working space must be measured from the enclosure front, not the live parts. ▶Figure 110–57

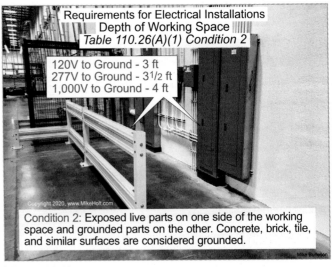

Condition 2: Exposed live parts on one side of the working space and grounded parts on the other. Concrete, brick, tile, and similar surfaces are considered grounded.

▶Figure 110–59

Author's Comment:

▶ If the working space is a platform, it must be sized to the working space requirements. ▶Figure 110–61

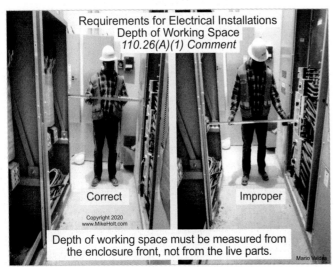

▶Figure 110–57

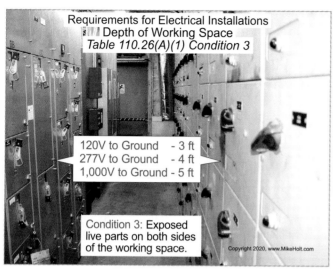

Requirements for Electrical Installations
Depth of Working Space
Table 110.26(A)(1) Condition 3

120V to Ground - 3 ft
277V to Ground - 4 ft
1,000V to Ground - 5 ft

Condition 3: Exposed
live parts on both sides
of the working space.

Copyright 2020, www.MikeHolt.com

▶Figure 110–60

Requirements for Electrical Installations
Depth of Working Space
110.26(A)(1) Comment

VIOLATION: If the working space is a platform, it
must be sized to the working space requirements.
In this case, the working platform is not 36 in.
deep per Table 110.26(A)(1) Condition 1.

Copyright 2020, www.MikeHolt.com

▶Figure 110–61

(a) Rear and Sides of Dead-Front Equipment. Working space is not required at the back or sides of equipment where all connections and all renewable, adjustable, or serviceable parts are accessible from the front. ▶Figure 110–62

Author's Comment:

▸ Sections of equipment that require rear or side access to make field connections must be marked by the manufacturer on the front of the equipment. See 408.18(C).

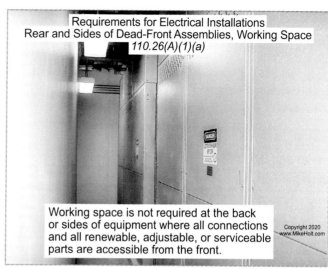

Requirements for Electrical Installations
Rear and Sides of Dead-Front Assemblies, Working Space
110.26(A)(1)(a)

Working space is not required at the back
or sides of equipment where all connections
and all renewable, adjustable, or serviceable
parts are accessible from the front.

Copyright 2020
www.MikeHolt.com

▶Figure 110–62

(c) Existing Buildings. If electrical equipment is being replaced, Condition 2 working space is permitted between dead-front switchboards, switchgear, panelboards, or motor control centers located across the aisle from each other where conditions of maintenance and supervision ensure that written procedures have been adopted to prohibit equipment on both sides of the aisle from being open at the same time, and only authorized, qualified persons will service the installation.

(2) Width of Working Space. The width of the working space must be a minimum of 30 in., but in no case less than the width of the equipment. ▶Figure 110–63

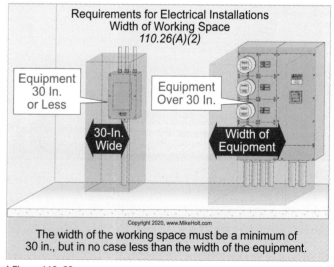

Requirements for Electrical Installations
Width of Working Space
110.26(A)(2)

Equipment
30 In.
or Less

Equipment
Over 30 In.

30-In.
Wide

Width of
Equipment

Copyright 2020, www.MikeHolt.com

The width of the working space must be a minimum of
30 in., but in no case less than the width of the equipment.

▶Figure 110–63

Author's Comment:

▶ The width of the working space can be measured from left-to-right, from right-to-left, or simply centered on the equipment and can overlap the working space for other electrical equipment. ▶Figure 110–64 and ▶Figure 110–65

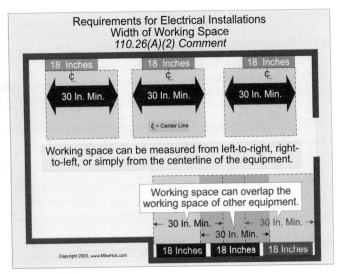

▶Figure 110–64

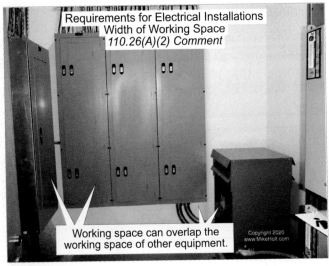

▶Figure 110–65

The working space must be of sufficient width, depth, and height to permit equipment doors to open at least 90 degrees. ▶Figure 110–66

(3) Height of Working Space. The height of the working space must be clear and extend from the grade, floor, or platform to a height of 6½ ft or the height of the equipment. ▶Figure 110–67

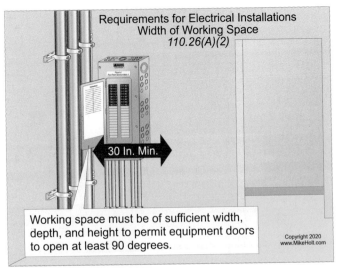

▶Figure 110–66

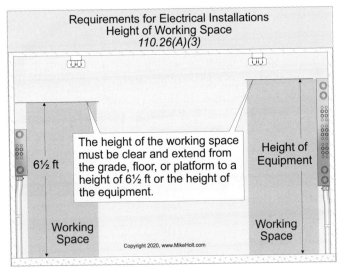

▶Figure 110–67

Other equipment such as raceways, cables, wireways, transformers, or support structures (such as concrete pads) are permitted to extend not more than 6 in. beyond the front of the electrical equipment. ▶Figure 110–68 and ▶Figure 110–69

Ex 2: The minimum height of working space does not apply to a service disconnect or panelboards rated 200A or less located in an existing dwelling unit.

Ex 3: Meters are permitted in the working space.

(4) Limited Access. Where equipment is likely to require examination, adjustment, servicing, or maintenance while energized is located above a suspended ceiling or crawl space, all the following conditions apply:

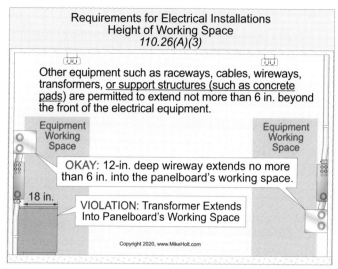

▶Figure 110–68

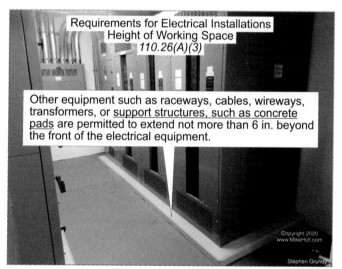

▶Figure 110–69

(1) Equipment installed above a suspended ceiling must have an access opening not smaller than 22 in. × 22 in., and equipment installed in a crawl space must have an accessible opening not smaller than 22 in. × 30 in.

(2) The width of the working space must be a minimum of 30 in., but in no case less than the width of the equipment.

(3) The working space must permit equipment doors to open 90 degrees.

(4) The working space in front of equipment must comply with the depth requirements of Table 110.26(A)(1). Horizontal ceiling structural members are permitted in this space.

(B) Clear Working Space. The working space required by this section must always be clear; therefore, this space is not permitted for storage. ▶Figure 110–70

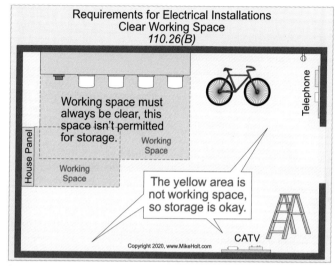

▶Figure 110–70

Caution

⚠ It is very dangerous to service energized parts in the first place, and unacceptable to be subjected to additional dangers by working around bicycles, boxes, crates, appliances, and other impediments.

When live parts are exposed for inspection or servicing, the working space (if in a passageway or open space) must be suitably guarded.

Author's Comment:

▶ When working in a passageway, the working space should be guarded from use by occupants. When working on electrical equipment in a passageway one must be mindful of a fire alarm. If one occurs, many people will need to be evacuated and will be congregating and moving through the area.

▶ Signaling and communications equipment are not permitted to be installed in a manner that encroaches on the working space of the electrical equipment. ▶Figure 110–71

(C) Access to and Egress from Working Space

(1) Minimum Required. At least one entrance large enough to give access to and egress from the working space must be provided.

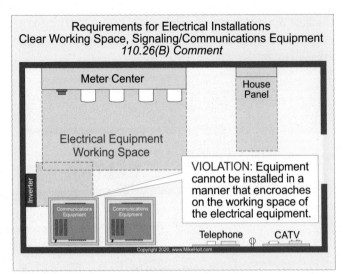

Author's Comment:

▸ Check to see what the authority having jurisdiction considers "large enough." Building *codes* contain minimum dimensions for doors and openings for personnel travel.

(2) Large Equipment. For large equipment containing overcurrent, switching, or control devices, an entrance to and egress from the required working space not less than 24 in. wide and 6½ ft high is required at each end of the working space. This requirement applies for either of the following conditions:

(1) Where equipment is over 6 ft wide rated 1,200A or more ▶Figure 110–72

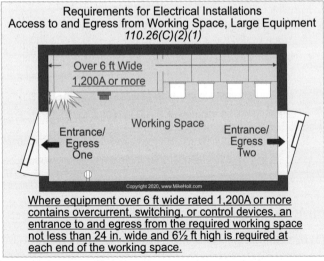

Where equipment over 6 ft wide rated 1,200A or more contains overcurrent, switching, or control devices, an entrance to and egress from the required working space not less than 24 in. wide and 6½ ft high is required at each end of the working space.

▶Figure 110–72

(2) Where the service disconnecting means installed in accordance with 230.71 has a combined rating of 1,200A or more and is over 6 ft wide ▶Figure 110–73

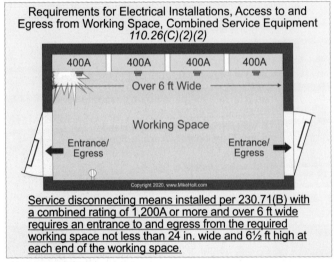

Service disconnecting means installed per 230.71(B) with a combined rating of 1,200A or more and over 6 ft wide requires an entrance to and egress from the required working space not less than 24 in. wide and 6½ ft high at each end of the working space.

▶Figure 110–73

Open equipment doors must not impede the entry to or egress from the working space.

A single entrance for access to and egress from the required working space is permitted where either of the following conditions are met:

(a) Unobstructed Egress. Where the location permits a continuous and unobstructed way of egress travel. ▶Figure 110–74

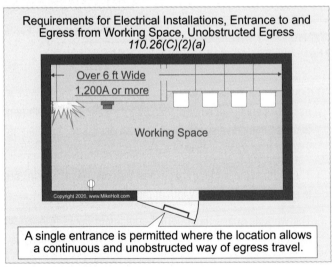

A single entrance is permitted where the location allows a continuous and unobstructed way of egress travel.

▶Figure 110–74

(b) Double Working Space. Where the required working space depth is doubled and the equipment is located so the edge of the entrance is no closer than the required working space distance. ▶Figure 110–75

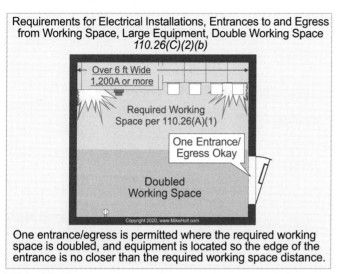

One entrance/egress is permitted where the required working space is doubled, and equipment is located so the edge of the entrance is no closer than the required working space distance.

▶Figure 110-75

(3) Fire Exit Hardware on Personnel Doors. Where equipment rated 800A or more contains overcurrent, switching, or control devices is installed and there is a personnel door(s) intended for entrance to and egress from the working space less than 25 ft from the nearest edge of the working space, the door(s) are required to open in the direction of egress and be equipped with listed panic <u>or listed fire exit hardware</u>. ▶Figure 110-76

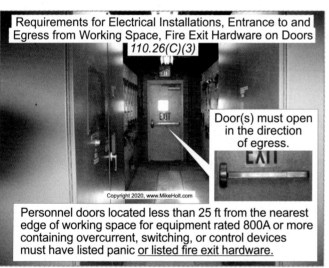

Personnel doors located less than 25 ft from the nearest edge of working space for equipment rated 800A or more containing overcurrent, switching, or control devices must have listed panic <u>or listed fire exit hardware.</u>

▶Figure 110-76

Author's Comment:

▶ History has shown that electricians who suffer burns on their hands in electrical arc flash or arc blast events often cannot open doors equipped with knobs that must be turned or doors that must be pulled open.

▶ Since this requirement is in the *NEC*, electrical contractors are responsible for ensuring panic hardware is installed where required. Some are offended at being held liable for nonelectrical responsibilities, but this rule is designed to save the lives of electricians. For this and other reasons, many construction professionals routinely hold "pre-construction" or "pre-con" meetings to review potential opportunities for miscommunication—before the work begins.

(D) Illumination. Illumination is required for all working spaces about service equipment, switchboards, switchgear, panelboards, or motor control centers installed indoors. Control by automatic means is not permitted <u>to control all illumination within the working space</u>. ▶Figure 110-77 and ▶Figure 110-78

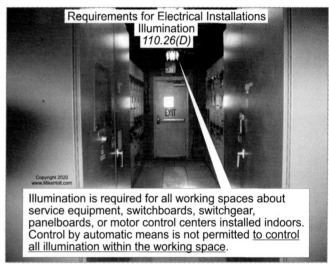

Illumination is required for all working spaces about service equipment, switchboards, switchgear, panelboards, or motor control centers installed indoors. Control by automatic means is not permitted <u>to control all illumination within the working space</u>.

▶Figure 110-77

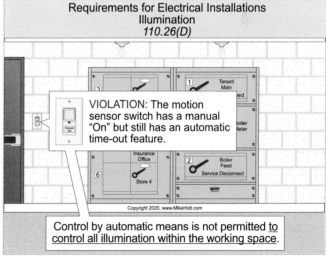

Control by automatic means is not permitted <u>to control all illumination within the working space</u>.

▶Figure 110-78

Additional lighting outlets are not required where the working space is illuminated by an adjacent light source, or as permitted by 210.70(A)(1) Ex 1 for switched receptacles.

(E) Dedicated Electrical Equipment Space. Switchboards and panelboards must have dedicated equipment space and be protected from damage that could result from condensation, leaks, breaks in the foreign systems, and vehicular traffic as follows:

(1) Indoors. Switchboards and panelboards installed indoors must comply with the following:

(a) Equipment Space. The footprint space (width and depth of the equipment) extending from the floor to a height of 6 ft above the equipment or to the structural ceiling, whichever is lower, must be dedicated for electrical equipment. ▶Figure 110–79

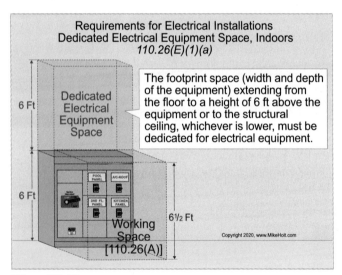

▶Figure 110–79

No piping, ducts, or other equipment foreign to the electrical system can be installed in this dedicated electrical equipment space. ▶Figure 110–80

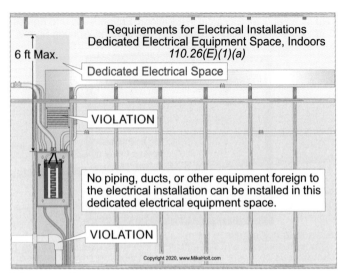

▶Figure 110–80

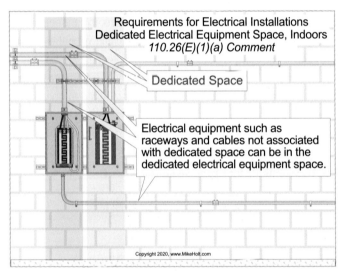

▶Figure 110–81

Ex: Suspended ceilings with removable panels can be within the dedicated space [110.26(E)(1)(d)].

(b) Foreign Systems. Foreign systems can be located above the dedicated space if protection is installed to prevent damage to the electrical equipment from condensation, leaks, or breaks in the foreign systems. Such protection can be as simple as a drip-pan. ▶Figure 110–82

(c) Sprinkler Protection. Sprinkler protection piping is not permitted in the dedicated space, but the *NEC* does not prohibit sprinklers from spraying water on electrical equipment.

(d) Suspended Ceilings. A dropped, suspended, or similar ceiling is not considered a structural ceiling. ▶Figure 110–83

(2) Outdoor. Outdoor installations for switchboards and panelboard must comply with the following:

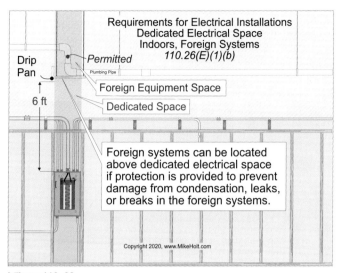

▶Figure 110–82

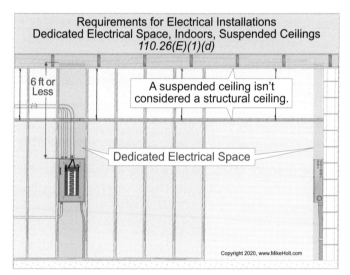

▶Figure 110–83

(a) Installation Requirements.

(1) Installed in identified enclosures

(2) Protected from accidental contact by unauthorized personnel or by vehicular traffic ▶Figure 110–84

(3) Protected from accidental spillage or leakage from piping systems

(b) Working Space. The working clearance space includes the zone described in 110.26(A). Architectural appurtenances or other equipment are not permitted within this zone.

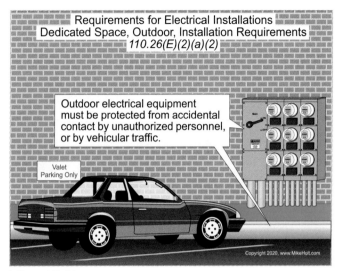

▶Figure 110–84

(c) Dedicated Equipment Space Outdoors. The footprint space (width and depth of the equipment) of the outdoor dedicated space extending from grade to a height of 6 ft above the equipment must be dedicated for electrical installations. No piping, ducts, or other equipment foreign to the electrical installation can be installed in this dedicated space. ▶Figure 110–85

▶Figure 110–85

(F) Locked Electrical Equipment Rooms or Enclosures. Rooms or enclosures containing electrical equipment controlled by a lock are considered accessible to qualified persons. ▶Figure 110–86

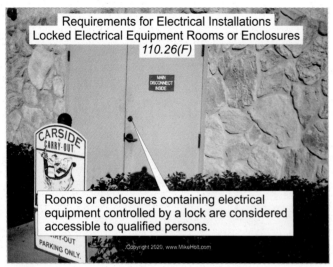

Requirements for Electrical Installations
Locked Electrical Equipment Rooms or Enclosures
110.26(F)

Rooms or enclosures containing electrical equipment controlled by a lock are considered accessible to qualified persons.

Copyright 2020, www.MikeHolt.com

▶Figure 110–86

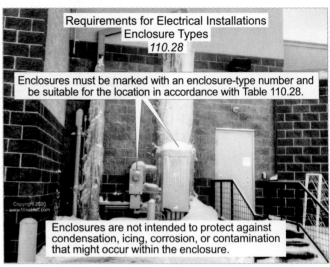

Requirements for Electrical Installations
Enclosure Types
110.28

Enclosures must be marked with an enclosure-type number and be suitable for the location in accordance with Table 110.28.

Enclosures are not intended to protect against condensation, icing, corrosion, or contamination that might occur within the enclosure.

Copyright 2020
www.MikeHolt.com

▶Figure 110–87

110.28 Enclosure Types

Enclosures must be marked with an enclosure-type number and be suitable for the location in accordance with Table 110.28. They are not intended to protect against condensation, icing, corrosion, or contamination that might occur within the enclosure or that enters via a raceway or unsealed openings. ▶Figure 110–87

Note 1: Raintight enclosures include Types 3, 3S, 3SX, 3X, 4, 4X, 6, and 6P; rainproof enclosures are Types 3R and 3RX; watertight enclosures are Types 4, 4X, 6, and 6P; driptight enclosures are Types 2, 5, 12, 12K, and 13; and dusttight enclosures are Types 3, 3S, 3SX, 3X, 4, 4X, 5, 6, 6P, 12, 12K, and 13.

Note 3: Dusttight enclosures are suitable for use in hazardous locations in accordance with 502.10(B)(4), 503.10(A)(2), and 506.15(C)(9).

Note 4: Dusttight enclosures are suitable for use in unclassified locations and in Class II, Division 2; Class III; and Zone 22 hazardous (classified) locations.

ARTICLE 110

PRACTICE QUESTIONS

Please use the 2020 *Code* book to answer the following questions.

Article 110—Requirements for Electrical Installations

1. General requirements for the examination and approval, installation and use, access to and spaces about electrical conductors and equipment; enclosures intended for personnel entry; and tunnel installations are within the scope of _____.

   (a) Article 800
   (b) Article 300
   (c) Article 110
   (d) Annex J

2. Listed or labeled equipment shall be installed and used in accordance with any instructions included in the listing or labeling.

   (a) True
   (b) False

3. Conductor sizes are expressed in American Wire Gage (AWG) or in _____.

   (a) inches
   (b) circular mils
   (c) square inches
   (d) cubic inches

4. Equipment not _____ for outdoor use or identified for indoor use such as "dry locations" or "indoor use only" shall be protected against damage from the weather during construction.

   (a) listed
   (b) identified
   (c) suitable
   (d) marked

5. The *NEC* requires that electrical equipment be _____.

   (a) installed in a neat and workmanlike manner
   (b) installed under the supervision of a licensed person
   (c) completed before being inspected
   (d) all of these

6. Cables and conductors installed exposed on the surfaces of ceilings and sidewalls shall be secured by hardware including straps, staples, cable ties, hangers, or _____ designed and installed so as not to damage the cable.

   (a) approved fittings
   (b) identified fittings
   (c) listed fittings
   (d) similar fittings

7. Connectors and terminals for conductors more finely stranded than Class B and Class C, as shown in Table 10 of Chapter 9, shall be _____ for the specific conductor class or classes.

   (a) listed
   (b) approved
   (c) identified
   (d) all of these

8. All _____ shall be covered with an insulation equivalent to that of the conductors or with an identified insulating device.

   (a) splices
   (b) joints
   (c) free ends of conductors
   (d) all of these

9. Conductors shall have their ampacity determined using the _____ column of Table 310.16 for circuits rated over 100A, or marked for conductors larger than 1 AWG, unless the equipment terminals are listed for use with higher temperature-rated conductors.

   (a) 30
   (b) 60
   (c) 75
   (d) 90

10. Tightening torque values for terminal connections shall be as indicated on equipment or in installation instructions provided by the manufacturer. An approved means shall be used to achieve the _____ torque value.

    (a) indicated
    (b) identified
    (c) maximum
    (d) minimum

11. Electrical equipment such as switchboards, switchgear, panelboards, industrial control panels, meter socket enclosures, and motor control centers, that are in other than dwelling units, and are likely to require _____ while energized, shall be field or factory marked to warn qualified persons of potential electric arc-flash hazards.

    (a) examination
    (b) adjustment
    (c) servicing or maintenance
    (d) any of these

12. NFPA 70E, *Standard for Electrical Safety in the Workplace*, provides guidance, such as determining severity of potential exposure, planning safe work practices, arc-flash labeling, and selecting _____.

    (a) personal protective equipment
    (b) coordinated overcurrent protective devices
    (c) emergency egress plans
    (d) fire suppression systems

13. Reconditioned equipment shall be marked with the _____ by which the organization responsible for reconditioning the electrical equipment can be identified, along with the date of the reconditioning.

    (a) name
    (b) trademark
    (c) descriptive marking
    (d) any of these

14. Reconditioned equipment original listing mark may include the mark of the certifying body and not the entire equipment label.

    (a) True
    (b) False

15. The *NEC* requires tested series-rated installations of circuit breakers or fuses to be legibly marked in the field to indicate the equipment has been applied with a series combination rating.

    (a) True
    (b) False

16. Working space is required for equipment operating at 1000 volts, nominal, or less to ground and likely to require _____ while energized.

    (a) examination
    (b) adjustment
    (c) servicing or maintenance
    (d) all of these

17. A minimum working space depth of _____ ft to live parts of equipment operating at 277 volts-to-ground is required where there are exposed live parts on one side and no live or grounded parts on the other side.

    (a) 2
    (b) 3
    (c) 4
    (d) 6

18. The required working space for access to live parts of equipment operating at 300 volts-to-ground, where there are exposed live parts on one side and grounded parts on the other side, is _____ ft.

    (a) 3
    (b) 3½
    (c) 4
    (d) 4½

19. The working space in front of the electric equipment shall not be less than _____ in. wide, or the width of the equipment, whichever is greater.

    (a) 15
    (b) 30
    (c) 40
    (d) 60

20. Where equipment operating at 1,000 volts, nominal, or less to ground and likely to require examination, adjustment, servicing, or maintenance while energized is required by installation instructions or function to be located in a space with limited access, the width of the working space shall be the width of the equipment enclosure or a minimum of _____ in., whichever is greater.

    (a) 12
    (b) 22
    (c) 26
    (d) 30

21. Working space shall not be used for _____.

    (a) storage
    (b) raceways
    (c) lighting
    (d) accessibility

22. For large equipment that contains overcurrent devices, switching devices, there shall be one entrance to and egress from the required working space not less than 24 in. wide and _____ ft high at each end of the working space.

    (a) 5½
    (b) 6
    (c) 6½
    (d) 7

23. Illumination shall be provided for all working spaces about service equipment, switchboards, switchgear, panelboards, or motor control centers _____.

    (a) over 600V
    (b) installed indoors
    (c) rated 1,200A or more
    (d) using automatic means of control

24. The area above the dedicated space required by 110.26(E)(1)(a) is permitted to contain foreign systems, provided protection is installed to avoid damage to the electrical equipment from condensation, leaks, or breaks in such foreign systems.

    (a) True
    (b) False

25. All switchboards, switchgear, panelboards, and motor control centers shall be located in dedicated spaces and protected from damage and the working clearance space for outdoor installations shall include the zone described in _____.

    (a) 110.26(A)
    (b) 110.26(B)
    (c) 110.26(C)
    (d) 110.26(D)

26. The term rainproof is typically used in conjunction with enclosure type(s) _____.

    (a) 3
    (b) 3R and 3RX
    (c) 4
    (d) 4R and 4RX

ARTICLE
250

GROUNDING AND BONDING

Introduction to Article 250—Grounding and Bonding

No other article can match this one for misapplication, violation, and misinterpretation. The terminology used in Article 250 has been a source of much confusion but has been improved during the last few *NEC* revisions. It is very important for you to understand the difference between grounding and bonding in order to correctly apply the provisions of this article. Pay careful attention to the definitions of important terms located in Article 100 that apply to grounding and bonding. Article 250 covers the grounding requirements for providing a path to the Earth to reduce overvoltage from lightning strikes, and the bonding requirements that establish a low-impedance fault current path back to the source of the electrical supply to facilitate the operation of overcurrent protective devices in the event of a ground fault.

This article is arranged in a logical manner as illustrated in Figure 250.1 in the *NEC*. It may be a good idea for you to just read through the entire article first to get a big picture overview. Then, study Article 250 closely so you understand the details and remember to check Article 100 for the definitions of terms that may be new to you. The illustrations that accompany the text in this textbook will help you better understand the key points.

Part I. General

250.1 Scope

Article 250 covers the general requirements for the grounding and bonding of electrical installations. ▶Figure 250–1

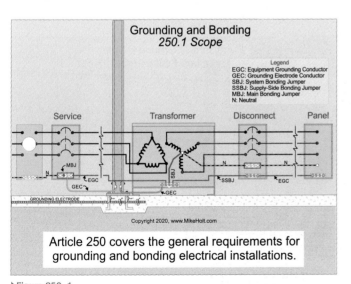

Grounding and Bonding
250.1 Scope

Legend
EGC: Equipment Grounding Conductor
GEC: Grounding Electrode Conductor
SBJ: System Bonding Jumper
SSBJ: Supply-Side Bonding Jumper
MBJ: Main Bonding Jumper
N: Neutral

Service   Transformer   Disconnect   Panel

Copyright 2020, www.MikeHolt.com

Article 250 covers the general requirements for grounding and bonding electrical installations.

▶Figure 250–1

Author's Comment:

▸ There are two completely different concepts being covered in this article; "Grounding" which is the connection to the Earth, and "Bonding" which is mechanically connecting electrically conductive components together to ensure electrical conductivity between metal parts [Article 100]. While these two systems overlap each other, that portion of the electrical system that needs to be able to carry fault current to the source must be heartier and capable of handling excessive amounts of current. This is called the "Effective Ground-Fault Current Path." The effective ground-fault current path needs a low-impedance fault current path to the source so fault current can rise as quickly as possible to operate the overcurrent protective device as soon as possible. Since fault current can be thousands of amperes, the effective ground-fault current path must be designed to safely handle those high current levels. ▶Figure 250–2

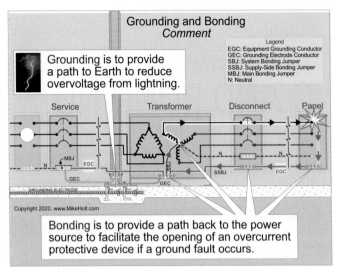

▶Figure 250–2

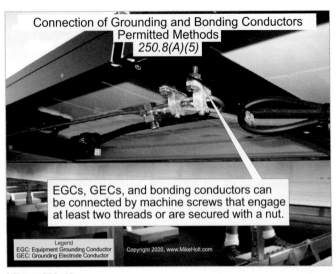

▶Figure 250–40

250.8 Connection of Grounding and Bonding Connectors

(A) Permitted Methods. Equipment grounding conductors, grounding electrode conductors, and bonding jumpers must be connected by one or more of the following methods:

(1) Listed pressure connectors

(2) Terminal bars

(3) Pressure connectors listed for grounding and bonding

(4) Exothermic welding

(5) Machine screws that engage at least two threads or are secured with a nut ▶Figure 250–40

(6) Self-tapping machine screws that engage at least two threads in the enclosure ▶Figure 250–41

(7) Connections that are part of a listed assembly

(8) Other listed means

250.10 Protection of Ground Clamps and Fittings

Ground clamps and fittings subject to physical damage must be protected. ▶Figure 250–42

▶Figure 250–41

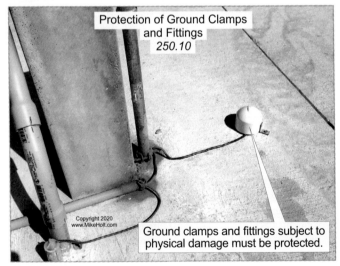

▶Figure 250–42

250.12 Clean Surfaces

Nonconductive coatings (such as paint) <u>on equipment to be grounded or bonded</u> must be removed to ensure good electrical continuity, or the termination fittings must be designed so to make such removal unnecessary [250.53(A) and 250.96(A)].

Author's Comment:

▸ Fittings such as locknuts are designed to cut through the nonconductive coating and establish the intended electrical continuity when they are properly tightened.

▸ Tarnish on copper water pipe need not be removed before making a termination.

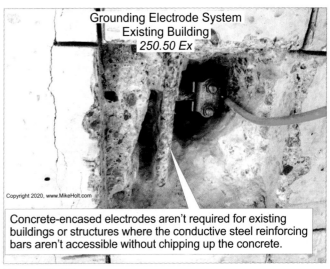

Concrete-encased electrodes aren't required for existing buildings or structures where the conductive steel reinforcing bars aren't accessible without chipping up the concrete.

▸Figure 250–105

Part III. Grounding Electrode System and Grounding Electrode Conductor

250.50 Grounding Electrode System

A grounding electrode system is comprised of bonding together the grounding electrodes described in 250.52(A)(1) through (A)(7) that are present at a building or structure. ▸Figure 250–104

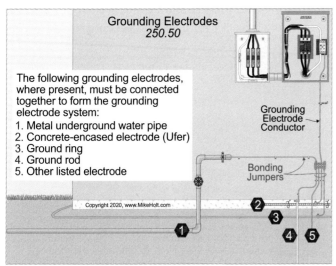

▸Figure 250–104

Ex: Concrete-encased electrodes are not required for existing buildings where the conductive steel reinforcing bars are not accessible without chipping up the concrete. ▸Figure 250–105

250.52 Grounding Electrode Types

(A) Electrodes.

(1) Underground Metal Water Pipe Electrode. Underground metal water pipe in direct contact with the Earth for 10 ft or more can serve as a grounding electrode. ▸Figure 250–106

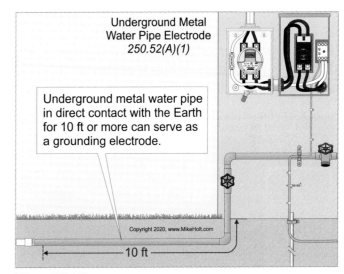

▸Figure 250–106

Author's Comment:

▸ Controversy about using metal underground water piping as a grounding electrode has existed since the early 1900s. The water industry believes that neutral current flowing on water piping corrodes the metal. For more information, contact the American Water Works Association about their report, *Effects of Electrical Grounding on Pipe Integrity and Shock Hazard*, Catalog No. 90702, 1.800.926.7337. ▸Figure 250–107

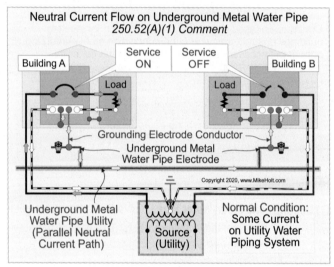

▸Figure 250–107

(2) Metal In-Ground Support Structure(s). Metal in-ground support structure(s) in direct contact with the Earth vertically for 10 ft or more can serve as a grounding electrode. ▸Figure 250–108

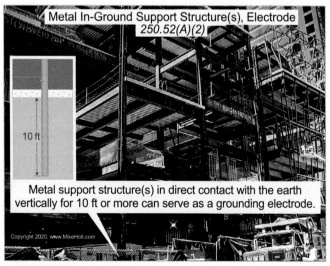

▸Figure 250–108

Note: Metal in-ground support structures include (but are not limited to) pilings, casings, and other structural metal.

(3) Concrete-Encased Electrode. Concrete-encased electrodes meeting the requirements of this subsection can serve as grounding electrodes. ▸Figure 250–109

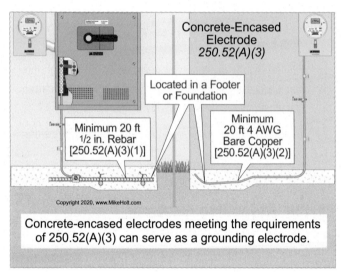

▸Figure 250–109

(1) One or more electrically conductive steel reinforcing bars (rebar) of not less than ½ in. in diameter that are mechanically connected by steel tie wires to create a 20 ft or greater in length of steel can serve as a grounding electrode. ▸Figure 250–110

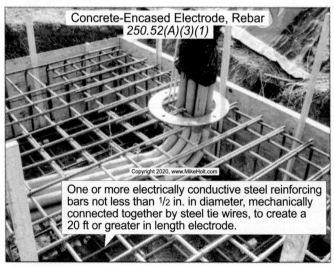

▸Figure 250–110

(2) A bare copper conductor not smaller than 4 AWG and 20 ft or greater in length can serve as a grounding electrode.

The rebar or bare copper conductor must be encased by at least 2 in. of concrete that is in direct contact with the Earth.

Where multiple concrete-encased electrodes are present at a building, only one is required to serve as a grounding electrode. ▶Figure 250–111

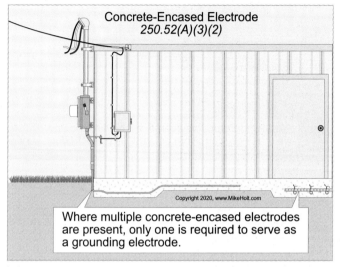

Concrete-Encased Electrode
250.52(A)(3)(2)

Where multiple concrete-encased electrodes are present, only one is required to serve as a grounding electrode.

Copyright 2020, www.MikeHolt.com

▶Figure 250–111

Note: Rebar in concrete that is not in direct contact with the Earth because of insulation, vapor barriers, or similar items is not considered to be a concrete-encased electrode. ▶Figure 250–112

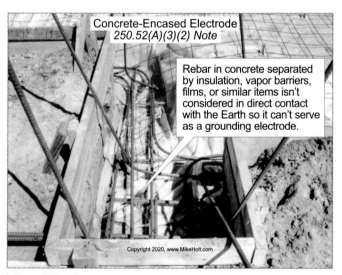

Concrete-Encased Electrode
250.52(A)(3)(2) Note

Rebar in concrete separated by insulation, vapor barriers, films, or similar items isn't considered in direct contact with the Earth so it can't serve as a grounding electrode.

Copyright 2020, www.MikeHolt.com

▶Figure 250–112

Author's Comment:

▶ A grounding electrode conductor to a concrete-encased grounding electrode is not required to be larger than 4 AWG copper [250.66(B)].

▶ A concrete-encased grounding electrode is also called a "Ufer Ground," named after a consultant working for the U.S. Army during World War II. The technique Herbert G. Ufer came up with was necessary because the site needing grounding had no underground water table and little rainfall. The desert site was a series of bomb storage vaults near of Flagstaff, Arizona. This type of grounding electrode generally offers the lowest ground resistance for the cost. In fact, Mr. Ufer's method is so effective that no other ground rods are necessary!

(4) Ground Ring. A direct buried bare copper conductor not smaller than 2 AWG encircling a building can serve as a grounding electrode. ▶Figure 250–113

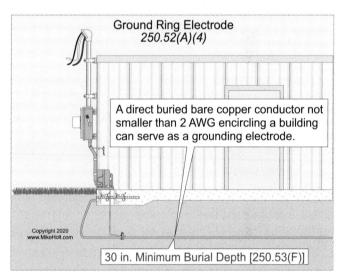

Ground Ring Electrode
250.52(A)(4)

A direct buried bare copper conductor not smaller than 2 AWG encircling a building can serve as a grounding electrode.

Copyright 2020 www.MikeHolt.com

30 in. Minimum Burial Depth [250.53(F)]

▶Figure 250–113

Author's Comment:

▶ A ground ring encircling a building must not be installed less than 30 in. below the surface of the Earth [250.53(F)].

(5) Ground Rod. Ground rods must have at least 8 ft in length in contact with the Earth [250.53(A)].

(b) Ground rods must have a diameter of at least ⅝ in., unless listed. ▶Figure 250–114

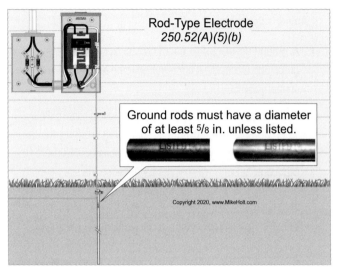

Rod-Type Electrode
250.52(A)(5)(b)

Ground rods must have a diameter of at least ⅝ in. unless listed.

Copyright 2020, www.MikeHolt.com

▶Figure 250–114

Metal Underground Systems
250.52(A)(8)

WELL AND SERVICE

Copyright 2020, www.MikeHolt.com

Metal underground systems, such as piping and well casings, can serve as grounding electrodes.

▶Figure 250–115

▶ The grounding electrode conductor, if it is the sole connection to the rod(s), is not required to be larger than 6 AWG copper [250.66(A)].

▶ The diameter of a ground rod has an insignificant effect on the contact resistance of a rod(s) to the Earth. However, larger diameter rods (¾ in. and 1 in.) are sometimes installed where mechanical strength is desired, or to compensate for the loss of the electrode's metal due to corrosion.

(6) Listed Electrode. Other listed grounding electrodes can serve as a grounding electrode.

(7) Plate Electrode. A bare or electrically conductive coated iron or a steel plate of not less than ¼ in. in thickness, or a solid uncoated copper metal plate not less than 0.06 in. in thickness, with an exposed surface area of not less than 2 sq ft can serve as a grounding electrode.

(8) Metal Underground Systems. Metal underground systems, piping, and well casings can serve as a grounding electrode. ▶Figure 250–115

Author's Comment:

▶ The grounding electrode conductor to the metal underground system must be sized in accordance with Table 250.66, based on the area of the largest phase conductor.

(B) Not Permitted for Use as a Grounding Electrode.

(1) Underground metal gas piping systems are not permitted to be used as a grounding electrode. ▶Figure 250–116

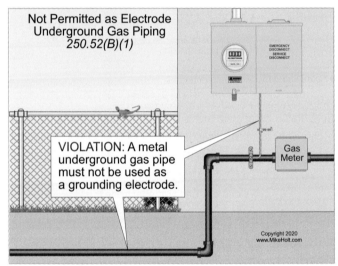

Not Permitted as Electrode
Underground Gas Piping
250.52(B)(1)

EMERGENCY DISCONNECT SERVICE DISCONNECT

VIOLATION: A metal underground gas pipe must not be used as a grounding electrode.

Gas Meter

Copyright 2020 www.MikeHolt.com

▶Figure 250–116

(2) Aluminum is not permitted to be used as a grounding electrode.

(3) The structures and structural reinforcing steel described in 680.26(B)(1) and (B)(2) are not permitted to be used as a grounding electrode. ▶Figure 250–117

250.53 Grounding Electrode Installation Requirements

(A) Ground Rods.

(1) Below Permanent Moisture Level. If practicable, rod, pipe, and plate electrodes must be embedded below the permanent moisture level and must be free from nonconductive coatings such as paint or enamel.

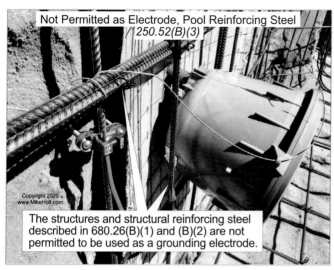

▶Figure 250–117

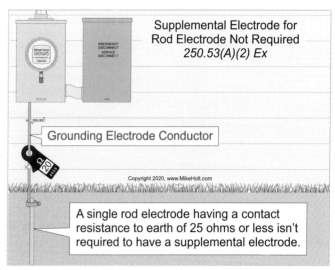

▶Figure 250–119

(2) Supplemental Electrode. A single ground rod must be supplemented by an additional electrode. The supplemental electrode must be bonded to: ▶Figure 250–118

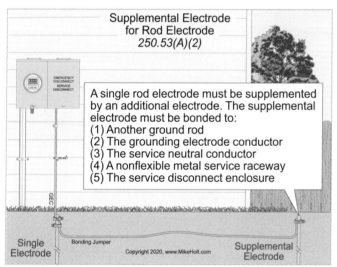

▶Figure 250–118

(1) Another ground rod

(2) The grounding electrode conductor

(3) The service neutral conductor

(4) A nonflexible metal service raceway

(5) The service-disconnect enclosure

Ex: A single ground rod electrode having a contact resistance to the Earth of 25 ohms or less is not required to have a supplemental electrode. ▶Figure 250–119

(3) Supplemental Ground Rod, Spacing. The supplemental electrode must be installed not less than 6 ft from the ground rod. ▶Figure 250–120

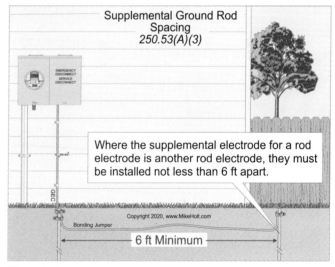

▶Figure 250–120

(4) Rod and Pipe Electrodes. The electrode must be installed such that at least 8 ft of length is in contact with the soil. It must be driven to a depth of not less than 8 ft except where rock bottom is encountered, the electrode must be driven at an oblique angle not to exceed 45 degrees from the vertical or, where rock bottom is encountered at an angle up to 45 degrees, the electrode is permitted to be buried in a trench that is at least 30 in. deep. ▶Figure 250–121

The upper end of the ground rod must be flush with or below ground level unless the grounding electrode conductor attachment is protected against physical damage as specified in 250.10. ▶Figure 250–122

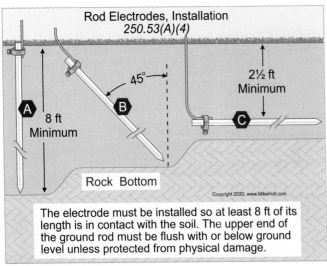

▶Figure 250–121

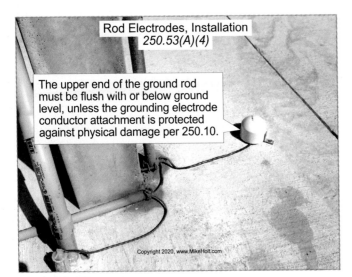

▶Figure 250–122

(B) Electrode Spacing. Electrodes for premises systems must be located no closer than 6 ft from lightning protection system grounding electrodes.

Two or more grounding electrodes that are bonded together are considered a single grounding electrode system. ▶Figure 250–123

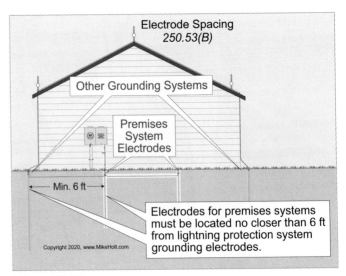

▶Figure 250–123

(C) Grounding Electrode Bonding Jumper. Grounding electrode bonding jumpers must be copper when within 18 in. of the Earth [250.64(A)]. Exposed grounding electrode bonding jumpers must be securely fastened to the surface and protected from physical damage [250.64(B)]. The bonding jumper to each electrode must be sized in accordance with 250.66, based on the area of the largest phase conductor. ▶Figure 250–124

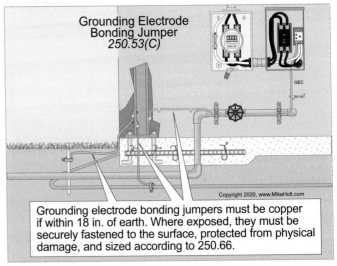

▶Figure 250–124

Author's Comment:

▶ Grounding electrode bonding jumpers must terminate by any of the following means in accordance with 250.8(A):

▶ Listed pressure connectors

▶ Terminal bars

▶ Pressure connectors listed as grounding and bonding equipment

- ▸ Exothermic welding
- ▸ Machine screw-type fasteners that engage not less than two threads or are secured with a nut
- ▸ Thread-forming machine screws that engage not less than two threads in the enclosure
- ▸ Connections that are part of a listed assembly
- ▸ Other listed means

When the grounding electrode conductor termination is encased in concrete or buried, the termination fittings must be listed for this purpose [250.70].

Rebar is not permitted to be used to interconnect the electrodes of grounding electrode systems.

(D) Underground Metal Water Pipe Electrode.

(1) Continuity. Continuity of the grounding path or the bonding connection to interior piping must not rely on water meters or filtering devices and similar equipment. ▸Figure 250–125

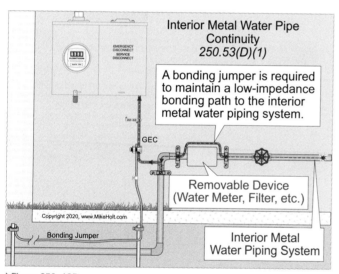

Interior Metal Water Pipe
Continuity
250.53(D)(1)

A bonding jumper is required to maintain a low-impedance bonding path to the interior metal water piping system.

GEC

Removable Device
(Water Meter, Filter, etc.)

Copyright 2020, www.MikeHolt.com

Bonding Jumper

Interior Metal
Water Piping System

▸Figure 250–125

(2) Water Pipe Supplemental Electrode. When an underground metal water pipe grounding electrode is present, it must be supplemented by any of the following electrodes:

- ▸ Metal frame of the building electrode [250.52(A)(2)]
- ▸ Concrete-encased electrode [250.52(A)(3)] ▸Figure 250–126
- ▸ Rod electrode [250.52(A)(5)]
- ▸ Other type of listed electrode [250.52(A)(6)]
- ▸ Metal underground piping electrode [250.52(A)(8)]

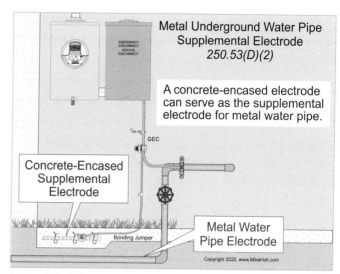

Metal Underground Water Pipe
Supplemental Electrode
250.53(D)(2)

A concrete-encased electrode can serve as the supplemental electrode for metal water pipe.

GEC

Concrete-Encased
Supplemental
Electrode

Bonding Jumper

Metal Water
Pipe Electrode

Copyright 2020, www.MikeHolt.com

▸Figure 250–126

The grounding electrode conductor for the supplemental electrode must terminate to any of the following: ▸Figure 250–127

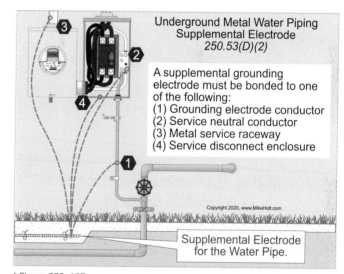

Underground Metal Water Piping
Supplemental Electrode
250.53(D)(2)

A supplemental grounding electrode must be bonded to one of the following:
(1) Grounding electrode conductor
(2) Service neutral conductor
(3) Metal service raceway
(4) Service disconnect enclosure

Copyright 2020, www.MikeHolt.com

Supplemental Electrode
for the Water Pipe.

▸Figure 250–127

(1) Grounding electrode conductor

(2) Service neutral conductor

(3) Metal service raceway

(4) Service-disconnect enclosure

Author's Comment:

- ▸ Because a metal underground waterpipe electrode could be replaced by a plastic water pipe, the supplemental electrode must be installed as if it is the only electrode for the system.

Ex: The supplemental electrode can be bonded to interior metal water piping located not more than 5 ft from the point of entrance to the building [250.68(C)(1)].

(E) Supplemental Rod Electrode. The grounding electrode conductor to a ground rod that serves as a supplemental electrode is not required to be larger than 6 AWG copper.

(F) Ground Ring. A ground ring encircling a building must be a bare 2 AWG or larger copper conductor installed not less than 30 in. below the surface of the Earth [250.52(A)(4)]. ▶Figure 250–128

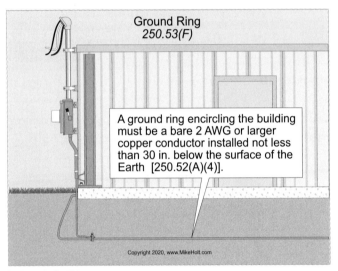

▶Figure 250–128

Measuring the Contact Resistance of Electrodes to Earth

A ground resistance clamp meter or a three-point fall-of-potential ground resistance meter can be used to measure the contact resistance of a grounding electrode to the Earth.

Ground Clamp Meter. The ground resistance clamp meter measures the contact resistance of the grounding electrode system to the Earth by injecting a high-frequency signal via the service neutral conductor to the serving electric utility's grounding system, and then measuring the strength of the return signal through the Earth to the grounding electrode being measured. ▶Figure 250–129

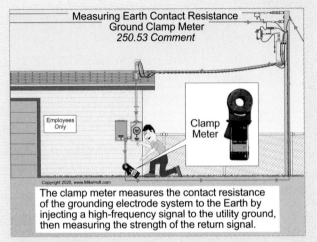

▶Figure 250–129

Fall-of-Potential Ground Resistance Meter. The three-point fall-of-potential ground resistance meter determines the contact resistance of a single grounding electrode to the Earth by using Ohm's Law where **Resistance = Voltage/Current**. ▶Figure 250–130

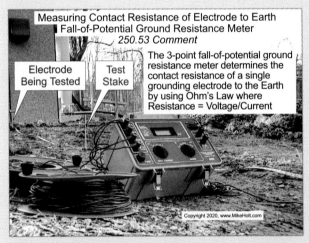

▶Figure 250–130

This meter divides the voltage difference between the electrode to be measured and a driven voltage test stake (P) by the current flowing between the electrode to be measured and a driven current test stake (C). The test stakes are typically made of ¼ in. diameter steel rods, 24 in. long, driven two-thirds of their length into the Earth.

The distance and alignment between the voltage and current test stakes, and the electrode, is extremely important to the validity of the Earth contact resistance measurements. For an 8-ft rod, the accepted practice is to space the current test stake (C) 80 ft from the electrode to be measured.

The voltage test stake (P) is positioned in a straight line between the electrode to be measured and the current test stake (C). The voltage test stake should be approximately 62 percent of the distance of where the current test stake is located from the electrode. If the current test stake (C) for an 8-ft ground rod is located 80 ft from the grounding electrode, the voltage test stake (P) will be about 50 ft from the electrode to be measured.

▶ Example

Question: *If the voltage between the ground rod and the voltage test stake (P) is 3V, and the current between the ground rod and the current test stake (C) is 0.20A, what will be the Earth contact resistance of the electrode to the Earth?* ▶Figure 250–131

(a) 3 ohms   (b) 5 ohms   (c) 10 ohms   (d) 15 ohms

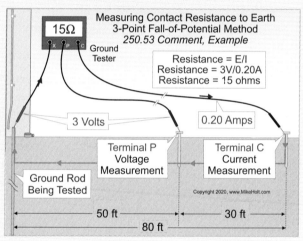

▶Figure 250–131

Solution:

Resistance = Voltage/Current
Voltage = 3V
Current = 0.20A

Resistance = 3V/0.20A
Resistance = 15 ohms

The Earth contact resistance of the electrode to the Earth will be 15 ohms.

Answer: *(d) 15 ohms*

Author's Comment:

▶ The three-point fall-of-potential meter should only be used to measure the contact resistance of one electrode to the Earth at a time, and that electrode must be independent and not connected to any part of the electrical system.

The contact resistance of two electrodes bonded together cannot measured until they have been separated. The contact resistance of two separate electrodes to the Earth can be thought of as two resistors in parallel if they are outside each other's sphere of influence.

Soil Resistivity

The contact resistance of an electrode to the Earth is impacted by soil resistivity, which varies throughout the world. Soil resistivity is influenced by electrolytes, which consist of moisture, minerals, and dissolved salts. Because soil resistivity changes with moisture content, the contact resistance of a grounding system to the Earth varies with the seasons.

Part VI. Equipment Grounding and Equipment Grounding Conductors

250.114 Equipment Connected by Cord and Plug

Exposed, normally noncurrent-carrying metal parts of cord-and-plug-connected equipment must be connected to the equipment grounding conductor of the circuit suppling the equipment under any of the following conditions:

Ex: Listed tools, listed appliances, and listed equipment covered in 250.114(2) through (4) are not required to be connected to an equipment grounding conductor where protected by a system of double insulation or its equivalent. Double insulated equipment must be distinctively marked.

(1) In hazardous (classified) locations. [Articles 500 through 517].

(2) Where operated at over 150V to ground.

Ex 1 to (2): Motors that are guarded.

Ex 2 to (2): Metal frames of exempted electrically heated appliances.

(3) In residential occupancies:

    a. Refrigerators, freezers, and air conditioners.

    b. Clothes-washing, clothes-drying, and dish-washing machines; ranges; kitchen waste disposers; IT equipment; sump pumps; and electrical aquarium equipment.

Author's Comment:

▸ Electric ranges and clothes dryers are shipped from the factory with a bonding strap that bonds the metal frame of the appliance to the neutral termination of the cord connection terminal block. This bonding strap may or may not have to be removed! The *Code* requires an insulated neutral for these appliances using a 4-wire branch circuit and the bonding strap should be removed, but that was not always the case. If an existing 3-wire branch circuit is to supply a replacement appliance, the factory-installed bonding strap must remain in place [250.140 Ex]. ▸Figure 250–208

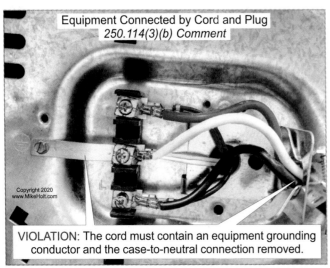

Equipment Connected by Cord and Plug
250.114(3)(b) Comment

Copyright 2020
www.MikeHolt.com

VIOLATION: The cord must contain an equipment grounding conductor and the case-to-neutral connection removed.

▸Figure 250–208

c. Hand-held, stationary or fixed, and light industrial motor-operated tools.

d. Motor-operated hedge clippers, lawn mowers, snow-blowers, and wet scrubbers.

e. Portable handlamps and portable luminaires.

(4) In other than residential occupancies:

a. Refrigerators, freezers, and air conditioners.

b. Clothes-washing, clothes-drying, and dish-washing machines; IT equipment; sump pumps; and electrical aquarium equipment.

c. Hand-held, stationary or fixed, and light industrial motor-operated tools.

d. Motor-operated hedge clippers, lawn mowers, snow-blowers, and wet scrubbers.

e. Portable handlamps and portable luminaires.

f. Appliances used in damp or wet locations or by persons standing on the ground, standing on metal floors, or working inside of metal tanks or boilers.

g. Tools likely to be used in wet or conductive locations

Ex: Tools and portable handlamps and portable luminaires likely to be used in wet or conductive locations are not required to be connected to an equipment grounding conductor where supplied through an isolating transformer with an ungrounded secondary not over 50V.

250.118 Types of Equipment Grounding Conductors

The equipment grounding conductor can be any one of the following types: ▸Figure 250–209

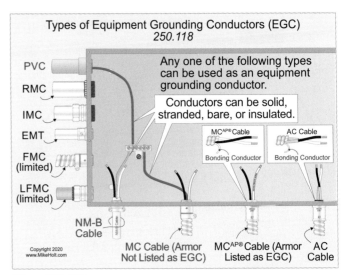

Types of Equipment Grounding Conductors (EGC)
250.118

Any one of the following types can be used as an equipment grounding conductor.

Conductors can be solid, stranded, bare, or insulated.

PVC
RMC
IMC
EMT
FMC (limited)
LFMC (limited)
NM-B Cable

MC^AP® Cable   AC Cable
Bonding Conductor   Bonding Conductor

MC Cable (Armor Not Listed as EGC)   MC^AP® Cable (Armor Listed as EGC)   AC Cable

Copyright 2020
www.MikeHolt.com

▸Figure 250–209

Note: The equipment grounding conductor is intended to serve as part of the effective ground-fault current path [Article 100]. ▸Figure 250–210

Author's Comment:

▸ The effective ground-fault current path [Article 100] is an intentionally constructed low-impedance conductive path designed to carry fault current from the point of a ground fault on a wiring system to the electrical supply source. Its purpose is to quickly remove dangerous voltage from a ground fault by opening the circuit overcurrent protective device. ▸Figure 250–211

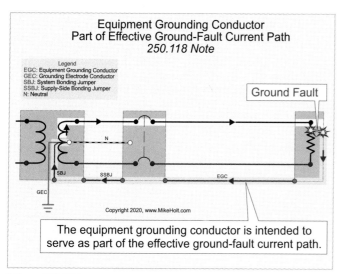

Equipment Grounding Conductor
Part of Effective Ground-Fault Current Path
250.118 Note

Legend
EGC: Equipment Grounding Conductor
GEC: Grounding Electrode Conductor
SBJ: System Bonding Jumper
SSBJ: Supply-Side Bonding Jumper
N: Neutral

Ground Fault

Copyright 2020, www.MikeHolt.com

The equipment grounding conductor is intended to serve as part of the effective ground-fault current path.

▶Figure 250–210

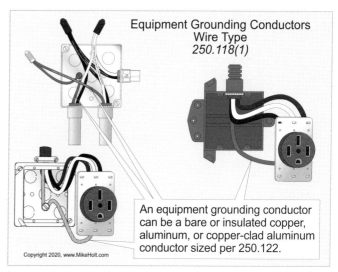

Equipment Grounding Conductors
Wire Type
250.118(1)

An equipment grounding conductor can be a bare or insulated copper, aluminum, or copper-clad aluminum conductor sized per 250.122.

Copyright 2020, www.MikeHolt.com

▶Figure 250–212

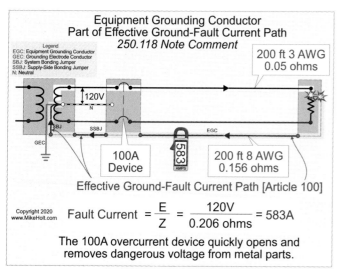

Equipment Grounding Conductor
Part of Effective Ground-Fault Current Path
250.118 Note Comment

Legend
EGC: Equipment Grounding Conductor
GEC: Grounding Electrode Conductor
SBJ: System Bonding Jumper
SSBJ: Supply-Side Bonding Jumper
N: Neutral

120V

200 ft 3 AWG
0.05 ohms

100A Device

583 AMPS

200 ft 8 AWG
0.156 ohms

Effective Ground-Fault Current Path [Article 100]

Copyright 2020
www.MikeHolt.com

$$\text{Fault Current} = \frac{E}{Z} = \frac{120V}{0.206 \text{ ohms}} = 583A$$

The 100A overcurrent device quickly opens and removes dangerous voltage from metal parts.

▶Figure 250–211

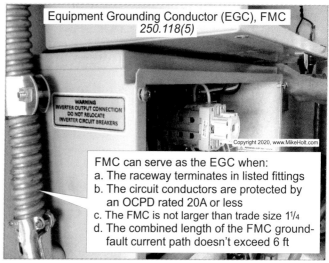

Equipment Grounding Conductor (EGC), FMC
250.118(5)

WARNING
INVERTER OUTPUT CONNECTION
DO NOT RELOCATE
INVERTER CIRCUIT BREAKERS

Copyright 2020, www.MikeHolt.com

FMC can serve as the EGC when:
a. The raceway terminates in listed fittings
b. The circuit conductors are protected by an OCPD rated 20A or less
c. The FMC is not larger than trade size 1¼
d. The combined length of the FMC ground-fault current path doesn't exceed 6 ft

▶Figure 250–213

(1) A bare or insulated copper, aluminum, or copper-clad aluminum conductor sized in accordance with 250.122. ▶Figure 250–212

(2) Rigid metal conduit.

(3) Intermediate metal conduit.

(4) Electrical metallic tubing.

(5) Listed flexible metal conduit where: ▶Figure 250–213

a. The raceway terminates in listed fittings.

b. The circuit conductors are protected by an overcurrent device rated 20A or less.

c. The size of the flexible metal conduit does not exceed 1¼.

d. The combined length of the flexible conduit in the same <u>effective ground-fault current path</u> does not exceed 6 ft.

e. If flexibility is required to minimize the transmission of vibration from equipment or to provide flexibility for equipment that requires movement after installation, an equipment grounding conductor of the <u>wire type</u> must be installed with the circuit conductors in accordance with 250.102(E). ▶Figure 250–214

(6) Listed liquidtight flexible metal conduit where: ▶Figure 250–215

a. The raceway terminates in listed fittings.

b. For ⅜ in. through ½ in., the circuit conductors are protected by overcurrent protective devices rated 20A or less.

c. For ¾ in. through 1¼ in., the circuit conductors are protected by overcurrent protective devices rated 60A or less.

d. The combined length of the flexible metal conduit in the same <u>effective ground-fault current path</u> does not exceed 6 ft.

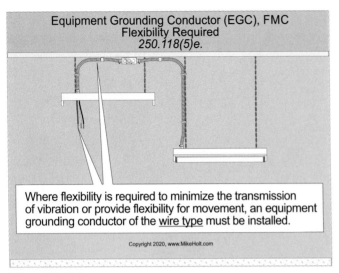

▶Figure 250–214

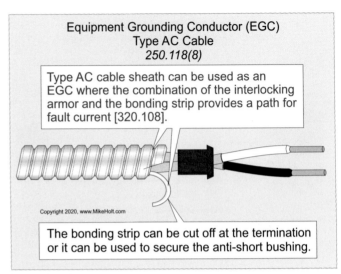

▶Figure 250–216

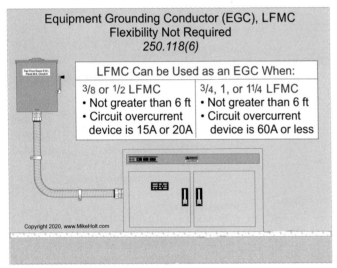

▶Figure 250–215

e. If flexibility is required to minimize the transmission of vibration from equipment or to provide flexibility for equipment that requires movement after installation, an equipment grounding conductor of the <u>wire type</u> must be installed with the circuit conductors in accordance with 250.102(E).

(8) The sheath of Type AC cable. ▶Figure 250–216

Author's Comment:

▶ The internal aluminum bonding strip is not an equipment grounding conductor, but it allows the interlocked armor of Type AC cable to serve as an equipment grounding conductor because it reduces the impedance of the armored spirals to ensure a ground fault will be cleared. It is the aluminum bonding strip in combination with the cable armor that creates the circuit equipment grounding conductor. Once the bonding strip exits the cable it can be cut off because it no longer serves any purpose.

(9) The sheath of Type MI cable.

(10) Type MC cable:

a. That contains an insulated or uninsulated equipment grounding conductor. ▶Figure 250–217

b. Where the metallic sheath and uninsulated equipment grounding/bonding conductor is listed and identified as an equipment grounding conductor. ▶Figure 250–218

Author's Comment:

▶ Once the bare aluminum grounding/bonding conductor of Type MC cable exits the cable it can be cut off because it no longer serves any purpose. The effective ground-fault current path must be maintained by the use of fittings specifically listed for Type MC^AP® cable [330.6]. See 300.12, 300.15, and 330.108. ▶Figure 250–219

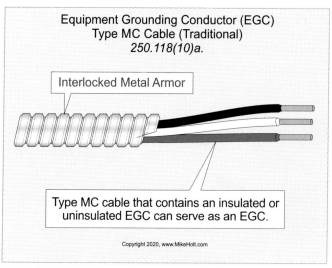

Equipment Grounding Conductor (EGC)
Type MC Cable (Traditional)
250.118(10)a.

Interlocked Metal Armor

Type MC cable that contains an insulated or uninsulated EGC can serve as an EGC.

Copyright 2020, www.MikeHolt.com

▶Figure 250–217

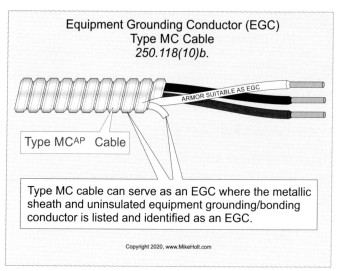

Equipment Grounding Conductor (EGC)
Type MC Cable
250.118(10)b.

ARMOR SUITABLE AS EGC

Type MC^AP Cable

Type MC cable can serve as an EGC where the metallic sheath and uninsulated equipment grounding/bonding conductor is listed and identified as an EGC.

Copyright 2020, www.MikeHolt.com

▶Figure 250–218

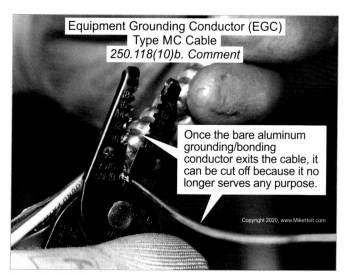

Equipment Grounding Conductor (EGC)
Type MC Cable
250.118(10)b. Comment

Once the bare aluminum grounding/bonding conductor exits the cable, it can be cut off because it no longer serves any purpose.

Copyright 2020, www.MikeHolt.com

▶Figure 250–219

c. When the metallic sheath of smooth or corrugated tube-type MC cable is listed and identified as an equipment grounding conductor it can serve as an equipment grounding conductor.

(11) Metal cable trays if continuous maintenance and supervision ensure only qualified persons will service the cable tray; the cable tray and fittings are identified for grounding; and the cable tray, fittings [392.10], and raceways are bonded together using bolted mechanical connectors or bonding jumpers sized and installed in accordance with 250.102 [392.60]. ▶Figure 250–220

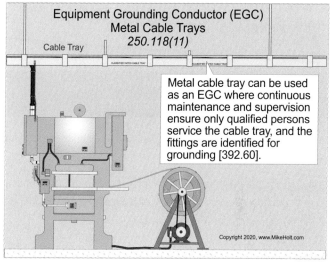

Equipment Grounding Conductor (EGC)
Metal Cable Trays
250.118(11)

Cable Tray

Metal cable tray can be used as an EGC where continuous maintenance and supervision ensure only qualified persons service the cable tray, and the fittings are identified for grounding [392.60].

Copyright 2020, www.MikeHolt.com

▶Figure 250–220

(13) Other listed electrically continuous metal raceways such as metal wireways [Article 376] or strut-type channel raceways [384.60]. ▶Figure 250–221

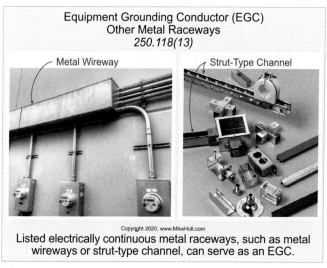

Equipment Grounding Conductor (EGC)
Other Metal Raceways
250.118(13)

Metal Wireway   Strut-Type Channel

Copyright 2020, www.MikeHolt.com

Listed electrically continuous metal raceways, such as metal wireways or strut-type channel, can serve as an EGC.

▶Figure 250–221

(14) Surface metal raceways listed for grounding [Article 386].

Note: For a definition of effective ground-fault current path, see Article 100.

Author's Comment:

▸ Listed offset nipples and metal fittings for metal cable, conduit, and tubing are considered suitable for grounding circuits where installed in accordance with the *NEC*, except as noted for flexible metal conduit fittings and liquid-tight flexible metal conduit fittings. See UL Product Spec™ *Guide, Information for "Conduit Fittings" (DWTT)*.

250.119 Identification of Equipment Grounding Conductors

Unless required to be insulated in this *Code*, equipment grounding conductors can be bare or covered.

Insulated equipment grounding conductors 6 AWG and smaller must have a continuous outer finish that is either green or green with one or more yellow stripes. ▸Figure 250–222

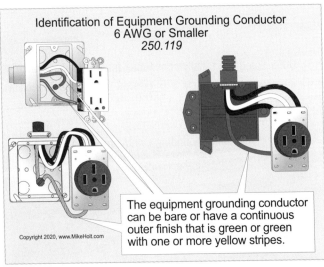

Identification of Equipment Grounding Conductor 6 AWG or Smaller
250.119

The equipment grounding conductor can be bare or have a continuous outer finish that is green or green with one or more yellow stripes.

Copyright 2020, www.MikeHolt.com

▸Figure 250–222

Conductors with insulation that is green, or green with one or more yellow stripes, are not permitted to be used for a phase or neutral conductor.

Author's Comment:

▸ The *NEC* neither requires nor prohibits the use of the color green for the identification of grounding electrode conductors. ▸Figure 250–223

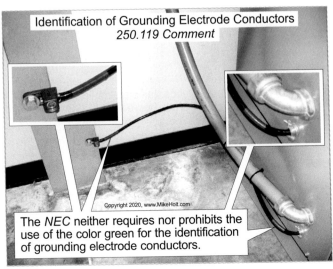

Identification of Grounding Electrode Conductors
250.119 Comment

The *NEC* neither requires nor prohibits the use of the color green for the identification of grounding electrode conductors.

Copyright 2020, www.MikeHolt.com

▸Figure 250–223

(A) Conductors 4 AWG and Larger.

(1) Identified Where Accessible. Insulated equipment grounding conductors 4 AWG and larger can be reidentified at the time of installation where the conductor is accessible. ▸Figure 250–224

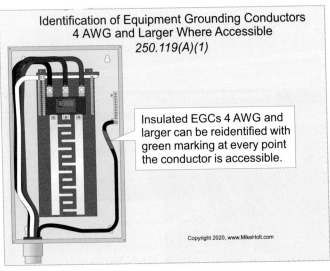

Identification of Equipment Grounding Conductors 4 AWG and Larger Where Accessible
250.119(A)(1)

Insulated EGCs 4 AWG and larger can be reidentified with green marking at every point the conductor is accessible.

Copyright 2020, www.MikeHolt.com

▸Figure 250–224

(2) Identification Methods. Identification must encircle the conductor and be accomplished by: ▸Figure 250–225

a. Removing the conductor insulation

b. Coloring the insulation green at termination

c. Marking the insulation at termination with green tape or green adhesive labels

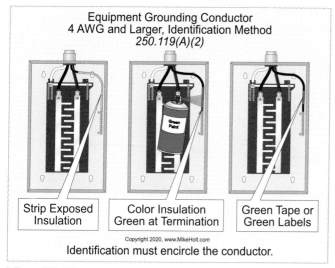

▶Figure 250–225

(B) Multiconductor Cable. One or more insulated conductors in a multiconductor cable, at the time of installation, are permitted to be permanently identified as equipment grounding conductors at each end and at every point where the conductors are accessible by one of the following means:

(1) Stripping the insulation from the entire exposed length.

(2) Coloring the exposed insulation green.

(3) Marking the exposed insulation with green tape or green adhesive labels. Identification must encircle the conductor.

250.120 Equipment Grounding Conductor Installation

An equipment grounding conductor must be installed as follows:

(A) Fittings Made Tight. For raceways, cable trays, cable armor, cablebus framework, or cable sheaths, the fittings and terminations must be made tight using suitable tools.

(B) Aluminum Conductors. Equipment grounding conductors of bare, covered, or insulated aluminum must be installed as follows:

(1) Unless part of a Chapter 3 wiring method, bare or covered conductors are not permitted to be installed where subject to corrosive conditions or in direct contact with concrete, masonry, or the Earth.

(2) Terminations made within outdoor enclosures that are listed and identified for the environment are permitted within 18 in. of the bottom of the enclosure.

(3) Aluminum conductors external to buildings or enclosures are not permitted to be terminated within 18 in. of the Earth, unless terminated within a listed wire connector system.

(C) Exposed. Exposed equipment grounding conductors 8 AWG and smaller for direct-current circuits [250.134(B) Ex.2], such as required by 690.45 for solar PV systems, are permitted to be run separately from the circuit conductors. 8 AWG or smaller exposed equipment grounding conductors must be protected from physical damage and must be installed within a raceway or cable.

250.121 Restricted Use of Equipment Grounding Conductors

(A) Grounding Electrode Conductor. An equipment grounding conductor is not permitted to be used as a grounding electrode conductor.
▶Figure 250–226

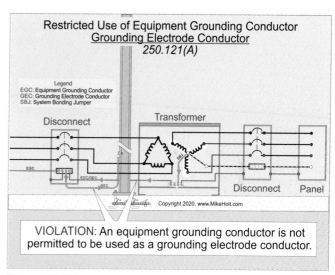

▶Figure 250–226

Ex: An equipment grounding conductor meeting the requirements for an equipment grounding conductor and grounding electrode conductor can be used as a grounding electrode conductor.

(B) Metal Frame of Building. The structural metal frame of a building must not be used as an equipment grounding conductor.

Author's Comment:

▶ Here is a perfect example of why it is so important for you have a complete understanding of the terminology used throughout the *Code*. While the structural metal frame of a building is not permitted to be used as an "equipment grounding conductor," the metal structure of a building is permitted to be used as a "grounding electrode conductor." Knowing the difference, is what makes the difference!

ARTICLE 250 PRACTICE QUESTIONS

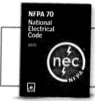

Please use the 2020 *Code* book to answer the following questions.

Article 250—Grounding and Bonding

1. Equipment grounding conductors, grounding electrode conductors, and bonding jumpers shall be connected by _____.

    (a) listed pressure connectors
    (b) terminal bars
    (c) exothermic welding
    (d) any of these

2. _____ on equipment to be grounded shall be removed from contact surfaces to ensure good electrical continuity.

    (a) Paint
    (b) Lacquer
    (c) Enamel
    (d) any of these

3. In order for a metal underground water pipe to be used as a grounding electrode, it shall be in direct contact with the earth for _____.

    (a) 5 ft
    (b) 10 ft or more
    (c) less than 10 ft
    (d) 20 ft or more

4. Reinforcing bars for use as a concrete-encased electrode can be bonded together by the usual steel tie wires or other effective means.

    (a) True
    (b) False

5. An electrode encased by at least 2 in. of concrete, located horizontally near the bottom or vertically and within that portion of a concrete foundation or footing that is in direct contact with the earth, shall be permitted as a grounding electrode when it consists of _____.

    (a) bare copper conductor not smaller than 8 AWG
    (b) bare copper conductor not smaller than 6 AWG
    (c) bare copper conductor not smaller than 4 AWG
    (d) bare copper conductor not smaller than 1/0 AWG

6. A ground ring encircling the building or structure can be used as a grounding electrode when the _____.

    (a) ring is in direct contact with the earth
    (b) ring consists of at least 20 ft of bare copper conductor
    (c) bare copper conductor is not smaller than 2 AWG
    (d) all of these

7. Grounding electrodes of the rod type less than _____ in. in diameter shall be listed.

    (a) ½
    (b) ⅝
    (c) ¾
    (d) 1

8. Grounding electrodes of bare or electrically conductive coated iron or steel plates shall be at least _____ in. thick.

    (a) ⅛
    (b) ¼
    (c) ½
    (d) ¾

9. _____ shall not be used as grounding electrodes.

   (a) Metal underground gas piping systems
   (b) Aluminum
   (c) Metal well casings
   (d) Metal underground gas piping systems and aluminum

10. Swimming pool structures and structural _____ [680.26(B)(1) and (B)(2)] shall not be used as a grounding electrode.

   (a) reinforcing steel
   (b) equipotential planes
   (c) pool shells
   (d) pool pump houses

11. Where the resistance-to-ground of 25 ohms or less is not achieved for a single rod electrode, _____.

   (a) other means besides electrodes shall be used in order to provide grounding
   (b) the single rod electrode shall be supplemented by one additional electrode
   (c) additional electrodes must be added until 25 ohms is achieved
   (d) any of these

12. A rod or pipe electrode shall be installed such that at least _____ of length is in contact with the soil.

   (a) 30 in.
   (b) 6 ft
   (c) 8 ft
   (d) 10 ft

13. Where rock bottom is encountered at an angle up to 45 degrees when driving a rod or pipe electrode, the electrode shall be permitted to be buried in a trench _____ deep.

   (a) 30 in.
   (b) 6 ft
   (c) 8 ft
   (d) 10 ft

14. Where a metal underground water pipe is used as a grounding electrode, the continuity of the grounding path or the bonding connection to interior piping shall not rely on _____ and similar equipment.

   (a) bonding jumpers
   (b) water meters or filtering devices
   (c) grounding clamps
   (d) all of these

15. Where the supplemental electrode is a rod, that portion of the bonding jumper that is the sole connection to the supplemental grounding electrode shall not be required to be larger than _____ AWG copper wire.

   (a) 8
   (b) 6
   (c) 4
   (d) 1

16. Exposed, normally noncurrent-carrying metal parts of cord-and-plug-connected equipment shall be connected to the equipment grounding conductor where operated at over _____ volts to ground.

   (a) 24
   (b) 50
   (c) 120
   (d) 150

17. Listed FMC can be used as the equipment grounding conductor if the length in any ground return path does not exceed 6 ft and the circuit conductors contained in the conduit are protected by overcurrent devices rated at _____ amperes or less.

   (a) 15
   (b) 20
   (c) 30
   (d) 60

18. Listed FMC and LFMC is permitted as an equipment grounding conductor at lengths, _____.

   (a) no greater than 2 ft
   (b) no greater than 3 ft
   (c) up to 6 ft
   (d) up to 10 ft

19. Type MC cable provides an effective ground-fault current path and is recognized by the *NEC* as an equipment grounding conductor when _____.

   (a) it contains an insulated or uninsulated equipment grounding conductor in compliance with 250.118(1)
   (b) the cable assembly contains a bare copper conductor
   (c) only when it is hospital grade Type MC cable
   (d) it is terminated with bonding bushings

20. An equipment grounding conductor shall be identified by _____.

    (a) a continuous outer finish that is green
    (b) being bare
    (c) a continuous outer finish that is green with one or more yellow stripes
    (d) any of these

21. An insulated or covered conductor _____ AWG and larger shall be permitted, at the time of installation, to be permanently identified as an equipment grounding conductor at each end and at every point where the conductor is accessible.

    (a) 8
    (b) 6
    (c) 4
    (d) 1/0

22. Where not routed with circuit conductors as permitted in 250.130(C) and 250.134(A) Exception No. 2, equipment grounding conductors smaller than _____ AWG shall be protected from physical damage by an identified raceway or cable armor.

    (a) 10
    (b) 8
    (c) 6
    (d) 4

23. The structural metal frame of a _____ shall not be used as an equipment grounding conductor.

    (a) roof or crawl space
    (b) wall or ceiling
    (c) building or structure
    (d) floor or window

ARTICLE 300

GENERAL REQUIREMENTS FOR WIRING METHODS AND MATERIALS

Introduction to Article 300—General Requirements for Wiring Methods and Materials

Article 300 contains the general requirements for all wiring methods included in the *NEC*. However, it does not apply to twisted-pair cable and coaxial cable (which are covered in Chapters 7 and 8) unless Article 300 is specifically referenced.

This article is primarily concerned with how to install, route, splice, protect, and secure conductors and raceways. How well you understand and apply the requirements of Article 300 will usually be evident in the finished work. Many of its requirements will affect the appearance, longevity, and even the safety of the installation. Imagine your surprise if you are shoveling some soil onto a plant in the garden and your shovel hits an electrical service cable! After studying and learning the rules in this article, you will immediately realize that the burial depth requirements of 300.5 were possibly overlooked or ignored. Even worse, they might not even have been known at the time of installation.

A good understanding of this article will start you on the path to correctly and safely installing the wiring methods included in Chapter 3. Be sure to carefully consider the accompanying illustrations and refer to the definitions in Article 100 as needed.

Part I. General Requirements

300.1 Scope

(A) All Wiring Installations. Article 300 contains the general requirements for wiring methods and materials for power and lighting. ▶Figure 300–1

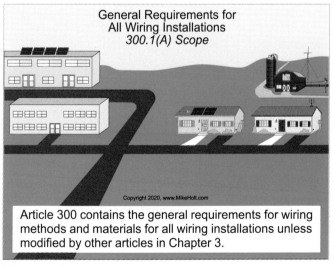

General Requirements for
All Wiring Installations
300.1(A) Scope

Copyright 2020, www.MikeHolt.com

Article 300 contains the general requirements for wiring methods and materials for all wiring installations unless modified by other articles in Chapter 3.

▶Figure 300–1

Author's Comment:

▶ The requirements contained in Article 300 do not apply to the wiring methods for Class 2 and 3 circuits, fire alarm circuits, and communications systems (twisted-pair conductors and coaxial cable). However, the chapters that contain the rules for such wiring methods (Chapters 7 and 8) may refer to Article 300 and those specific references will then apply.

(B) Integral Parts of Equipment. The requirements contained in Article 300 do not apply to the integral parts of electrical equipment. ▶Figure 300–2

Author's Comment:

▶ Integral wiring of equipment is covered by various product standards and not the *NEC*. It is the intent of this *Code* that the factory-installed internal wiring of equipment processed by a qualified testing laboratory does not need to be inspected [90.7].

(C) Trade Sizes. Designators for raceway trade sizes are given in Table 300.1(C).

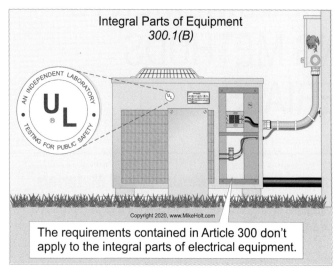

Integral Parts of Equipment
300.1(B)

The requirements contained in Article 300 don't apply to the integral parts of electrical equipment.

▶Figure 300-2

Author's Comment:

▶ Industry practice is to describe raceways using inch sizes, such as ½ in., 2 in., and so on; however, the proper reference is to use "Trade Size ½," or "Trade Size 2." In this textbook we use the proper reference and identify raceway sizes using the phrase "Trade Size."

300.3 Conductors

(A) Single Conductors. Conductors must be installed in a Chapter 3 wiring method such as in a raceway, cable, or enclosure. ▶Figure 300-3

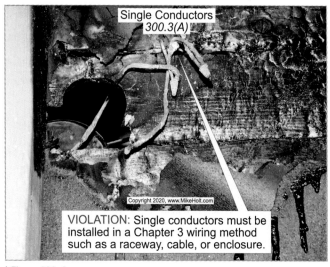

Single Conductors
300.3(A)

VIOLATION: Single conductors must be installed in a Chapter 3 wiring method such as a raceway, cable, or enclosure.

▶Figure 300-3

(B) Circuit Conductors Grouped Together. All conductors of a circuit, including the neutral and equipment grounding conductors, must be installed together in the same raceway, cable, trench, cord, or cable tray; except as permitted by (1) through (4). ▶Figure 300-4 and ▶Figure 300-5

Circuit Conductors Grouped Together
300.3(B)

VIOLATION: All conductors of a circuit, including the neutral and equipment grounding conductors, must be installed together in the same raceway, cable, trench, cord, or cable tray.

▶Figure 300-4

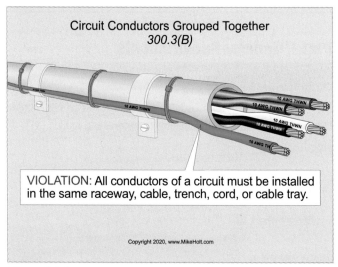

Circuit Conductors Grouped Together
300.3(B)

VIOLATION: All conductors of a circuit must be installed in the same raceway, cable, trench, cord, or cable tray.

▶Figure 300-5

(1) Paralleled Installations. Conductors installed in parallel in accordance with 310.10(G) must have all circuit conductor sets grouped together within the same raceway, cable tray, trench, or cable. ▶Figure 300-6

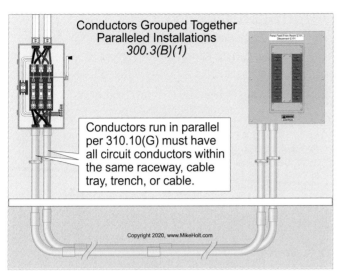

▶Figure 300-6

Author's Comment:

▶ Grouping of all conductors of the circuit is to minimize heating of surrounding ferrous metal raceways and enclosures by induction for alternating-current circuits. See 300.20(A). ▶Figure 300-7

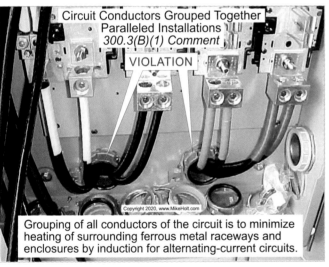

▶Figure 300-7

Connections, taps, or extensions made from paralleled conductors must connect to all conductors of the paralleled set.

Ex: Parallel phase and neutral conductors can be installed in individual underground nonmetallic raceways (Phase A in raceway 1, Phase B in raceway 2, and so forth) as permitted by 300.5(I) Ex 2 if the installation complies with 300.20(B). ▶Figure 300-8

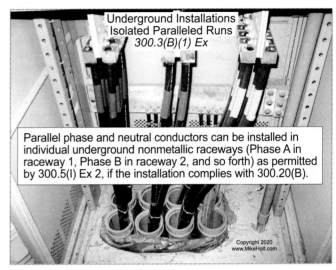

▶Figure 300-8

(2) Outside a Raceway or an Enclosure. Equipment bonding jumpers can be located outside of a raceway if the bonding jumper is installed in accordance with 250.102(E)(2). ▶Figure 300-9

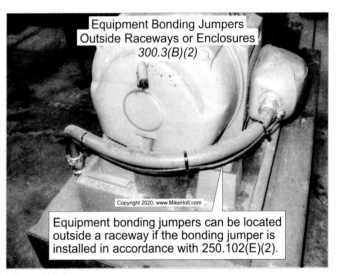

▶Figure 300-9

For direct-current circuits, the equipment grounding conductor can be run separately from the circuit conductors in accordance with 250.134(2) Ex 2. ▶Figure 300-10

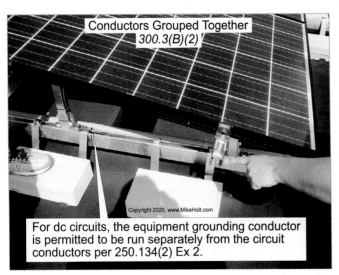

▶Figure 300–10

For dc circuits, the equipment grounding conductor is permitted to be run separately from the circuit conductors per 250.134(2) Ex 2.

(C) Conductors of Different Systems.

(1) Mixing. Power conductors rated 1,000V or less can occupy the same raceway, cable, or enclosure if all conductors have an insulation voltage rating not less than the maximum circuit voltage. ▶Figure 300–11

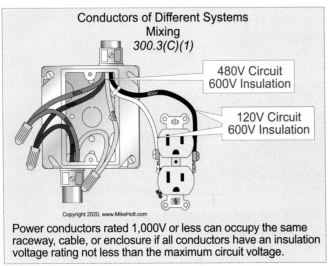

Power conductors rated 1,000V or less can occupy the same raceway, cable, or enclosure if all conductors have an insulation voltage rating not less than the maximum circuit voltage.

▶Figure 300–11

Author's Comment:

▶ Control, signaling, and communications wiring must be separated from power and lighting circuits so the higher-voltage conductors do not accidentally energize the control, signaling, or communications wiring: ▶Figure 300–12

  ▶ Class 1 Control circuits, 725.48
  ▶ Class 2 Control Circuits, 725.136(A)
  ▶ Communications Circuits, 805.133(A)(1)(c)

  ▶ Coaxial Cable, 820.133(A)
  ▶ Fire Alarm Circuits, 760.136(A)
  ▶ Sound Circuits, 640.9(C)

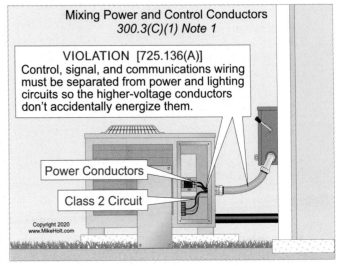

▶Figure 300–12

Author's Comment:

▶ Class 1 circuit conductors can be installed with associated power conductors [725.48(B)(1)] if all conductors have an insulation voltage rating not less than the maximum circuit voltage [300.3(C)(1)].

▶ A Class 2 circuit that has been reclassified as a Class 1 circuit [725.130(A) Ex 2] can be installed with associated power conductors [725.48(B)(1)] if all conductors have an insulation voltage rating not less than the maximum circuit voltage [300.3(C)(1)]. ▶Figure 300–13

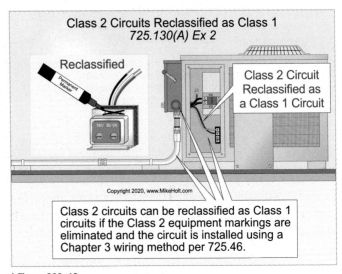

Class 2 circuits can be reclassified as Class 1 circuits if the Class 2 equipment markings are eliminated and the circuit is installed using a Chapter 3 wiring method per 725.46.

▶Figure 300–13

300.4 Protection Against Physical Damage

Where subject to physical damage, conductors, raceways, and cables must be protected in accordance with (A) through (H).

(A) Cables and Raceways Through Wood Members.

Author's Comment:

▶ When the following wiring methods are installed through wood members, they must comply with 300.4(A)(1) or (2). ▶Figure 300–14

- ▹ Armored Cable, Article 320
- ▹ Electrical Nonmetallic Tubing, Article 362
- ▹ Flexible Metal Conduit, Article 348
- ▹ Liquidtight Flexible Metal Conduit, Article 350
- ▹ Liquidtight Flexible Nonmetallic Conduit, Article 356
- ▹ Metal-Clad Cable, Article 330
- ▹ Nonmetallic-Sheathed Cable, Article 334
- ▹ Service-Entrance Cable, Article 338
- ▹ Underground Feeder and Branch-Circuit Cable, Article 340

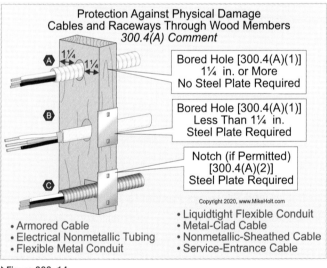

▶Figure 300–14

(1) Bored Holes in Wood Members. Holes through wood framing members for the above cables or raceways must be not less than 1¼ in. from the edge of the wood member. If the edge of a drilled hole in a wood framing member is less than 1¼ in. from the edge, a ¹/₁₆ in. thick steel plate of enough length and width must be installed to protect the wiring method from screws and nails. ▶Figure 300–15

If the edge of a drilled hole in a wood framing member is less than 1¼ in. from the edge, a ¹/₁₆ in. thick steel plate must be installed to protect the wiring method from screws and nails.

▶Figure 300–15

Ex 1: A steel plate is not required to protect rigid metal conduit, intermediate metal conduit, PVC conduit, or electrical metallic tubing.

(2) Notches in Wood Members. If notching of wood framing members for cables and raceways is permitted by the building code, a ¹/₁₆ in. thick steel plate of enough length and width must be installed to protect the wiring method laid in those wood notches from screws and nails. ▶Figure 300–16

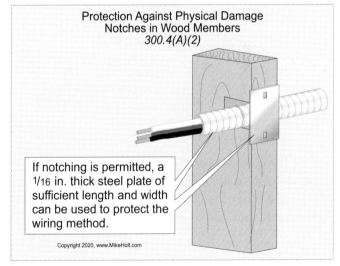

If notching is permitted, a ¹/₁₆ in. thick steel plate of sufficient length and width can be used to protect the wiring method.

▶Figure 300–16

Ex 1: A steel plate is not required to protect rigid metal conduit, intermediate metal conduit, PVC conduit, or electrical metallic tubing.

Caution

⚡ Many wood and metal framing members (especially joists and beams) have specific drilling and/or notching instructions meant to maintain structural integrity. Be sure to check with the building official for building code requirements.

(B) Nonmetallic-Sheathed Cable and Electrical Nonmetallic Tubing Through Metal Framing Members.

(1) Type NM Cable, Metal Framing Members. If Type NM cables pass through factory or field-made openings in metal framing members, the cable must be protected by listed bushings or listed grommets that cover all metal edges. The protection fitting must be securely fastened in the opening before the installation of the cable. ▶Figure 300–17

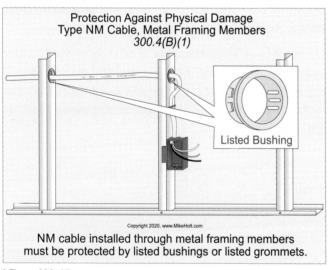

Protection Against Physical Damage
Type NM Cable, Metal Framing Members
300.4(B)(1)

Listed Bushing

Copyright 2020, www.MikeHolt.com

NM cable installed through metal framing members must be protected by listed bushings or listed grommets.

▶Figure 300–17

(2) Type NM Cable and Electrical Nonmetallic Tubing. If nails or screws are likely to penetrate Type NM cable or electrical nonmetallic tubing, a steel sleeve, steel plate, or steel clip not less than $^1/_{16}$ in. in thickness must be installed to protect the cable or tubing.

Ex: A listed and marked steel plate less than $^1/_{16}$ in. thick that provides equal or better protection against nail or screw penetration is permitted.

(C) Behind Suspended Ceilings. Wiring methods such as boxes, enclosures, cables, or raceways, installed behind panels designed to allow access must be supported in accordance with its applicable article. ▶Figure 300–18

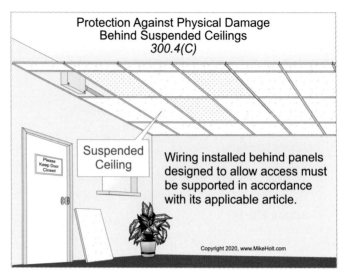

Protection Against Physical Damage
Behind Suspended Ceilings
300.4(C)

Please Keep Door Closed

Suspended Ceiling

Wiring installed behind panels designed to allow access must be supported in accordance with its applicable article.

Copyright 2020, www.MikeHolt.com

▶Figure 300–18

Author's Comment:

▶ Requirements for the support of various wiring methods in suspended ceilings can be found in 300.11(B). Check each applicable wiring method in Chapter 3 for additional support requirements.

▶ Similar support requirements are contained in Chapters 6, 7, and 8 as follows:

  ▶ Audio Cable, 640.5 and 640.6(A)

  ▶ Communications (twisted pair) Cable and Coaxial Cable, 800.21 and 800.24

  ▶ Control and Signaling Cable, 725.21 and 725.24

  ▶ Fire Alarm Cable, 760.21 and 760.24

  ▶ Optical Fiber Cable, 770.21 and 770.24

(D) Cables and Raceways Parallel to Framing Members and Furring Strips. Cables or raceways run parallel to framing members or furring strips must be protected by installing the wiring method not less than 1¼ in. from the nearest edge of the framing member or furring strip. If the edge of the framing member or furring strip is less than 1¼ in. away, a $^1/_{16}$ in. thick steel plate of enough length and width must be installed to protect the wiring method from screws and nails. ▶Figure 300–19

Ex 1: Protection is not required for rigid metal conduit, intermediate metal conduit, PVC conduit, or electrical metallic tubing.

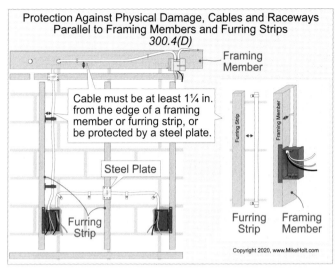

Protection Against Physical Damage, Cables and Raceways Parallel to Framing Members and Furring Strips
300.4(D)

Framing Member

Cable must be at least 1¼ in. from the edge of a framing member or furring strip, or be protected by a steel plate.

Furring Strip

Framing Member

Steel Plate

Furring Strip

Furring Strip

Framing Member

Copyright 2020, www.MikeHolt.com

▶Figure 300-19

(E) Wiring Under Roof Decking. Cables, raceways, and enclosures under metal-corrugated sheet roof decking are not permitted to be located within 1½ in. of the roof decking measured from the lowest surface of the roof decking to the top of the cable, raceway, or box.
▶Figure 300-20

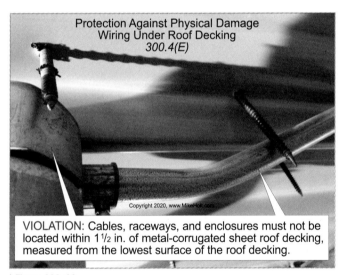

Protection Against Physical Damage
Wiring Under Roof Decking
300.4(E)

Copyright 2020, www.MikeHolt.com

VIOLATION: Cables, raceways, and enclosures must not be located within 1½ in. of metal-corrugated sheet roof decking, measured from the lowest surface of the roof decking.

▶Figure 300-20

Author's Comment:

▶ A similar requirement applies to luminaires installed in or under roof decking [410.10(F)].

Note: Raceways or cables installed under metal roof decking may be penetrated by screws or other mechanical devices designed to "hold down" the waterproof membrane or roof insulating material.

Ex: Spacing from roof decking does not apply to rigid metal conduit and intermediate metal conduit.

(G) Fittings. Raceways containing insulated circuit conductors 4 AWG and larger that enter a cabinet, box, enclosure, or raceway, must have the conductors protected as follows:

(1) A fitting providing a smoothly rounded insulating surface ▶Figure 300-21

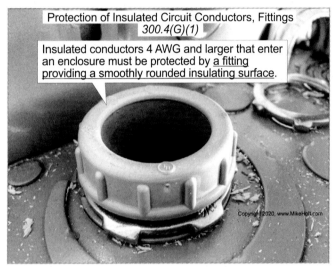

Protection of Insulated Circuit Conductors, Fittings
300.4(G)(1)

Insulated conductors 4 AWG and larger that enter an enclosure must be protected by a fitting providing a smoothly rounded insulating surface.

Copyright 2020, www.MikeHolt.com

▶Figure 300-21

(2) A listed metal fitting that has smoothly rounded edges ▶Figure 300-22

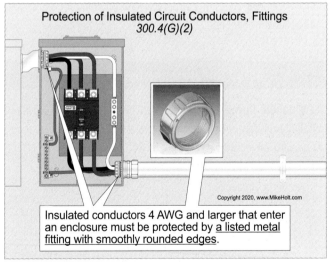

Protection of Insulated Circuit Conductors, Fittings
300.4(G)(2)

Copyright 2020, www.MikeHolt.com

Insulated conductors 4 AWG and larger that enter an enclosure must be protected by a listed metal fitting with smoothly rounded edges.

▶Figure 300-22

(3) Separation from the fitting or raceway using an identified insulating material securely fastened in place

(4) Threaded hubs or bosses that are an integral part of a cabinet, box, enclosure, or raceway that provide a smoothly rounded or flared entry for conductors. ▶Figure 300–23

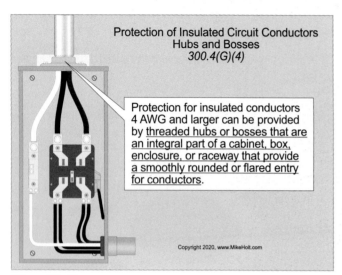

Protection of Insulated Circuit Conductors
Hubs and Bosses
300.4(G)(4)

Protection for insulated conductors 4 AWG and larger can be provided by threaded hubs or bosses that are an integral part of a cabinet, box, enclosure, or raceway that provide a smoothly rounded or flared entry for conductors.

Copyright 2020, www.MikeHolt.com

▶Figure 300–23

Author's Comment:

▶ If IMC or RMC enters an enclosure without a connector, a bushing must be provided regardless of the conductor size [342.46 and 344.46].

(H) Structural Joints. A listed expansion/deflection fitting, or other means approved by the authority having jurisdiction, must be used where a raceway crosses a structural joint intended for expansion, contraction, or deflection.

300.5 Underground Installations

(A) Minimum Cover Requirements. When cables or raceways are installed underground, they must have a minimum cover in accordance with Table 300.5. ▶Figure 300–24

Author's Comment:

▶ Table 300.5 Note 1 defines "Cover" as the shortest distance in in. measured between the top of any direct-buried conductor, cable, or raceway to the surface of the finished grade, concrete, or similar cover. ▶Figure 300–25 and ▶Figure 300–26

Underground Installations
Minimum Cover Requirements
Table 300.5

	Column 1 UF or USE Cables or Conductors	Column 2 RMC or IMC	Column 3 Nonmetallic Raceways not Encased in Concrete	Column 4 Residential 15A & 20A GFCI 120V Branch Ckts
Dwelling Unit Driveway and Parking Area	18 in.	18 in.	18 in.	12 in.
Under Roadway Driveway Parking Lot	24 in.	24 in.	24 in.	24 in.
Other Locations	24 in.	6 in.	18 in.	12 in.

Copyright 2020, www.MikeHolt.com

▶Figure 300–24

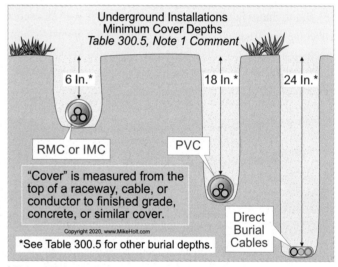

Underground Installations
Minimum Cover Depths
Table 300.5, Note 1 Comment

6 In.*

18 In.*

24 In.*

RMC or IMC

PVC

"Cover" is measured from the top of a raceway, cable, or conductor to finished grade, concrete, or similar cover.

Direct Burial Cables

Copyright 2020, www.MikeHolt.com

*See Table 300.5 for other burial depths.

▶Figure 300–25

Minimum Cover Depths, Under a Building
Table 300.5 Comment

Copyright 2020, www.MikeHolt.com

There are no cover requirements for raceways under a building.

▶Figure 300–26

Table 300.5 Minimum Cover Requirements in Inches			
Location	Column 1 Buried Cables	Column 2 RMC or IMC	Column 3 Nonmetallic Raceways
Under Building	0	0	0
Dwelling Unit	24/12*	18/12*	18/12*
Dwelling Unit Driveway	18/12*	6	18/12*
Under Roadway	24	24	24
Other Locations	18/12*	6	18/12*

*Residential branch circuits rated 120V or less with GFCI protection and maximum protection of 20A.

See the table in the NEC for full details.

b. A depth of 6 in. is permitted for pool, spa, and fountain lighting wiring installed in a nonmetallic raceway, where part of a listed 30V or less lighting system. ▶**Figure 300–27**

Note 1 to Table 300.5: "Cover" is defined as the shortest distance from the top of the underground cable or raceway to the top surface of finished grade.

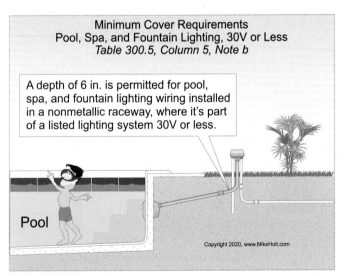

Minimum Cover Requirements
Pool, Spa, and Fountain Lighting, 30V or Less
Table 300.5, Column 5, Note b

A depth of 6 in. is permitted for pool, spa, and fountain lighting wiring installed in a nonmetallic raceway, where it's part of a listed lighting system 30V or less.

Pool

Copyright 2020, www.MikeHolt.com

▶Figure 300–27

Author's Comment:

▶ The cover requirements contained in 300.5 do not apply to signaling, communications, and other power-limited wiring systems: ▶**Figure 300–28**

  ▷ Class 2 and 3 Circuits, 725.3

  ▷ Communications Cables and Raceways, 90.3

  ▷ Coaxial Cable, 90.3

  ▷ Fire Alarm Circuits, 760.3

  ▷ Optical Fiber Cables and Raceways, 770.3

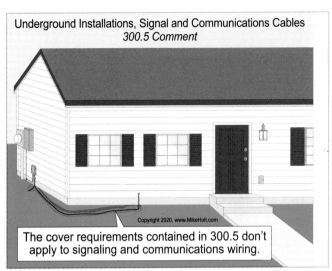

Underground Installations, Signal and Communications Cables
300.5 Comment

Copyright 2020, www.MikeHolt.com

The cover requirements contained in 300.5 don't apply to signaling and communications wiring.

▶Figure 300–28

(B) Wet Locations. Cables and insulated conductors installed in underground enclosures or raceways must be listed as suitable for a wet location [310.10(C)]. ▶**Figure 300–29**

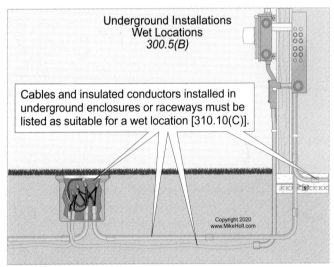

Underground Installations
Wet Locations
300.5(B)

Cables and insulated conductors installed in underground enclosures or raceways must be listed as suitable for a wet location [310.10(C)].

Copyright 2020
www.MikeHolt.com

▶Figure 300–29

Author's Comment:

▶ According to Article 100, a "Wet Location" includes installations underground, in concrete slabs in direct contact with the Earth, locations subject to saturation with water, and unprotected locations exposed to weather. See 300.9 for raceways in wet locations above ground.

(C) Cables and Conductors Under Buildings. Cables and conductors installed under a building must be installed within a raceway that extends past the outside walls of the building. ▶**Figure 300–30**

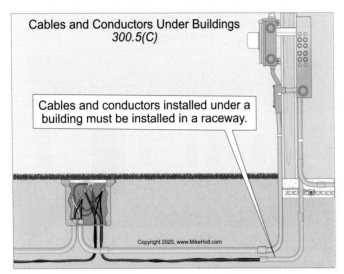

▶Figure 300–30

Ex 2: Type MC Cable listed for direct burial or concrete encasement is permitted under a building without installation within a raceway [330.10(A)(5) and 330.10(A)(11)]. ▶Figure 300–31

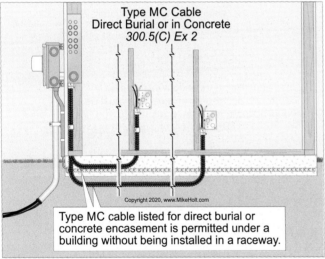

▶Figure 300–31

(D) Protecting Underground Cables and Conductors. Direct-buried conductors and cables such as Types MC, UF, and USE installed underground must be protected from damage in accordance with (1) through (4).

(1) Emerging from Grade. Direct-buried cables and conductors that emerge from grade must be protected against physical damage. Protection is not required to extend more than 18 in. below grade, and protection above ground must extend to a height of not less than 8 ft. ▶Figure 300–32

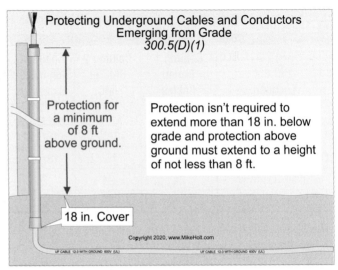

▶Figure 300–32

(2) Conductors Entering Buildings. Underground conductors and cables that enter a building must be protected to the point of entrance.

(3) Underground Service Conductors. Underground service conductors must have their location identified by a warning ribbon placed in the trench at least 12 in. above the underground conductor installation. ▶Figure 300–33

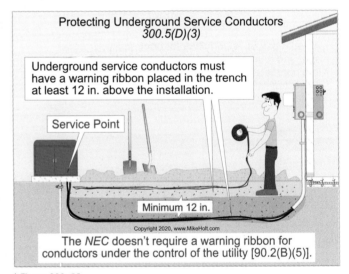

▶Figure 300–33

Author's Comment:

▶ The *NEC* does not require a warning ribbon for conductors under the exclusive control of the utility [90.2(B)(5)].

(4) Raceway Damage. Where a raceway is subject to physical damage, the conductors must be installed in EMT, RMC, IMC, RTRC-XW, or Schedule 80 PVC conduit.

(E) Underground Splices and Taps. Direct-buried conductors or cables can be spliced or tapped underground without a splice box [300.15(G)] if the splice or tap is made in accordance with 110.14(B). ▶Figure 300–34

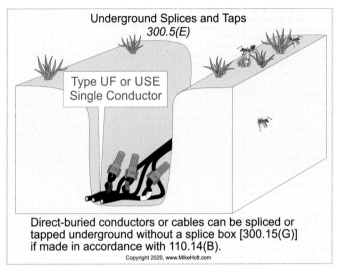

Underground Splices and Taps
300.5(E)

Type UF or USE
Single Conductor

Direct-buried conductors or cables can be spliced or tapped underground without a splice box [300.15(G)] if made in accordance with 110.14(B).
Copyright 2020, www.MikeHolt.com

▶Figure 300–34

(F) Backfill. Backfill material for underground wiring is not permitted to damage underground raceways, cables, or conductors. ▶Figure 300–35

Author's Comment:

▸ Large rocks, chunks of concrete, steel rods, mesh, and other sharp-edged objects are not permitted to be used for backfilling material because they can damage the underground conductors, cables, or raceways.

(G) Raceway Seals. If moisture could contact energized live parts through an underground raceway, a seal identified for use with the cable or conductor insulation must be installed at either or both ends of the raceway [225.27 and 230.8]. ▶Figure 300–36

Author's Comment:

▸ Moisture is a common problem for equipment located downhill from the supply, or in underground equipment rooms.

(H) Bushing. Raceways that terminate underground must have a bushing or fitting at the end of the raceway to protect emerging cables or conductors. ▶Figure 300–37

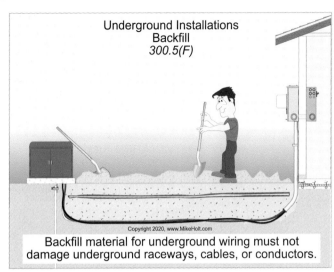

Underground Installations
Backfill
300.5(F)

Copyright 2020, www.MikeHolt.com

Backfill material for underground wiring must not damage underground raceways, cables, or conductors.

▶Figure 300–35

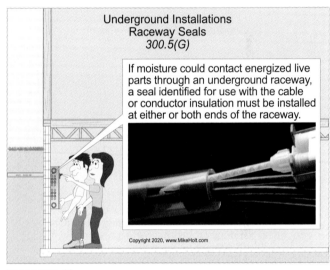

Underground Installations
Raceway Seals
300.5(G)

If moisture could contact energized live parts through an underground raceway, a seal identified for use with the cable or conductor insulation must be installed at either or both ends of the raceway.

Copyright 2020, www.MikeHolt.com

▶Figure 300–36

(I) Conductors of the Same Circuit. Underground conductors of the same circuit (including the equipment grounding conductor) must be installed inside the same raceway, multiconductor cable, or near each other in the same trench. See 300.3(B). ▶Figure 300–38

Ex 2: Underground parallel conductors can have the conductors of each phase or neutral installed in separate nonmetallic raceways where inductive heating at raceway terminations is reduced by the use of aluminum locknuts and by cutting a slot between the individual holes through which the conductors pass as required by 300.20(B). ▶Figure 300–39

▶Figure 300–37

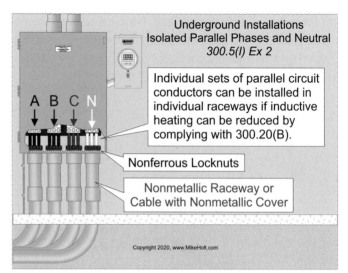

▶Figure 300–39

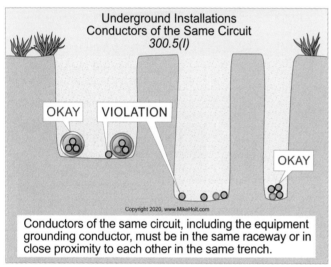

▶Figure 300–38

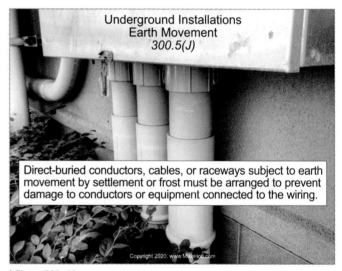

▶Figure 300–40

Author's Comment:

▶ Separating phase and neutral conductors in individual PVC conduits makes it easier to terminate larger parallel installations, but it also results in elevated electromagnetic fields (EMF). Keeping the phase and neutral conductors close to each other helps reduce circuit impedance.

(J) Earth Movement. Direct-buried conductors, cables, or raceways that are subject to movement by settlement or frost must be arranged to prevent damage to conductors or equipment connected to the wiring. ▶Figure 300–40

300.6 Protection Against Corrosion and Deterioration

Raceways, cable trays, cablebus, cable armor, boxes, cable sheathing, cabinets, elbows, couplings, fittings, supports, and support hardware must be suitable for the environment. ▶Figure 300–41

Author's Comment:

▶ Section 110.11 has similar requirements regarding deteriorating agents.

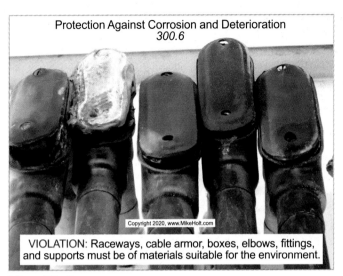

VIOLATION: Raceways, cable armor, boxes, elbows, fittings, and supports must be of materials suitable for the environment.

▶Figure 300–41

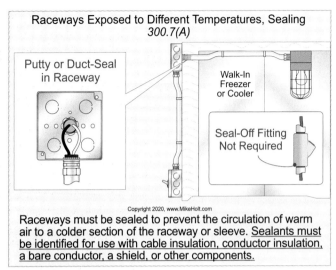

Raceways must be sealed to prevent the circulation of warm air to a colder section of the raceway or sleeve. Sealants must be identified for use with cable insulation, conductor insulation, a bare conductor, a shield, or other components.

▶Figure 300–42

(A) Ferrous Metal Equipment. Ferrous metal raceways, enclosures, cables, cable trays, fittings, and support hardware must be protected against corrosion by a coating of listed corrosion-resistant material. Where conduit is threaded in the field, the threads must be coated with an approved electrically conductive, corrosion-resistant compound such as zinc galvanizing or KOPR-Shield®.

Note: Field-cut threads are those threads that are cut anywhere other than at the factory.

Author's Comment:

▶ Ferrous metals are those that are prone to higher degrees of oxidation or ferrous oxide; most commonly called "rust." The use of nonferrous materials is preferred in locations and environments that lead to this type of deterioration.

▶ Nonferrous metal raceways, such as aluminum rigid metal conduit, do not have to meet the provisions of this section. See 300.6(B).

300.7 Raceways Exposed to Different Temperatures

(A) Sealing. If a raceway is subjected to different temperatures, and where condensation is known to be a problem, the raceway must be filled with a material approved by the authority having jurisdiction that will prevent the circulation of warm air to a colder section of the raceway. Sealants must be identified for use with cable insulation, conductor insulation, a bare conductor, a shield, or other components. ▶Figure 300–42

Author's Comment:

▶ One common product used for this is electrical duct seal and it is so identified. There are other identified products such as Polywater's FST Duct Sealant. Typical expanding foams used to seal buildings are not identified for this application.

(B) Expansion, Expansion-Deflection, and Deflection Fittings. Raceways must be provided with expansion, expansion-deflection, or deflection fittings where necessary to compensate for thermal expansion, deflection, and contraction. ▶Figure 300–43

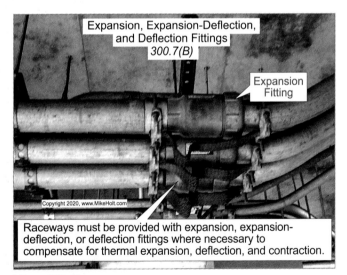

Raceways must be provided with expansion, expansion-deflection, or deflection fittings where necessary to compensate for thermal expansion, deflection, and contraction.

▶Figure 300–43

Note: Table 352.44 provides the expansion characteristics for PVC conduit. The expansion characteristics for steel conduit are determined by multiplying the values from Table 352.44 by 0.20, and those for aluminum raceways are determined by multiplying the values from Table 352.44 by 0.40. Table 355.44 provides the expansion characteristics for reinforced thermosetting resin conduit (RTRC). ▶Figure 300–44

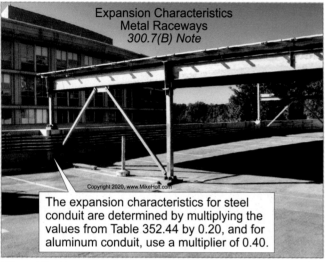

Expansion Characteristics
Metal Raceways
300.7(B) Note

The expansion characteristics for steel conduit are determined by multiplying the values from Table 352.44 by 0.20, and for aluminum conduit, use a multiplier of 0.40.

▶Figure 300–44

300.9 Raceways in Wet Locations Above Grade

The interior of raceways installed in wet locations above ground is considered a wet location. Insulated conductors and cables installed in raceways in aboveground wet locations must be listed for use in wet locations in accordance with 310.10(C). ▶Figure 300–45

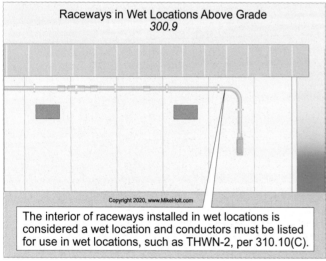

Raceways in Wet Locations Above Grade
300.9

The interior of raceways installed in wet locations is considered a wet location and conductors must be listed for use in wet locations, such as THWN-2, per 310.10(C).

▶Figure 300–45

Author's Comment:

▶ In addition to 310.10(C), Table 310.4(A) can be used to find other insulation types permitted in wet locations.

300.10 Electrical Continuity

Metal raceways, cable armor, and other metal enclosures must be metallically joined into a continuous electrical conductor to provide effective electrical continuity [110.10 and 250.4(A)]. ▶Figure 300–46

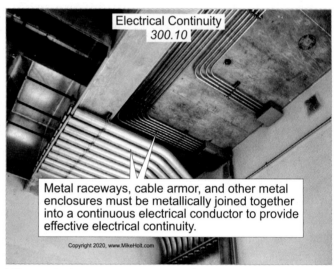

Electrical Continuity
300.10

Metal raceways, cable armor, and other metal enclosures must be metallically joined together into a continuous electrical conductor to provide effective electrical continuity.

▶Figure 300–46

Author's Comment:

▶ The purpose of electrical continuity between metal parts is to establish the effective ground-fault current path necessary to facilitate the operation of the circuit overcurrent protective device in the event of a ground fault [250.4(A)(5)]. ▶Figure 300–47

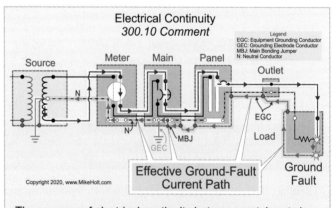

Electrical Continuity
300.10 Comment

The purpose of electrical continuity between metal parts is to establish the effective ground-fault current path necessary to facilitate the operation of the circuit overcurrent protective device in the event of a ground fault [250.4(A)(5)].

▶Figure 300–47

Ex 1: Short lengths of metal raceways used for the support or protection of cables are not required to be electrically continuous, nor are they required to be connected to an equipment grounding conductor [250.86 Ex 2 and 300.12 Ex 1]. ▶Figure 300–48

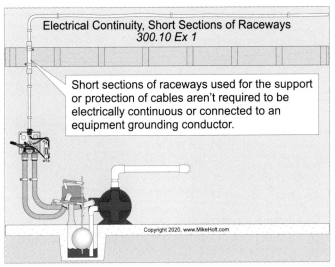

Electrical Continuity, Short Sections of Raceways
300.10 Ex 1

Short sections of raceways used for the support or protection of cables aren't required to be electrically continuous or connected to an equipment grounding conductor.

Copyright 2020, www.MikeHolt.com

▶Figure 300–48

300.11 Securing and Supporting

(A) Secured in Place. Raceways, cable assemblies, and enclosures must be securely fastened in place.

(B) Wiring Systems Installed Above Suspended Ceilings. Ceiling-support wires or the ceiling grid is not permitted to support raceways or cables. Independent support wires secured at both ends can be used to support raceways or cables. ▶Figure 300–49

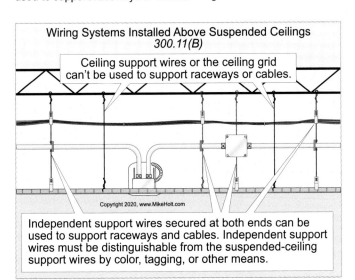

Wiring Systems Installed Above Suspended Ceilings
300.11(B)

Ceiling support wires or the ceiling grid can't be used to support raceways or cables.

Copyright 2020, www.MikeHolt.com

Independent support wires secured at both ends can be used to support raceways and cables. Independent support wires must be distinguishable from the suspended-ceiling support wires by color, tagging, or other means.

▶Figure 300–49

(1) Fire-Rated Assemblies. Electrical wiring within the cavity of a fire-rated ceiling assembly can be supported by independent support wires attached to the ceiling assembly. The independent support wires must be distinguishable from the suspended-ceiling support wires by color, tagging, or other effective means.

Author's Comment:

▸ Outlet boxes [314.23(D)] and luminaires can be secured to the suspended-ceiling grid if the luminaire is securely fastened to the ceiling-framing members by mechanical means such as bolts, screws, or rivets, or by the use of clips or other securing means identified for use with the type of ceiling-framing member(s) used [410.36(B)].

(C) Raceways Used for Support. Raceways are not permitted to support other wiring methods, except as follows: ▶Figure 300–50 and ▶Figure 300–51

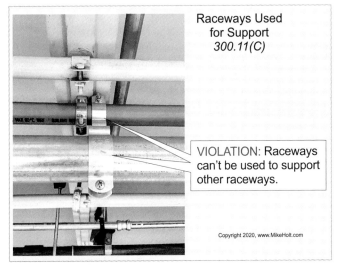

Raceways Used
for Support
300.11(C)

VIOLATION: Raceways can't be used to support other raceways.

Copyright 2020, www.MikeHolt.com

▶Figure 300–50

(1) Identified. If the raceway or means of support is identified as a means of support.

(2) Class 2 and 3 Circuits. Class 2 and 3 cables can be supported by the raceway that supplies power to the equipment controlled by the Class 2 or 3 circuit. ▶Figure 300–52

(D) Cables Not Used as Means of Support. Cables are not permitted to support other wiring methods. ▶Figure 300–53

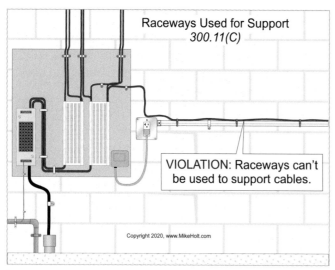

Raceways Used for Support
300.11(C)

VIOLATION: Raceways can't be used to support cables.

▶Figure 300–51

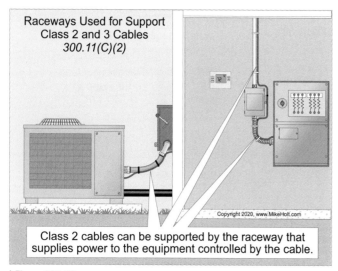

Raceways Used for Support
Class 2 and 3 Cables
300.11(C)(2)

Class 2 cables can be supported by the raceway that supplies power to the equipment controlled by the cable.

▶Figure 300–52

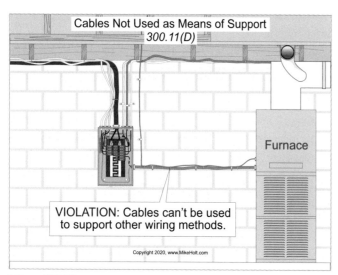

Cables Not Used as Means of Support
300.11(D)

Furnace

VIOLATION: Cables can't be used to support other wiring methods.

▶Figure 300–53

300.12 Mechanical Continuity

Raceways and cable sheaths must be mechanically continuous between boxes, cabinets, and fittings. ▶Figure 300–54 and ▶Figure 300–55

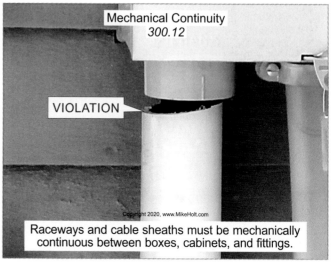

Mechanical Continuity
300.12

VIOLATION

Raceways and cable sheaths must be mechanically continuous between boxes, cabinets, and fittings.

▶Figure 300–54

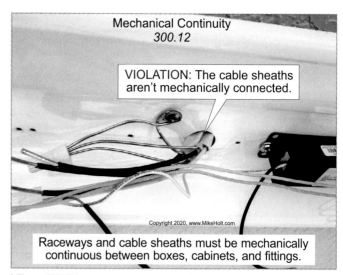

Mechanical Continuity
300.12

VIOLATION: The cable sheaths aren't mechanically connected.

Raceways and cable sheaths must be mechanically continuous between boxes, cabinets, and fittings.

▶Figure 300–55

Ex 1: Short sections of raceways used to provide support or protection of cables from physical damage are not required to be mechanically continuous [250.86 Ex 2 and 300.10 Ex 1]. ▶Figure 300–56

Ex 2: Raceways and cables installed into the bottom of open-bottom equipment such as switchboards, motor control centers, and floor or pad-mounted transformers are not required to be mechanically secured to the equipment. ▶Figure 300–57

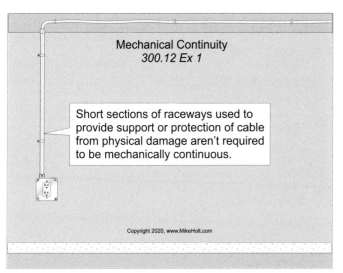

Mechanical Continuity
300.12 Ex 1

Short sections of raceways used to provide support or protection of cable from physical damage aren't required to be mechanically continuous.

Copyright 2020, www.MikeHolt.com

▶Figure 300–56

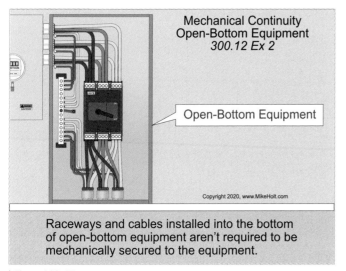

Mechanical Continuity
Open-Bottom Equipment
300.12 Ex 2

Open-Bottom Equipment

Copyright 2020, www.MikeHolt.com

Raceways and cables installed into the bottom of open-bottom equipment aren't required to be mechanically secured to the equipment.

▶Figure 300–57

300.13 Mechanical and Electrical Continuity—Conductors

(A) Conductor Splices. Conductor splices and taps must be made inside enclosures in accordance with 300.15. Splices are not permitted in raceways, except as permitted for wireways in 376.56. ▶Figure 300–58

(B) Device Removal—Neutral Continuity. Continuity of the neutral conductor of a multiwire branch circuit is not permitted to be interrupted by the removal of a wiring device.

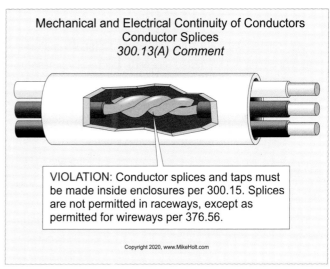

Mechanical and Electrical Continuity of Conductors
Conductor Splices
300.13(A) Comment

VIOLATION: Conductor splices and taps must be made inside enclosures per 300.15. Splices are not permitted in raceways, except as permitted for wireways per 376.56.

Copyright 2020, www.MikeHolt.com

▶Figure 300–58

Author's Comment:

▶ This means that (for multiwire applications) the neutral conductors must be spliced together, and a pigtail must be provided for the wiring device. ▶Figure 300–59

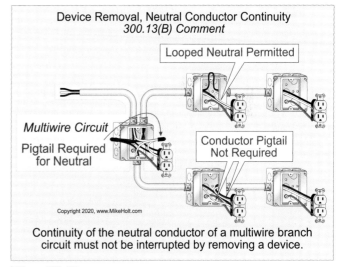

Device Removal, Neutral Conductor Continuity
300.13(B) Comment

Looped Neutral Permitted

Multiwire Circuit

Pigtail Required for Neutral

Conductor Pigtail Not Required

Copyright 2020, www.MikeHolt.com

Continuity of the neutral conductor of a multiwire branch circuit must not be interrupted by removing a device.

▶Figure 300–59

▶ The opening of the phase conductors, or the neutral conductor of a 2-wire circuit while a device is replaced does not cause a safety hazard, so pigtailing these conductors is not required [110.14(B)].

<ins>Caution</ins>

⚠ If the continuity of the neutral conductor of a multiwire circuit is interrupted (opened), the resulting over- or undervoltage can cause a fire and/or destruction of electrical equipment.

▶ **Hazard of Open Neutral Example**

Example: *If the neutral conductor is interrupted on a 3-wire, 120/240V multiwire circuit that supplies a 1,200W, 120V hair dryer and a 600W, 120V television, it will cause the 120V television to momentarily operate at 160V before it burns up. This can be determined as follows:* ▶**Figure 300–60** *and* ▶**Figure 300–61**

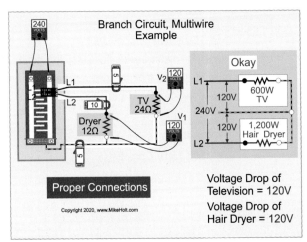

▶Figure 300–60

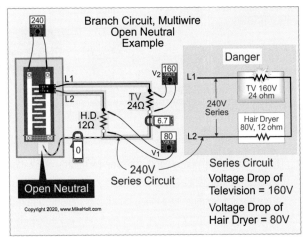

▶Figure 300–61

Step 1: Determine the resistance of each appliance.

$R = E^2/P$

R of the hair dryer = $120V^2/1,200W$
R of the hair dryer = 12 ohms

R of the television = $120V^2/600W$
R of the television = 24 ohms

Step 2: Determine the current of the circuit.

I = Volts/Resistance

Volts = 240V
R = 36 ohms (12 ohms + 24 ohms)

I = 240V/36 ohms
I = 6.70A

Step 3: Determine the operating voltage for each appliance.

Volts = I × R

I = 6.70A
R = 12 ohms for the hair dryer and 24 ohms for the TV.

Voltage of hair dryer = 6.70A × 12 ohms
Voltage of hair dryer = 80V

Voltage of television = 6.70A × 24 ohms
Voltage of television = 160V

300.14 Length of Free Conductors

At least 6 in. of conductor, measured from the point in the box where the conductors enter the enclosure, must be available at each point for conductor splices or terminations. ▶Figure 300–62

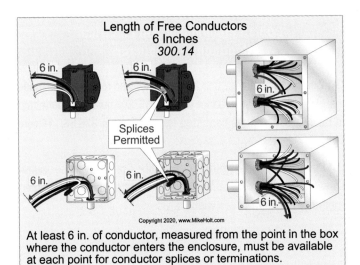

At least 6 in. of conductor, measured from the point in the box where the conductor enters the enclosure, must be available at each point for conductor splices or terminations.

▶Figure 300–62

Boxes with openings less than 8 in. at any dimension must have at least 6 in. of conductor, measured from the point where the conductors enter the box, and at least 3 in. of conductor outside the box. ▶Figure 300–63

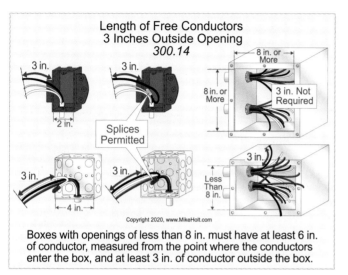

Length of Free Conductors
3 Inches Outside Opening
300.14

Boxes with openings of less than 8 in. must have at least 6 in. of conductor, measured from the point where the conductors enter the box, and at least 3 in. of conductor outside the box.

▶Figure 300–63

300.15 Boxes or Fittings

A box must be installed at each splice or termination point, except as permitted by 300.15(A) through (L): ▶Figure 300–64 and ▶Figure 300–65

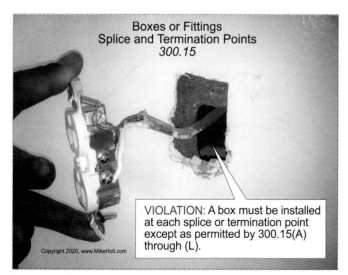

Boxes or Fittings
Splice and Termination Points
300.15

VIOLATION: A box must be installed at each splice or termination point except as permitted by 300.15(A) through (L).

▶Figure 300–64

Author's Comment:

▶ Conductors can be spliced in a conduit body in accordance with 314.16(C). ▶Figure 300–66

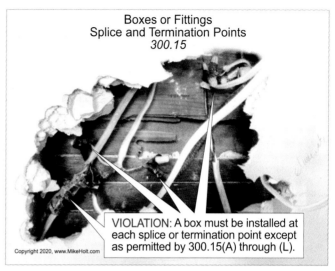

Boxes or Fittings
Splice and Termination Points
300.15

VIOLATION: A box must be installed at each splice or termination point except as permitted by 300.15(A) through (L).

▶Figure 300–65

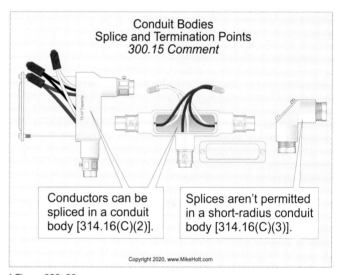

Conduit Bodies
Splice and Termination Points
300.15 Comment

Conductors can be spliced in a conduit body [314.16(C)(2)].

Splices aren't permitted in a short-radius conduit body [314.16(C)(3)].

▶Figure 300–66

Fittings <u>and connectors</u> can only be used with the specific wiring methods for which they are <u>designed and</u> listed. ▶Figure 300–67

Author's Comment:

▶ Type NM cable connectors are not permitted to be used with Type AC cable, and electrical metallic tubing fittings are not permitted to be used with rigid metal conduit or intermediate metal conduit unless listed for the purpose

▶ PVC conduit couplings and connectors are permitted with electrical nonmetallic tubing if the proper glue is used in accordance with manufacturer's instructions [110.3(B)]. See 362.48.

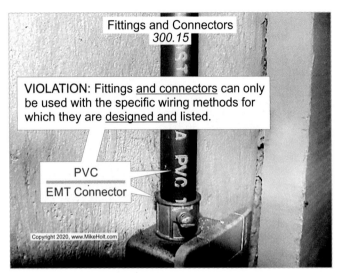

▶Figure 300–67

(A) Wiring Methods with Interior Access. A box is not required for wiring methods with removable covers such as wireways, multioutlet assemblies, and surface raceways.

(C) Raceways for Support or Protection. When a raceway is used for the support or protection of cables, a fitting to reduce the potential for abrasion must be placed at the location the cables enter the raceway. ▶Figure 300–68

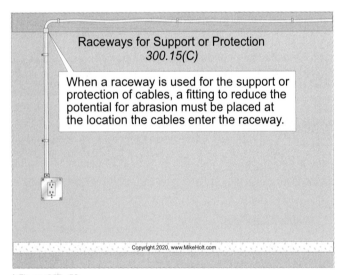

▶Figure 300–68

▸ Boxes are not required for the following signaling and communications cables or raceways: ▶**Figure 300–69**

  ▸ Class 2 and 3 Control and Signaling, 725.3
  ▸ Communications, 90.3
  ▸ Coaxial Cable, 90.3
  ▸ Optical Fiber, 770.3

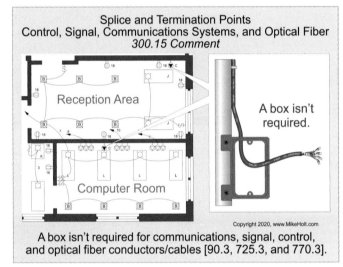

A box isn't required for communications, signal, control, and optical fiber conductors/cables [90.3, 725.3, and 770.3].

▶Figure 300–69

(F) Fittings. A fitting identified for the use is permitted instead of a box or conduit body where conductors are not spliced or terminated within the fitting. The fitting must be accessible after installation, unless it is listed for concealed installation. ▶Figure 300–70

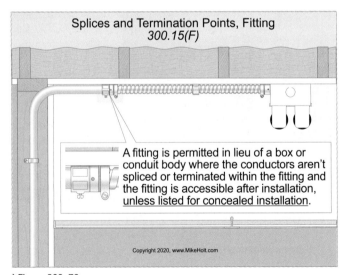

▶Figure 300–70

(G) Underground Splices. A box is not required where a splice is made underground if the conductors are spliced with a splicing device listed for direct burial. See 110.14(B) and 300.5(E).

(H) Type NM Cable Interconnector Device. A box is not required where a listed nonmetallic-sheathed cable interconnector device is used for exposed cable wiring or concealed repair wiring in an existing building in accordance with 334.40(B). ▶Figure 300-71

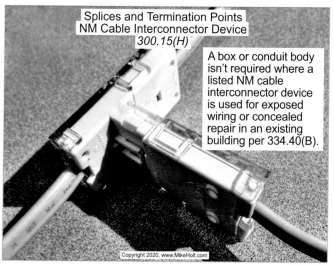

Splices and Termination Points
NM Cable Interconnector Device
300.15(H)

A box or conduit body isn't required where a listed NM cable interconnector device is used for exposed wiring or concealed repair in an existing building per 334.40(B).

Copyright 2020, www.MikeHolt.com

▶Figure 300-71

(I) Enclosures. A box or conduit body is not required where a splice is made in a cabinet containing switches or overcurrent protective devices if the splices or taps do not fill the wiring space at any cross section to more than 75 percent, and the wiring at any cross section does not exceed 40 percent. See 312.8 and 404.3(B). ▶Figure 300-72

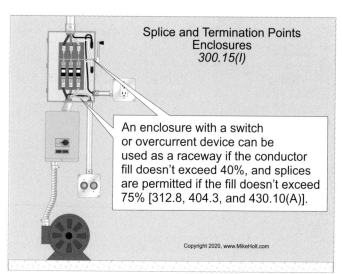

Splice and Termination Points
Enclosures
300.15(I)

An enclosure with a switch or overcurrent device can be used as a raceway if the conductor fill doesn't exceed 40%, and splices are permitted if the fill doesn't exceed 75% [312.8, 404.3, and 430.10(A)].

Copyright 2020, www.MikeHolt.com

▶Figure 300-72

(L) Handhole Enclosures. A box is not required for conductors installed in a handhole enclosure installed in accordance with 314.30. ▶Figure 300-73

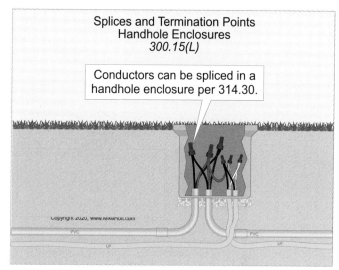

Splices and Termination Points
Handhole Enclosures
300.15(L)

Conductors can be spliced in a handhole enclosure per 314.30.

Copyright 2020, www.MikeHolt.com

PVC   PVC
UF   UF

▶Figure 300-73

Author's Comment:

▶ A handhole enclosure is used for underground wiring and designed to allow persons to reach into but not enter the enclosure [Article 100].

▶ Equipment used for splices or terminations in a handhole enclosure must be listed for wet locations [110.14(B) and 314.30(C)].

300.17 Number and Size of Conductors in a Raceway

Raceways must be large enough to permit the installation and removal of conductors without damaging the conductors' insulation.

Note: See the "xxx.22" section of the specific wiring method for more information about the number of conductors permitted.

Author's Comment:

▶ When all conductors within a raceway are the same size and of the same insulation type, the number of conductors permitted, or the raceway size can be determined using Annex C.

▶ **Example**

Question: How many 12 THHN conductors can be installed in trade size ¾ electrical metallic tubing (EMT)? ▶**Figure 300–74**

(a) 10   (b) 12   (c) 14   (d) 16

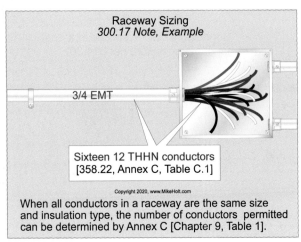

▶Figure 300–74

Answer: (d) 16 [Annex C, Table C.1]

Author's Comment:

▶ When different size conductors are installed in a raceway, conductor fill is limited to the percentages in Table 1 and Note (6) of Chapter 9. ▶**Figure 300–75**

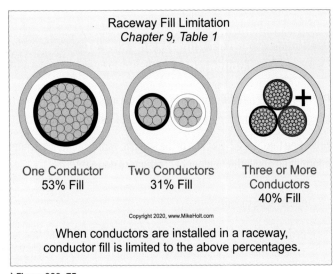

▶Figure 300–75

Chapter 9, Table 1	
Number	**Percent Fill**
1 Conductor	53%
2 Conductors	31%
3 or More	40%

The above percentages are based on conditions where the length of the conductor and number of raceway bends are within reasonable limits [Chapter 9, Table 1, Table Note 1].

Author's Comment:

▶ Follow these steps for sizing raceways:

  ▶ **Step 1:** When sizing a raceway, first determine the total area needed for the conductors (Chapter 9, Table 5 for insulated conductors and Chapter 9, Table 8 for bare conductors). ▶**Figure 300–76**

  ▶ **Step 2:** Select the raceway from Chapter 9, Table 4 in accordance with the percent fill listed in Chapter 9, Table 1. ▶**Figure 300–77**

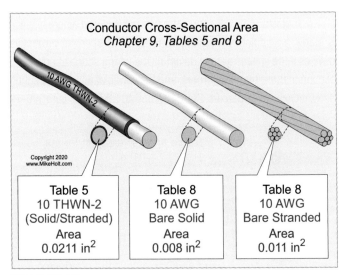

▶Figure 300–76

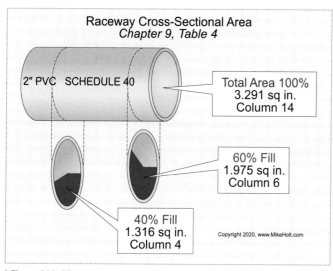

▶Figure 300–77

▶ Example

Question: What size Schedule 40 PVC conduit is required for the following conductors? ▶Figure 300–78

- 3–500 THHN
- 1–250 THHN
- 1–3 THHN

(a) Trade Size 1   (b) Trade Size 2
(c) Trade Size 3   (d) Trade Size 4

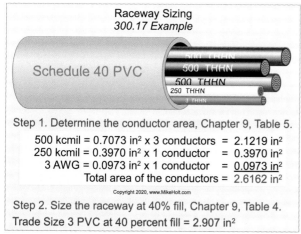

Raceway Sizing
300.17 Example

Schedule 40 PVC

500 THHN
500 THHN
500 THHN
250 THHN
3 THHN

Step 1. Determine the conductor area, Chapter 9, Table 5.

500 kcmil = 0.7073 in² x 3 conductors = 2.1219 in²
250 kcmil = 0.3970 in² x 1 conductor   = 0.3970 in²
3 AWG = 0.0973 in² x 1 conductor   = 0.0973 in²
                  Total area of the conductors = 2.6162 in²

Copyright 2020, www.MikeHolt.com

Step 2. Size the raceway at 40% fill, Chapter 9, Table 4.
Trade Size 3 PVC at 40 percent fill = 2.907 in²

▶Figure 300–78

Solution:

Step 1: Determine the total area needed for the conductors [Chapter 9, Table 5].

500 THHN	0.7073 × 3 =	2.1219 in.²
250 THHN	0.3970 × 1 =	0.3970 in.²
3 THHN	0.0973 × 1 =	+ 0.0973 in.²
Total Area =		2.6162 in.²

Step 2: Select the raceway at 40 percent fill [Chapter 9, Table 1 and Table Note (6), and Table 4].

Use trade size 3 Schedule 40 PVC because there are 2.907 sq in. of conductor fill at 40 percent.

Answer: (c) Trade Size 3

300.18 Inserting Conductors in Raceways

(A) Complete Runs. To protect conductor insulation from abrasion during installation, raceways must be mechanically completed between the pulling points before conductors are installed. See 300.10 and 300.12. ▶Figure 300–79

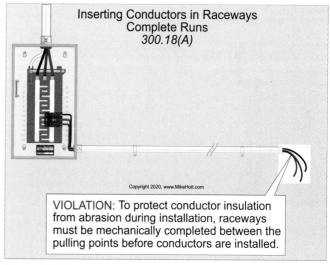

Inserting Conductors in Raceways
Complete Runs
300.18(A)

Copyright 2020, www.MikeHolt.com

VIOLATION: To protect conductor insulation from abrasion during installation, raceways must be mechanically completed between the pulling points before conductors are installed.

▶Figure 300–79

Ex: Short sections of raceways used for the protection of cables from physical damage are not required to be complete. ▶Figure 300–80

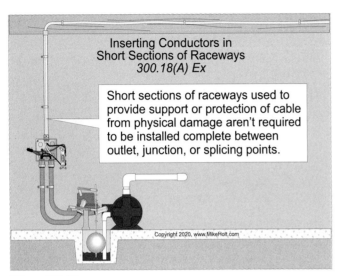

Inserting Conductors in
Short Sections of Raceways
300.18(A) Ex

Short sections of raceways used to provide support or protection of cable from physical damage aren't required to be installed complete between outlet, junction, or splicing points.

Copyright 2020, www.MikeHolt.com

▶Figure 300–80

raceway were released from the pulling "basket" or "grip" (at the top) without being secured. Sheer weight and gravity take over, accelerating the conductors down and out of the raceway and injuring those at the bottom of the installation.

300.20 Induced Alternating Currents in Ferrous Metal Parts

(A) Conductors Grouped Together. To minimize the induction heating of ferrous metal raceways and enclosures, and to maintain an effective ground-fault current path, all conductors of a circuit (including any neutral and equipment grounding conductors) must be installed in the same raceway, cable, trench, cord, or cable tray. See 250.102(E), 300.3(B), 300.5(I), and 392.20(C). ▶Figure 300–82 and ▶Figure 300–83

300.19 Supporting Conductors in Vertical Raceways

(A) Spacing Intervals. If the vertical rise of a raceway exceeds the values of Table 300.19(A), each conductor must be supported at the top or as close to the top as practical. Intermediate support must also be provided in increments not exceeding the values of Table 300.19(A). ▶Figure 300–81

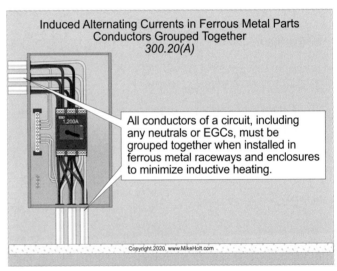

Induced Alternating Currents in Ferrous Metal Parts
Conductors Grouped Together
300.20(A)

All conductors of a circuit, including any neutrals or EGCs, must be grouped together when installed in ferrous metal raceways and enclosures to minimize inductive heating.

Copyright 2020, www.MikeHolt.com

▶Figure 300–82

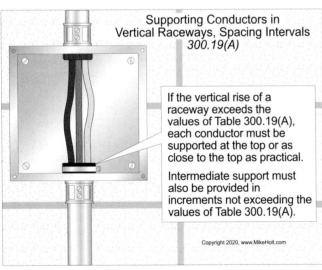

Supporting Conductors in
Vertical Raceways, Spacing Intervals
300.19(A)

If the vertical rise of a raceway exceeds the values of Table 300.19(A), each conductor must be supported at the top or as close to the top as practical.

Intermediate support must also be provided in increments not exceeding the values of Table 300.19(A).

Copyright 2020, www.MikeHolt.com

▶Figure 300–81

Author's Comment:

▶ A great deal of weight accumulates in long vertical runs of conductors and can cause them to drop out of the raceway (sometimes called a "runaway") if they are not properly secured. There have been many cases where conductors in a vertical

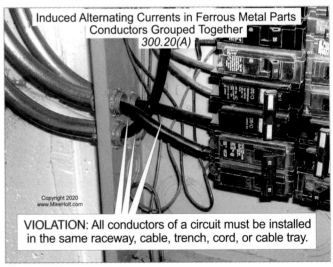

Induced Alternating Currents in Ferrous Metal Parts
Conductors Grouped Together
300.20(A)

Copyright 2020
www.MikeHolt.com

VIOLATION: All conductors of a circuit must be installed in the same raceway, cable, trench, cord, or cable tray.

▶Figure 300–83

Author's Comment:

▸ When alternating current flows through a conductor, a pulsating or varying magnetic field is created around the conductor. This magnetic field is constantly expanding and contracting with the amplitude of the alternating current. In the United States, the frequency is 60 cycles per second (Hz). Since alternating current reverses polarity 120 times per second, the magnetic field that surrounds the conductor also reverses direction 120 times per second. This expanding and collapsing magnetic field induces eddy currents in the ferrous metal parts that surround the conductors, causing them to heat up due to hysteresis heating.

▸ Magnetic materials naturally resist rapidly changing magnetic fields. The resulting friction produces its own heat (hysteresis heating) in addition to eddy current heating. A metal which offers high resistance is said to have high magnetic "permeability." Permeability can vary on a scale of 100 to 500 for magnetic materials; nonmagnetic materials have a permeability of one.

▸ Simply put, the molecules of steel and iron align to the polarity of the magnetic field and when it reverses, the molecules reverse their polarity as well. This back-and-forth alignment of the molecules heats up the metal. The more the current flows, the more the heat increases in ferrous metal parts. ▸Figure 300–84

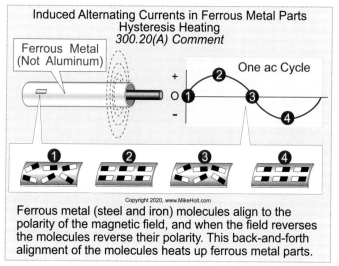

▸Figure 300–84

Author's Comment:

▸ When conductors of the same circuit are grouped together, the magnetic fields of the different conductors tend to cancel each other out, resulting in a reduced magnetic field around them. The smaller magnetic field reduces induced currents in ferrous metal raceways or enclosures, which reduces the hysteresis heating of the surrounding metal enclosure.

(B) Single Conductors. Where a single conductor carrying alternating current passes through metal with magnetic properties, the inductive effect must be minimized by either cutting slots in the metal between the individual holes through which the individual conductors pass, or passing all the conductors in the circuit through an insulating wall large enough for all the conductors of the circuit

Author's Comment:

▸ When single conductors are installed in nonmetallic raceways as permitted in 300.5(I) Ex 2, the inductive heating of the metal enclosure can be minimized by using aluminum locknuts and by cutting a slot between the individual holes through which the conductors pass. ▸Figure 300–85

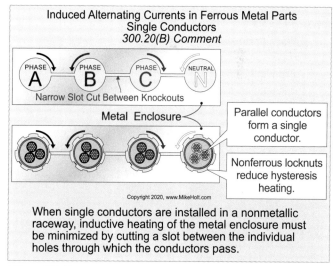

▸Figure 300–85

Note: Because aluminum is a nonmagnetic metal, aluminum parts do not heat up due to hysteresis heating.

300.21 Spread of Fire or Products of Combustion

Electrical circuits and equipment must be installed in such a way that the spread of fire or products of combustion will not be substantially increased. Openings around electrical penetrations into or through fire-resistant-rated walls, partitions, floors, or ceilings must be firestopped using approved methods to maintain the fire-resistance rating. ▶Figure 300–86

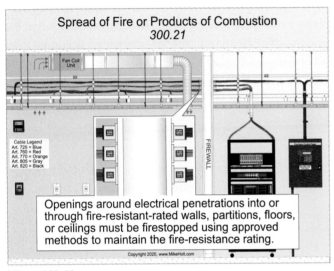

▶Figure 300–86

Author's Comment:

▶ Fire-stopping materials are listed for the specific types of wiring methods and the construction of the assembly they penetrate. ▶Figure 300–87

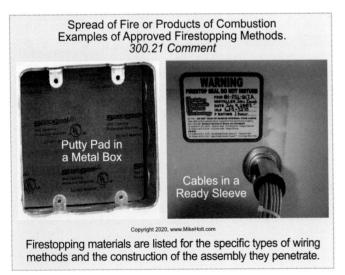

Firestopping materials are listed for the specific types of wiring methods and the construction of the assembly they penetrate.

▶Figure 300–87

Note: Directories of electrical construction materials published by recognized testing laboratories contain listing and installation restrictions necessary to maintain the fire-resistive rating of assemblies. Building codes also have restrictions on penetrations on opposite sides of a fire-resistance rated wall. Outlet boxes must have a horizontal separation of not less than 24 in. when installed in a fire-rated assembly, unless an outlet box is listed for closer spacing or protected by fire-resistant "putty pads" in accordance with manufacturer's instructions. ▶Figure 300–88 and ▶Figure 300–89

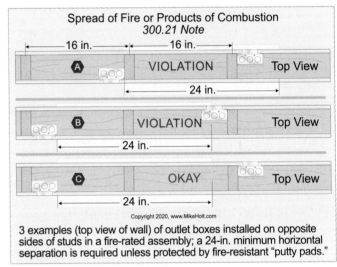

3 examples (top view of wall) of outlet boxes installed on opposite sides of studs in a fire-rated assembly; a 24-in. minimum horizontal separation is required unless protected by fire-resistant "putty pads."

▶Figure 300–88

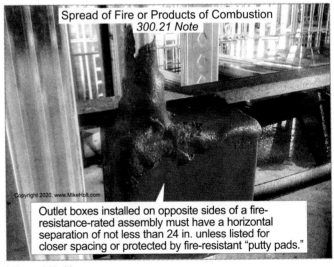

Outlet boxes installed on opposite sides of a fire-resistance-rated assembly must have a horizontal separation of not less than 24 in. unless listed for closer spacing or protected by fire-resistant "putty pads."

▶Figure 300–89

Author's Comment:

▶ Boxes installed in fire-resistance rated assemblies must be listed for the purpose. If steel boxes are used, they must be secured to the framing member; cut-in type boxes are not permitted (UL White Book, *Guide Information for Electrical Equipment*).

▶ This requirement also applies to control, signaling, and communications cables or raceways.

    ▶ Communications and Coaxial Cable, 800.26

    ▶ Control and Signaling, 725.3(B)

    ▶ Fire Alarms, 760.3(A)

    ▶ Optical Fiber, 770.26

    ▶ Sound Systems, 640.3(A)

300.22 Wiring in Ducts and Plenum Spaces

This section applies to the installation and uses of electrical wiring and equipment in ducts used for dust, loose stock, or vapor removal; ducts specifically fabricated for environmental air; and plenum spaces used for environmental air.

(A) Ducts Used for Dust, Loose Stock, or Vapor. Wiring methods are not permitted to be installed in ducts that transport dust, loose stock, or flammable vapors. ▶Figure 300–90

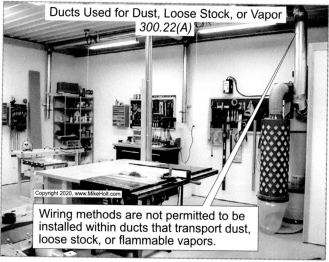

Ducts Used for Dust, Loose Stock, or Vapor
300.22(A)

Wiring methods are not permitted to be installed within ducts that transport dust, loose stock, or flammable vapors.

▶Figure 300–90

(B) Ducts Fabricated for Environmental Air. Equipment is only permitted within a duct fabricated to transport environmental air if the equipment is necessary for the direct action upon, or sensing of, the contained air. ▶Figure 300–91

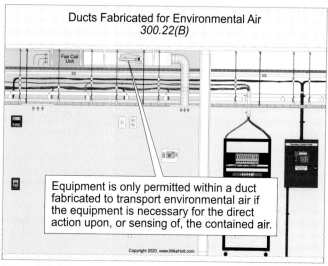

Ducts Fabricated for Environmental Air
300.22(B)

Equipment is only permitted within a duct fabricated to transport environmental air if the equipment is necessary for the direct action upon, or sensing of, the contained air.

▶Figure 300–91

Type MC Cable without an overall nonmetallic covering and metal raceways can be installed in ducts fabricated to transport environmental air. Flexible metal conduit in lengths not exceeding 4 ft can be used to connect physically adjustable equipment and devices within the fabricated duct.

(C) Plenum Spaces for Environmental Air. This section applies only to the space above a suspended ceiling or below a raised floor used for environmental air. It does not apply to habitable rooms or areas of buildings, the prime purpose of which is not air handling.

Note 1: The spaces or cavities above a suspended ceiling and below a raised floor used for environmental air are examples of the type of plenum space to which this section applies. ▶Figure 300–92

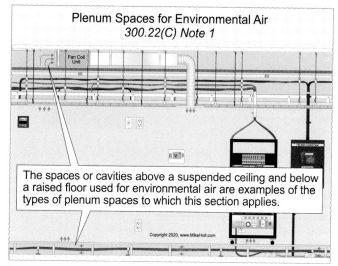

Plenum Spaces for Environmental Air
300.22(C) Note 1

The spaces or cavities above a suspended ceiling and below a raised floor used for environmental air are examples of the types of plenum spaces to which this section applies.

▶Figure 300–92

(1) Wiring Methods. Metal raceways, Type AC cable, and Type MC cable without a nonmetallic cover, electrical metallic tubing, intermediate metal conduit, rigid metal conduit, flexible metal conduit, or (where accessible) surface metal raceways or metal wireways with metal covers. ▶Figure 300–93

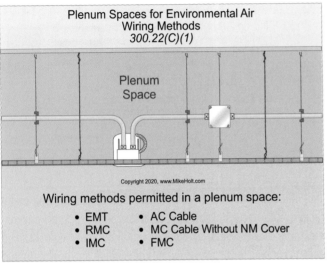

▶Figure 300–93

Cable ties for securing and supporting must be listed for use in a plenum space ▶Figure 300–94

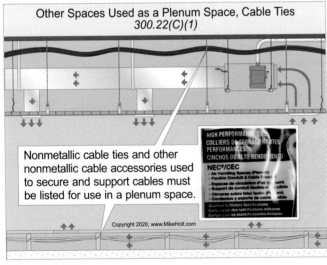

▶Figure 300–94

Author's Comment:

▶ Plenum-rated control, signaling, and communications cables and raceways are permitted in plenum spaces according to the following: ▶Figure 300–95

▶ Communications Cable and Coaxial Cable, 800.3(C) and Table 800.154(a)
▶ Control and Signaling, 725.3(C) Ex 2 and Table 725.154
▶ Fire Alarms, 760.3(B) Ex 2 and Table 760.154
▶ Optical Fiber Cables and Raceways, Table 770.154(a)
▶ Sound Systems, 640.9(C) and Table 725.154

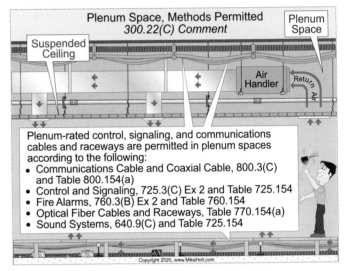

▶Figure 300–95

(2) Cable Tray Systems.

(a) Metal Cable Tray Systems. Metal cable tray systems can be installed to support the wiring methods and equipment permitted to be installed in a plenum space. ▶Figure 300–96

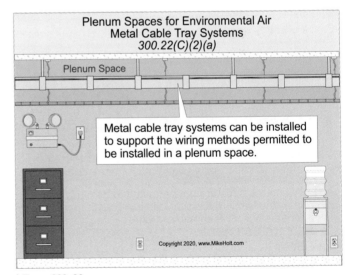

▶Figure 300–96

(3) Equipment. Electrical equipment with a metal enclosure or a nonmetallic enclosure listed for use in an air-handling space can be installed in a plenum space. ▶Figure 300–97

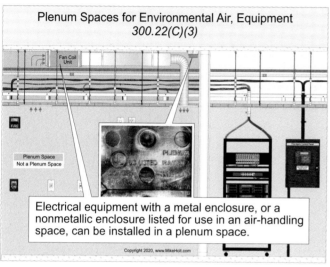

▶Figure 300–97

Author's Comment:

▶ Examples of electrical equipment permitted in plenum spaces are air handlers, junction boxes, and dry-type transformers; however, transformers are not permitted to be rated over 50 kVA when located in hollow spaces [450.13(B)].

300.23 Panels Designed to Allow Access

Cables, raceways, and equipment installed behind panels must be located so the panels can be removed to give access to electrical equipment. ▶Figure 300–98

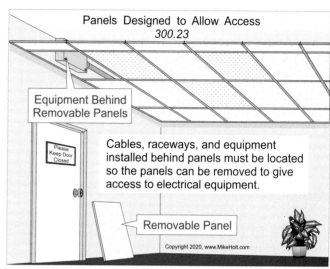

▶Figure 300–98

Author's Comment:

▶ Access to equipment is not permitted to be hindered by an accumulation of cables that prevent the removal of suspended-ceiling panels. Control, signaling, and communications cables must be located and supported so the suspended-ceiling panels can be moved to provide access to electrical equipment.

- ▹ Communications Cable and Coaxial Cable, 800.21
- ▹ Control and Signaling Cable, 725.21
- ▹ Fire Alarm Cable, 760.21
- ▹ Optical Fiber Cable, 770.21
- ▹ Audio Cable, 640.5

ARTICLE
300 PRACTICE QUESTIONS

Please use the 2020 *Code* book to answer the following questions.

Article 300—General Requirements for Wiring Methods and Materials

1. The provisions of Article 300 apply to the conductors that form an integral part of equipment or listed utilization equipment.

   (a) True
   (b) False

2. Connections, taps, or extensions made from paralleled conductors shall connect to all conductors of the paralleled set.

   (a) True
   (b) False

3. Where cables or nonmetallic raceways are installed through bored holes in joists, rafters, or wood members, holes shall be bored so that the edge of the hole is _____ the nearest edge of the wood member.

   (a) not less than 1¼ in. from
   (b) immediately adjacent to
   (c) not less than ¹⁄₁₆ in. from
   (d) 90 degrees away from

4. Where Type NM cables pass through cut or drilled slots or holes in metal members, the cable shall be protected by _____ which are installed in the opening prior to the installation of the cable and which securely cover all metal edges.

   (a) anti-shorts
   (b) sleeves
   (c) plates
   (d) listed bushings or grommets

5. A cable, raceway, or box installed under metal-corrugated sheet roof decking shall be supported so the top of the cable, raceway, or box is not less than _____ in. from the lowest surface of the roof decking to the top of the cable, raceway, or box.

   (a) ½
   (b) 1
   (c) 1½
   (d) 2

6. Where raceways contain insulated circuit conductors _____ and larger, the conductors shall be protected from abrasion during and after installation by an identified fitting providing a smoothly rounded insulating surface.

   (a) 8 AWG
   (b) 6 AWG
   (c) 4 AWG
   (d) 2 AWG

7. What is the minimum cover requirement for direct burial Type UF cable installed outdoors that supplies a 120V, 30A circuit?

   (a) 6 in.
   (b) 12 in.
   (c) 18 in.
   (d) 24 in.

8. What is the minimum cover requirement for Type UF cable supplying power to a 120V, 15A GFCI-protected circuit outdoors under a driveway of a one-family dwelling?

   (a) 6 in.
   (b) 12 in.
   (c) 16 in.
   (d) 24 in.

9. _____ is defined as the shortest distance measured between a point on the top surface of direct-burial cable and the top surface of the finished grade.

(a) Notch
(b) Cover
(c) Gap
(d) Spacing

10. Type MC Cable listed for _____ is permitted to be installed underground under a building without installation in a raceway.

(a) direct burial
(b) damp/wet locations
(c) rough service
(d) encasement in concrete

11. Backfill used for underground wiring shall not damage _____ or prevent adequate compaction of fill or contribute to corrosion.

(a) raceways
(b) cables
(c) conductors
(d) all of these

12. A/(An) _____, with an integral bushed opening shall be used at the end of a conduit or other raceway that terminates underground where the conductors or cables emerge as a direct burial wiring method.

(a) splice kit
(b) connector
(c) adapter
(d) bushing or terminal fitting

13. Direct-buried conductors, cables, or raceways, which are subject to movement by settlement or frost, shall be arranged to prevent damage to the _____ or to equipment connected to the raceways.

(a) siding of the building mounted on
(b) landscaping around the cable or raceway
(c) enclosed conductors
(d) expansion fitting

14. Which of the following metal parts shall be protected from corrosion?

(a) ferrous metal raceways
(b) ferrous metal elbows
(c) ferrous boxes
(d) all of these

15. Raceways shall be provided with expansion, expansion-deflection, or deflection fittings where necessary to compensate for thermal expansion, deflection, and contraction.

(a) True
(b) False

16. Where raceways are installed in wet locations above grade, the interior of these raceways shall be considered a _____ location.

(a) wet
(b) dry
(c) damp
(d) corrosive

17. Where independent support wires of a suspended ceiling assembly are used to support raceways, cable assemblies, or boxes above a ceiling, they shall be secured at _____ end(s).

(a) one
(b) both
(c) the line and load
(d) at the attachment to the structural member

18. Cable wiring methods shall not be used as a means of support for _____.

(a) other cables
(b) raceways
(c) nonelectrical equipment
(d) all of these

19. In multiwire branch circuits, the continuity of the _____ shall not be dependent upon the device connections.

(a) ungrounded conductor
(b) grounded conductor
(c) grounding electrode
(d) raceway

20. A box or conduit body shall not be required where cables enter or exit from conduit or tubing that is used to provide cable support or protection against physical damage.

(a) True
(b) False

21. The number and size of conductors permitted in a raceway is limited to _____.

(a) permit heat to dissipate
(b) prevent damage to insulation during installation
(c) prevent damage to insulation during removal of conductors
(d) all of these

22. Short sections of raceways used for _____ shall not be required to be installed complete between outlet, junction, or splicing points.

    (a) meter to service enclosure connection
    (b) protection of cables from physical damage
    (c) nipples
    (d) separately derived systems

23. Conductors in ferrous metal raceways or enclosures shall be arranged so as to avoid heating the surrounding ferrous metal by alternating-current induction. To accomplish this, the _____ conductor(s) shall be grouped together.

    (a) phase
    (b) grounded
    (c) equipment grounding
    (d) all of these

24. Openings around electrical penetrations into or through fire-resistant-rated walls, partitions, floors, or ceilings shall _____ to maintain the fire-resistance rating.

    (a) be documented
    (b) not be permitted
    (c) be firestopped using approved methods
    (d) be enlarged

25. Wiring methods that are permitted to be installed in ducts fabricated for environmental air include _____.

    (a) MC cable without an overall nonmetallic covering
    (b) EMT (electrical metallic tubing)
    (c) RMC (rigid metal conduit)
    (d) all of these

26. Section 300.22(C) applies to spaces not specifically fabricated for environmental air-handling purposes but used for air-handling purposes such as the space over a hung ceiling.

    (a) True
    (b) False

27. Wiring methods permitted in the ceiling areas used for environmental air include _____.

    (a) electrical metallic tubing
    (b) FMC of any length
    (c) RMC without an overall nonmetallic covering
    (d) all of these

28. Wiring methods and equipment installed behind suspended-ceiling panels shall be arranged and secured to allow access to the electrical equipment.

    (a) True
    (b) False

ARTICLE 310

CONDUCTORS FOR GENERAL WIRING

Introduction to Article 310—Conductors for General Wiring

This article contains the general requirements for conductors such as their insulation markings, ampacity ratings, and conditions of use. It does not apply to conductors that are part of flexible cords, fixture wires, or to those that are an integral part of equipment [90.7 and 300.1(B)].

Why does Article 310 contain so many tables? Why does Table 310.17 list the ampacity of 6 THHN as 105A, while Table 310.16 lists the same conductor as having an ampacity of only 75A? To answer that, go back to Article 100, review the definition of "Ampacity" and notice the phrase "conditions of use." These tables set a maximum current value at which premature failure of the conductor insulation should not occur during normal use, under the conditions described in the tables. Tables throughout the *NEC* are accompanied by a section of text with information about that table. For example, section 310.16 says that Table 310.16 applies to conductors carrying voltages rated 0V through 2,000V. It can be easy to overlook that limitation if you are not careful! It is imperative for you to read the *Code* section pertaining to each table and any of the Table's footnotes before you decide what is necessary for your particular application.

THHN, THWN-2, RHH, and so on, are insulation types. Those containing a "W" are suitable for use in wet locations. Every type of insulation has a limit as to how much heat it can withstand. When current flows through a conductor, it creates heat. How well the insulation around a conductor can dissipate that heat depends on factors such as whether the conductor is in free air or not. Think about what happens when you put on a sweater, a jacket, and then a coat—all at the same time. You heat up. Your skin cannot dissipate heat with all that clothing on nearly as well as it can in free air. The same principle applies to conductors.

Conductor insulation degrades with age and is called "aging." Its failure takes decades under normal use and becomes a maintenance issue for the appropriate personnel to manage. However, if a conductor is forced to exceed the ampacity listed in the appropriate table (and as a result its design temperature is exceeded) insulation failure happens much sooner and is often catastrophic. Consequently, exceeding the ampacity of a conductor is a serious safety issue.

Part I. General

310.1 Scope

Article 310 contains the general requirements for conductors rated up to and including 2,000V, including their insulation markings, ampacity ratings, and use. ▶Figure 310–1

Note: For flexible cords and cable, see Article 400. For fixture wires, see Article 402.

310.3 Conductors

(A) Minimum Size Conductors. The minimum sizes of conductors are 14 AWG copper or 12 AWG aluminum or copper-clad aluminum, except as permitted elsewhere in this *Code*.

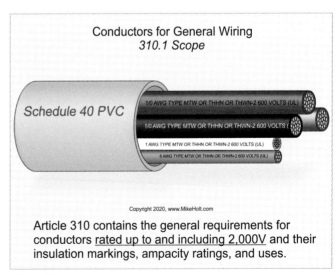

Conductors for General Wiring
310.1 Scope

Schedule 40 PVC

1/0 AWG TYPE MTW OR THHN OR THWN-2 600 VOLTS (UL)
1/0 AWG TYPE MTW OR THHN OR THWN-2 600 VOLTS
1 AWG TYPE MTW OR THHN OR THWN-2 600 VOLTS (UL)
6 AWG TYPE MTW OR THHN OR THWN-2 600 VOLTS (UL)

Copyright 2020, www.MikeHolt.com

Article 310 contains the general requirements for conductors rated up to and including 2,000V and their insulation markings, ampacity ratings, and uses.

▶Figure 310–1

▸ There is a misconception that 12 AWG copper is the smallest conductor permitted for commercial or industrial facilities. Although it is not true based on *NEC* rules, it might be a job specification or local code requirement.

▸ Conductors smaller than 14 AWG are permitted for Class 1 remote-control circuits [725.43], fixture wire [402.6], and motor control circuits [Table 430.72(B)].

(C) Stranded Conductors. Conductors 8 AWG and larger installed in a raceway <u>must be stranded, unless</u> specifically permitted or required elsewhere in this *Code* to be solid. ▸Figure 310–2

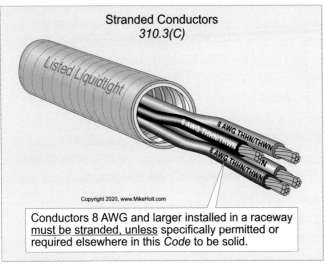

Stranded Conductors
310.3(C)

Copyright 2020, www.MikeHolt.com

Conductors 8 AWG and larger installed in a raceway <u>must be stranded, unless</u> specifically permitted or required elsewhere in this *Code* to be solid.

▸Figure 310–2

▸ According to 250.120(C), exposed equipment grounding conductors 8 AWG and smaller for direct-current circuits [250.134(2) Ex 2], such as those required by 690.45 for solar PV systems, are permitted to be run separately from the circuit conductors. Where an 8 AWG or smaller exposed equipment grounding conductor is subject to physical damage, it must be installed in a raceway or cable.

▸ A grounding electrode conductor is an example where an 8 AWG and larger solid conductor can be installed in a raceway when it is required to be protected from physical damage [250.64(B)].

(D) Insulated. Conductors must be insulated, unless specifically permitted to be bare. ▸Figure 310–3

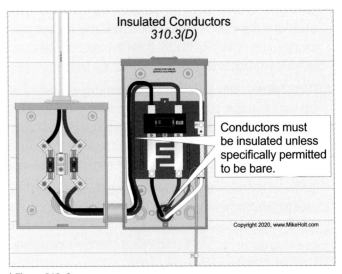

Insulated Conductors
310.3(D)

Conductors must be insulated unless specifically permitted to be bare.

Copyright 2020, www.MikeHolt.com

▸Figure 310–3

ARTICLE
310
PRACTICE QUESTIONS

Article 310—Conductors for General Wiring

1. The minimum size copper conductor permitted for voltage ratings up to 2,000V _____ AWG.

   (a) 14
   (b) 12
   (c) 10
   (d) 8

2. In general, where installed in raceways, conductors _____ AWG and larger shall be stranded.

   (a) 2
   (b) 4
   (c) 6
   (d) 8

3. Where installed in raceways, conductors _____ AWG and larger shall be stranded, unless specifically permitted or required elsewhere in the *NEC*.

   (a) 10
   (b) 8
   (c) 6
   (d) 4

4. Conductors for general wiring not specifically permitted elsewhere in this *Code* to be covered or bare shall _____.

   (a) not be permitted
   (b) be insulated
   (c) be rated
   (d) be listed

ARTICLE 314

OUTLET, PULL, AND JUNCTION BOXES; CONDUIT BODIES; AND HANDHOLE ENCLOSURES

Introduction to Article 314—Outlet, Pull, and Junction Boxes; Conduit Bodies; and Handhole Enclosures

Article 314 contains the installation requirements for outlet boxes, pull and junction boxes, conduit bodies, and handhole enclosures. As with the cabinets covered in Article 312, the conditions of use have a bearing on the type of material and equipment selected for the installation.

The information contained in this article will help you size an outlet box using the proper cubic-inch capacity as well as calculating the minimum dimensions for pull boxes. There are limits on the amount of weight that can be supported by an outlet box, and rules on how to support a device or outlet box to various surfaces. Article 314 will help you understand these rules so your installation will be compliant with the *NEC*. As always, the clear illustrations will help you visualize the finished installation.

Part I. Scope and General

314.1 Scope

Article 314 contains the installation requirements for outlet boxes, pull and junction boxes, conduit bodies, and handhole enclosures. ▶Figure 314–1

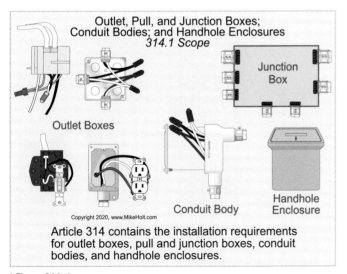

▶Figure 314–1

314.3 Nonmetallic Boxes

Nonmetallic boxes can only be used with nonmetallic cables and raceways.

Ex 1: Metal raceways and cables can be used with nonmetallic boxes if the raceways and cables are bonded together in the nonmetallic box. ▶Figure 314–2

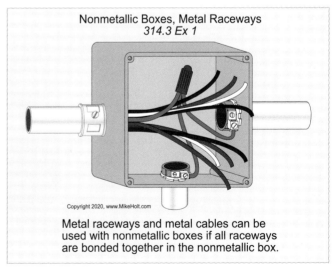

▶Figure 314–2

314.4 Metal Boxes

Metal boxes must be connected to an equipment grounding conductor in accordance with 250.148. ▶Figure 314–3

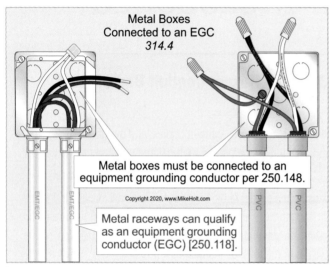

Metal Boxes
Connected to an EGC
314.4

Metal boxes must be connected to an equipment grounding conductor per 250.148.

Copyright 2020, www.MikeHolt.com

Metal raceways can qualify as an equipment grounding conductor (EGC) [250.118].

▶Figure 314–3

Part II. Installation

314.15 Damp or Wet Locations

Boxes, conduit bodies, and fittings in damp or wet locations must be listed for use in wet locations. ▶Figure 314–4 and ▶Figure 314–5

Damp or Wet Locations
Boxes, Conduit Bodies, and Fittings
314.15

Boxes, conduit bodies, and fittings in damp or wet locations must be listed for wet locations.

▶Figure 314–4

Damp or Wet Locations
Boxes, Conduit Bodies, and Fittings
314.15

Copyright 2020, www.MikeHolt.com

VIOLATION: Boxes and fittings in damp or wet locations must prevent moisture or water from entering or accumulating within the enclosure.

▶Figure 314–5

314.16 Sizing Outlet Boxes

Boxes containing 6 AWG and smaller conductors must be sized in an approved manner to provide free space for all conductors, devices, and fittings. In no case can the volume of the box, as calculated in 314.16(A), be less than the volume requirement as calculated in 314.16(B). ▶Figure 314–6 and ▶Figure 314–7

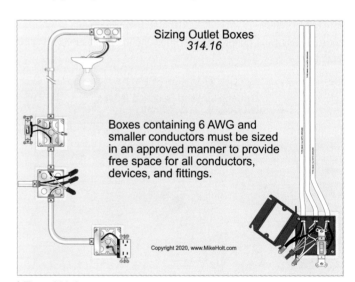

Sizing Outlet Boxes
314.16

Boxes containing 6 AWG and smaller conductors must be sized in an approved manner to provide free space for all conductors, devices, and fittings.

Copyright 2020, www.MikeHolt.com

▶Figure 314–6

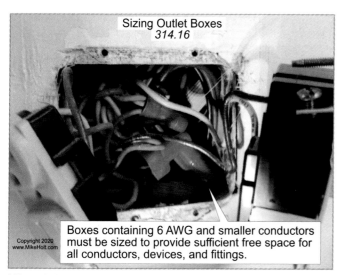

Sizing Outlet Boxes
314.16

Boxes containing 6 AWG and smaller conductors must be sized to provide sufficient free space for all conductors, devices, and fittings.

▶Figure 314–7

Author's Comment:

▶ The requirements for sizing boxes and conduit bodies containing conductors 4 AWG and larger are in 314.28, and those for sizing handhole enclosures are contained in 314.30(A). An outlet box is generally used for the attachment of devices and luminaires and has a specific amount of space (volume) for conductors, devices, and fittings. The volume taken up by conductors, devices, and fittings in a box must not exceed the box fill capacity.

Boxes and conduit bodies enclosing conductors 4 AWG or larger must also comply with the provisions of 314.28.

(A) Box Volume Calculations. The volume of a box is the total volume of its assembled parts including plaster rings, raised covers, and extension rings. The total volume includes only those parts marked with their volumes in cubic inches (cu in.) [314.16(A)] or included in Table 314.16(A). ▶Figure 314–8

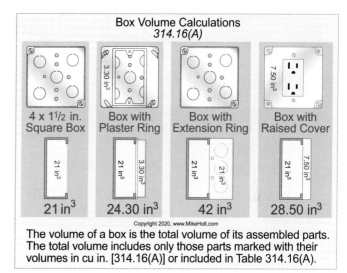

Box Volume Calculations
314.16(A)

4 x 1½ in. Square Box	Box with Plaster Ring	Box with Extension Ring	Box with Raised Cover
21 in³	24.30 in³	42 in³	28.50 in³

Copyright 2020, www.MikeHolt.com

The volume of a box is the total volume of its assembled parts. The total volume includes only those parts marked with their volumes in cu in. [314.16(A)] or included in Table 314.16(A).

▶Figure 314–8

Table 314.16(A) Metal Boxes

Box Trade Size		Minimum Volume	Maximum Number of Conductors (arranged by AWG size)					
in.	Box Shape	in³	18	16	14	12	10	8
(4 × 1¼)	round/octagonal	12.50	8	7	6	5	5	5
(4 × 1½)	round/octagonal	15.50	10	8	7	6	6	5
(4 × 2⅛)	round/octagonal	21.50	14	12	10	9	8	7
(4 × 1¼)	square	18.00	12	10	9	8	7	6
(4 × 1½)	square	21.00	14	12	10	9	8	7
(4 × 2⅛)	square	30.30	20	17	15	13	12	10
(4¹¹⁄₁₆ × 1¼)	square	25.50	17	14	12	11	10	8
(4¹¹⁄₁₆ × 1½)	square	29.50	19	16	14	13	11	9
(4¹¹⁄₁₆ × 2⅛)	square	42.00	28	24	21	18	16	14

▶ Example

Question: *What is the total box volume for a 4 × 4 × 1½ outlet box and a 4 × 4 × 1½ extension box with a domed cover marked with a 7.50 cu in. volume?* ▶Figure 314–9

(a) *44.50 cu in.*   (b) *46.50 cu in.*
(c) *47.50 cu in.*   (d) *49.50 cu in.*

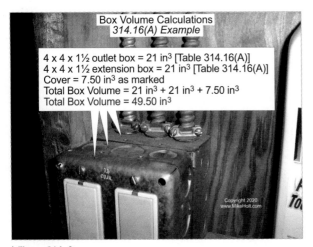

▶Figure 314–9

Solution:

Volume of 4 × 4 × 1½ outlet box = 21 cu in. [Table 314.16(A)]
Volume of 4 × 4 × 1½ extension box = 21 cu in. [Table 314.16(A)]

Cover Volume = 7.50 cu in. as marked

Total Volume = 21 cu in. + 21 cu in. + 7.50 cu in.
Total Volume = 49.50 cu in.

Do not calculate the actual volume of a box contained in Table 314.16(A) since the table volume is based on the inside dimensions of the box, not the outside dimensions.

Answer: *(d) 49.50 cu in.*

Where a box is provided with barriers, the volume is apportioned to each of the resulting spaces. Each barrier, if not marked with its volume, is considered to take up ½ cu in. if metal and 1 cu in. if nonmetallic. ▶Figure 314–10

Author's Comment:

▸ When all the conductors in an outlet box are the same size (insulation does not matter), Table 314.16(A) can be used to determine the number of conductors permitted in the outlet box, or to determine the required outlet box size for the given number of conductors.

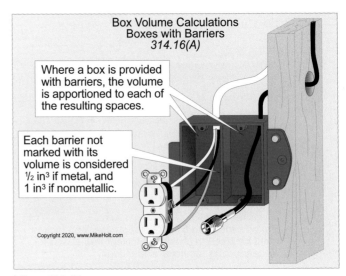

▶Figure 314–10

▸ If the outlet box contains switches, receptacles, luminaire studs, luminaire hickeys, cable clamps, or equipment grounding conductors, then allowance must be made for these items which are not reflected in Table 314.16(A).

▶ Table 314.16(A) Example

Question: *Which 4-in. square outlet box will be required for three 12 THW and six 12 THHN conductors?* ▶Figure 314–11

(a) *4 × 1¼ in. square*   (b) *4 × 1½ in. square*
(c) *4 × 2⅛ in. square*   (d) *4 × 2⅛ in. with extension*

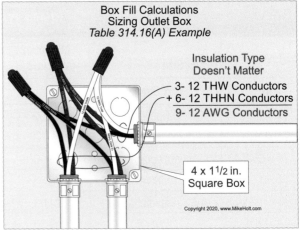

▶Figure 314–11

Answer: *(b) 4 × 1½ in. square*

(B) Box Fill Calculations. Table 314.16(A) does not consider switches, receptacles, luminaire studs, luminaire hickeys, cable clamps, or equipment grounding conductors. The calculated conductor volumes determined by 314.16(B)(1) through (B)(5) are added together to determine the total volume of the conductors, devices, and fittings. ▶Figure 314-12

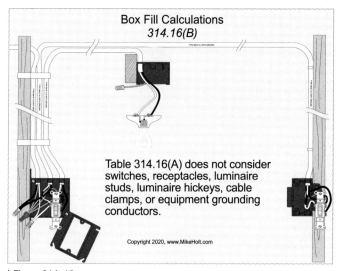

Box Fill Calculations
314.16(B)

Table 314.16(A) does not consider switches, receptacles, luminaire studs, luminaire hickeys, cable clamps, or equipment grounding conductors.

Copyright 2020, www.MikeHolt.com

▶Figure 314-12

Raceway and cable fittings, including locknuts and bushings, are not counted for box fill calculations. ▶Figure 314-13

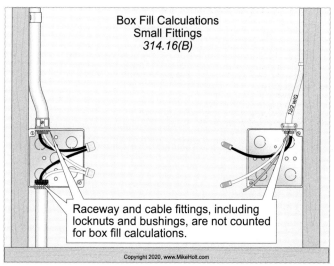

Box Fill Calculations
Small Fittings
314.16(B)

Raceway and cable fittings, including locknuts and bushings, are not counted for box fill calculations.

Copyright 2020, www.MikeHolt.com

▶Figure 314-13

Each space within a box with a barrier must be calculated separately. ▶Figure 314-14

(1) Conductor Volume. Each conductor that originates outside the box and terminates or is spliced inside the box counts as a single conductor volume as shown in Table 314.16(B). ▶Figure 314-15

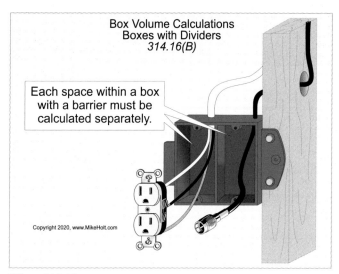

Box Volume Calculations
Boxes with Dividers
314.16(B)

Each space within a box with a barrier must be calculated separately.

Copyright 2020, www.MikeHolt.com

▶Figure 314-14

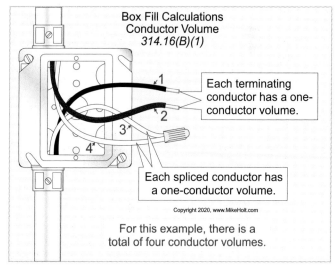

Box Fill Calculations
Conductor Volume
314.16(B)(1)

Each terminating conductor has a one-conductor volume.

Each spliced conductor has a one-conductor volume.

Copyright 2020, www.MikeHolt.com

For this example, there is a total of four conductor volumes.

▶Figure 314-15

Author's Comment:

▸ Table 314.16(B) lists the conductor cu in. volumes for 18 AWG through 6 AWG. For example, one 14 AWG conductor has a volume of 2 cu in. If a box has four 14 AWG conductors, the conductor volume is 8 cu in.

▸ Conductor insulation is not a factor for box fill calculations.

Table 314.16(B) Volume Allowance Required per Conductor

Conductor AWG Size	Free Space Required for Each Conductor (cu in.)
18	1.50
16	1.75
14	2.00
12	2.25
10	2.50
8	3.00
6	5.00

Each conductor loop having a total length of less than 12 in. is considered a single conductor volume, and each conductor loop having a length of at least 12 in. is considered as two conductor volumes in accordance with Table 314.16(B) [300.14]. ▶Figure 314–16

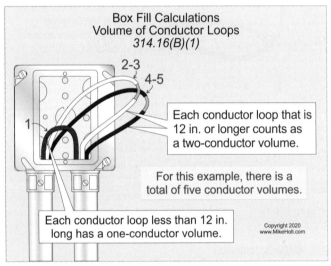

▶Figure 314–16

Author's Comment:

▶ At least 6 in. of conductor, measured from the point in the box where the conductor enters the enclosure, must be available at each point for conductor splices or terminations. ▶Figure 314–17

▶ Boxes that have openings of less than 8 in. in any dimension must have at least 6 in. of conductor, measured from the point where the conductor enters the box, and at least 3 in. of conductor outside the box. ▶Figure 314–18

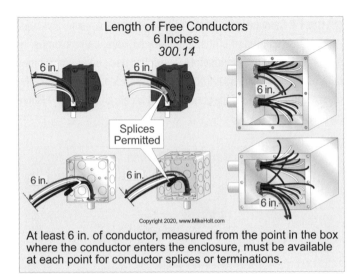

At least 6 in. of conductor, measured from the point in the box where the conductor enters the enclosure, must be available at each point for conductor splices or terminations.

▶Figure 314–17

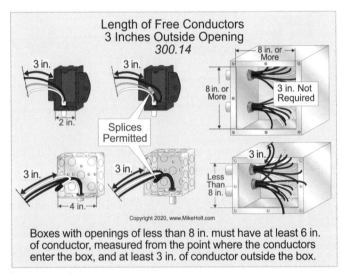

Boxes with openings of less than 8 in. must have at least 6 in. of conductor, measured from the point where the conductors enter the box, and at least 3 in. of conductor outside the box.

▶Figure 314–18

Conductors that originate and terminate within the box, such as pigtails and bonding jumpers, are not counted as a conductor volume. ▶Figure 314–19

Ex: Equipment grounding conductors and not more than four fixture wires are not counted as a conductor volume if they enter the box from a domed luminaire or similar canopy, such as a ceiling paddle fan canopy. ▶Figure 314–20

(2) Cable Clamp Volume. Cable clamps that are part of the outlet box are counted as a single conductor volume based on the largest conductor in the box in accordance with Table 314.16(B). ▶Figure 314–21

(3) Support Fitting Volume. Each luminaire stud or luminaire hickey counts as a single conductor volume based on the largest conductor that enters the box in accordance with Table 314.16(B). ▶Figure 314–22

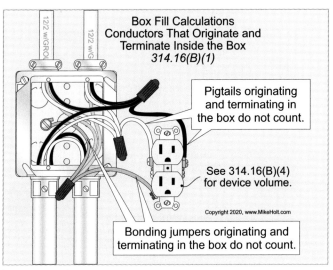

Box Fill Calculations
Conductors That Originate and
Terminate Inside the Box
314.16(B)(1)

Pigtails originating and terminating in the box do not count.

See 314.16(B)(4) for device volume.

Copyright 2020, www.MikeHolt.com

Bonding jumpers originating and terminating in the box do not count.

▶Figure 314–19

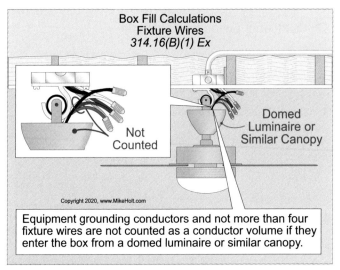

Box Fill Calculations
Fixture Wires
314.16(B)(1) Ex

Not Counted

Domed Luminaire or Similar Canopy

Copyright 2020, www.MikeHolt.com

Equipment grounding conductors and not more than four fixture wires are not counted as a conductor volume if they enter the box from a domed luminaire or similar canopy.

▶Figure 314–20

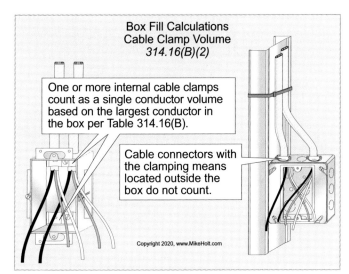

Box Fill Calculations
Cable Clamp Volume
314.16(B)(2)

One or more internal cable clamps count as a single conductor volume based on the largest conductor in the box per Table 314.16(B).

Cable connectors with the clamping means located outside the box do not count.

Copyright 2020, www.MikeHolt.com

▶Figure 314–21

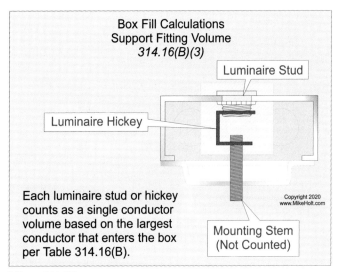

Box Fill Calculations
Support Fitting Volume
314.16(B)(3)

Luminaire Stud

Luminaire Hickey

Copyright 2020
www.MikeHolt.com

Mounting Stem (Not Counted)

Each luminaire stud or hickey counts as a single conductor volume based on the largest conductor that enters the box per Table 314.16(B).

▶Figure 314–22

(4) Device Yoke Volume. Each single-gang device yoke counts as two conductor volumes based on the largest conductor that terminates on the device in accordance with Table 314.16(B). ▶Figure 314–23

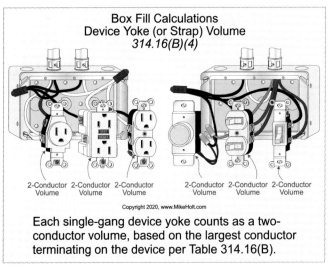

Box Fill Calculations
Device Yoke (or Strap) Volume
314.16(B)(4)

2-Conductor Volume | 2-Conductor Volume | 2-Conductor Volume | 2-Conductor Volume | 2-Conductor Volume | 2-Conductor Volume

Copyright 2020, www.MikeHolt.com

Each single-gang device yoke counts as a two-conductor volume, based on the largest conductor terminating on the device per Table 314.16(B).

▶Figure 314–23

Author's Comment:

▶ A device yoke (also called a "strap") is the mounting structure for a receptacle, switch, switch with pilot light, switch/receptacle, and so forth. ▶Figure 314–24

Each device yoke wider than 2 in. counts as a two-conductor volume for each gang required for mounting, based on the largest conductor that terminates on the device in accordance with Table 314.16(B). ▶Figure 314–25

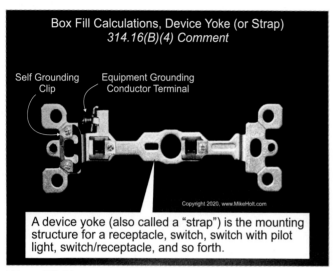

Box Fill Calculations, Device Yoke (or Strap)
314.16(B)(4) Comment

Self Grounding Clip

Equipment Grounding Conductor Terminal

Copyright 2020, www.MikeHolt.com

A device yoke (also called a "strap") is the mounting structure for a receptacle, switch, switch with pilot light, switch/receptacle, and so forth.

▶Figure 314–24

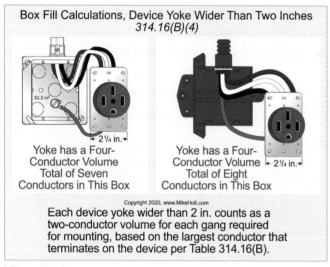

Box Fill Calculations, Device Yoke Wider Than Two Inches
314.16(B)(4)

30.3 in³

◄ 2¼ in. ▶

Yoke has a Four-Conductor Volume Total of Seven Conductors in This Box

Yoke has a Four-Conductor Volume Total of Eight Conductors in This Box

◄ 2¼ in. ▶

Copyright 2020, www.MikeHolt.com

Each device yoke wider than 2 in. counts as a two-conductor volume for each gang required for mounting, based on the largest conductor that terminates on the device per Table 314.16(B).

▶Figure 314–25

(5) Equipment Grounding Conductor Volume. Up to four equipment grounding conductors count as a single conductor volume, based on the largest equipment grounding conductor that enters the box in accordance with Table 314.16(B).

A ¼ volume allowance applies for each additional equipment grounding conductor or equipment bonding jumper that enters the box, based on the largest equipment grounding or bonding conductor. ▶Figure 314–26

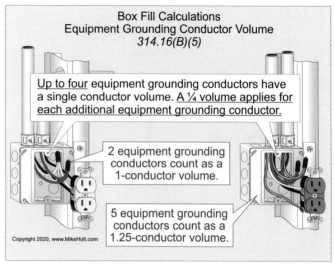

Box Fill Calculations
Equipment Grounding Conductor Volume
314.16(B)(5)

Up to four equipment grounding conductors have a single conductor volume. A ¼ volume applies for each additional equipment grounding conductor.

2 equipment grounding conductors count as a 1-conductor volume.

5 equipment grounding conductors count as a 1.25-conductor volume.

Copyright 2020, www.MikeHolt.com

▶Figure 314–26

▶ Number of Conductors Example

Question: What is the total number of conductors used for box fill calculations in a 4-in. square × 2⅛ in. deep box with two internal cable clamps, one single-pole switch, one duplex receptacle, one 14/3 with ground NM cable, and one 14/2 with ground NM cable? ▶Figure 314–27

(a) 5 conductors   (b) 7 conductors
(c) 9 conductors   (d) 11 conductors

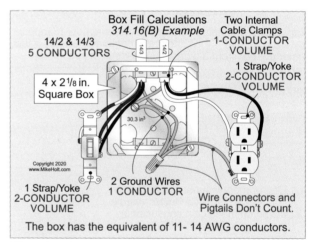

Box Fill Calculations
314.16(B) Example

Two Internal Cable Clamps
1-CONDUCTOR VOLUME

14/2 & 14/3
5 CONDUCTORS

4 x 2⅛ in. Square Box

30.3 in³

1 Strap/Yoke
2-CONDUCTOR VOLUME

1 Strap/Yoke
2-CONDUCTOR VOLUME

2 Ground Wires
1 CONDUCTOR

Wire Connectors and Pigtails Don't Count.

Copyright 2020 www.MikeHolt.com

The box has the equivalent of 11- 14 AWG conductors.

▶Figure 314–27

Solution:

Switch and Conductors	5–14 AWG conductors [†]
Receptacles and Conductors	4–14 AWG conductors [††]
Equipment Grounding Conductor	1–14 AWG conductor
Cable Clamps	+ 1–14 AWG conductor
Total	11–14 AWG conductors

†Two conductors for the device and three conductors terminating

††Two conductors for the device and two conductors terminating

Each 14 AWG conductor counts as 2 cu in. [Table 314.16(B)].
11 conductors × 2 cu in. = 22 cu in.

If the cubic-inch volume of the plaster ring is not stamped on it, or given in the problem, it cannot be included in the box volume. Without knowing the plaster ring volume, a 4 in. square by 2⅛ in. deep box is the minimum required for this example.

Answer: (d) 11 conductors

▶ Box Fill Example

Question: How many 14 AWG conductors can be pulled through a 4-in. square × 2⅛ in. deep box with a plaster ring with a marking of 3.60 cu in.? The box contains two receptacles, five 12 AWG conductors, and two 12 AWG equipment grounding conductors. ▶Figure 314–28

(a) 4 conductors   (b) 5 conductors
(c) 6 conductors   (d) 7 conductors

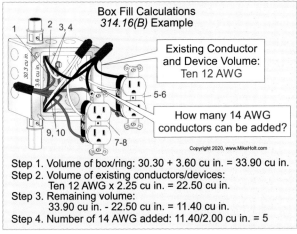

Box Fill Calculations
314.16(B) Example

Existing Conductor and Device Volume:
Ten 12 AWG

How many 14 AWG conductors can be added?

Step 1. Volume of box/ring: 30.30 + 3.60 cu in. = 33.90 cu in.
Step 2. Volume of existing conductors/devices:
Ten 12 AWG x 2.25 cu in. = 22.50 cu in.
Step 3. Remaining volume:
33.90 cu in. - 22.50 cu in. = 11.40 cu in.
Step 4. Number of 14 AWG added: 11.40/2.00 cu in. = 5

Copyright 2020, www.MikeHolt.com

▶Figure 314–28

Solution:

Step 1: Determine the volume of the box assembly [314.16(A)].

Box Assembly Volume = Box 30.30 cu in. + 3.60 cu in. plaster ring
Box Assembly Volume = 33.90 cu in.

Step 2: Determine the volume of the devices and conductors in the box:

Two–receptacles	4–12 AWG
Five–12 AWG conductors	5–12 AWG
Two–12 AWG equipment grounding conductors	1–12 AWG

Total Device Volume and Conductors = Ten–12 AWG × 2.25 cu in.
Total Device Volume and Conductors = 22.50 cu in.

Step 3: Determine the remaining volume permitted for the 14 AWG conductors (volume of the box minus the volume of the conductors).

Remaining Volume = 33.90 cu in. – 22.50 cu in.
Remaining Volume = 11.40 cu in.

Step 4: Determine the number of 14 AWG conductors (at 2.00 cu in. each) permitted in the remaining volume of 11.40 cu in.:

14 AWG = 2.00 cu in. each [Table 314.16(B)]
11.40 cu in./2.00 cu in. = 5 conductors

Five 14 AWG conductors can be pulled through.

Answer: (b) 5 conductors

(C) Conduit Bodies

(2) Splices. Splices are permitted in conduit bodies that are legibly marked by the manufacturer with their volume. The maximum number of conductors permitted in a conduit body is limited in accordance with 314.16(B).

▶ Number of Conductors in Conduit Body Example

Example: How many 12 AWG conductors can be spliced in an 11.80 cu in. conduit body? ▶Figure 314–29

(a) four conductors   (b) five conductors
(c) six conductors   (d) seven conductors

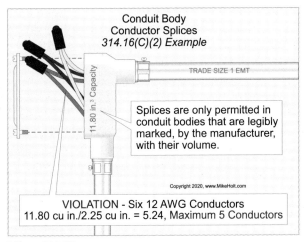

Conduit Body
Conductor Splices
314.16(C)(2) Example

TRADE SIZE 1 EMT

11.80 in.³ Capacity

Splices are only permitted in conduit bodies that are legibly marked, by the manufacturer, with their volume.

Copyright 2020, www.MikeHolt.com

VIOLATION - Six 12 AWG Conductors
11.80 cu in./2.25 cu in. = 5.24, Maximum 5 Conductors

▶Figure 314–29

• • •

Solution:

12 AWG = 2.25 cu in. [Table 314.16(B)]

11.80 cu in./2.25 cu in. = 5.24 conductors

Answer: *(b) five conductors*

(3) Short Radius Conduit Bodies. Capped elbows, handy ells, and service-entrance elbows are not permitted to contain any splices. ▶Figure 314–30

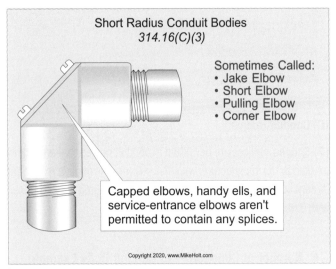

Short Radius Conduit Bodies
314.16(C)(3)

Sometimes Called:
• Jake Elbow
• Short Elbow
• Pulling Elbow
• Corner Elbow

Capped elbows, handy ells, and service-entrance elbows aren't permitted to contain any splices.

Copyright 2020, www.MikeHolt.com

▶Figure 314–30

314.17 Conductors That Enter Boxes or Conduit Bodies

(A) Openings to be Closed. Unused openings through which conductors enter a box must be closed in an approved manner identified for the application. ▶Figure 314–31

Author's Comment:

▶ Unused cable or raceway openings must be effectively closed by fittings that provide protection substantially equivalent to the wall of the equipment [110.12(A)].

(B) Boxes. The installation of the conductors in boxes must comply with the following:

(2) Conductors Entering Through Cable Clamps. Where cable assemblies (Type NM or UF) are used, the sheath must extend not less than ¼ in. inside the box and beyond any cable clamp. ▶Figure 314–32

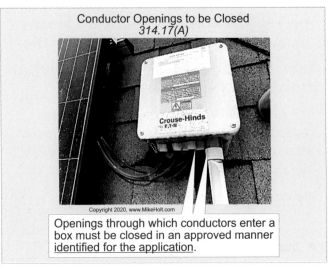

Conductor Openings to be Closed
314.17(A)

Copyright 2020, www.MikeHolt.com

Openings through which conductors enter a box must be closed in an approved manner identified for the application.

▶Figure 314–31

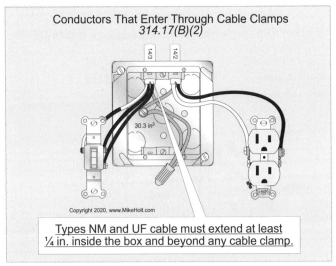

Conductors That Enter Through Cable Clamps
314.17(B)(2)

30.3 in³

Copyright 2020, www.MikeHolt.com

Types NM and UF cable must extend at least ¼ in. inside the box and beyond any cable clamp.

▶Figure 314–32

Author's Comment:

▶ Two Type NM cables can terminate in a single cable clamp if it is listed for this purpose [UL White Book].

Ex: Type NM cable terminating to a single-gang nonmetallic box is not required to be secured to the box if the cable is securely fastened within 8 in. of the box and the sheath extends at least ¼ in. inside the box. ▶Figure 314–33

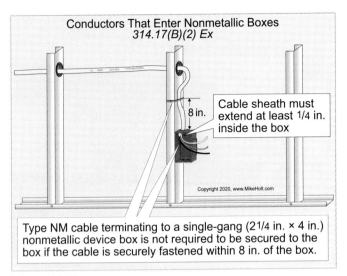

Conductors That Enter Nonmetallic Boxes
314.17(B)(2) Ex

Cable sheath must extend at least 1/4 in. inside the box

8 in.

Type NM cable terminating to a single-gang (2¼ in. × 4 in.) nonmetallic device box is not required to be secured to the box if the cable is securely fastened within 8 in. of the box.

▶Figure 314–33

314.20 Flush-Mounted Box Installations

Installation within walls or ceilings constructed of noncombustible material must have the front edge of the box, plaster ring, extension ring, or listed extender set back no more than ¼ in. from the finished surface. ▶Figure 314–34

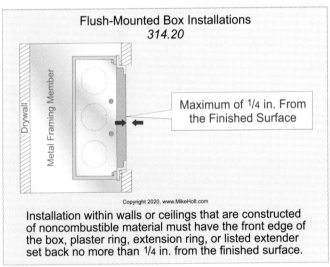

Flush-Mounted Box Installations
314.20

Maximum of ¼ in. From the Finished Surface

Installation within walls or ceilings that are constructed of noncombustible material must have the front edge of the box, plaster ring, extension ring, or listed extender set back no more than ¼ in. from the finished surface.

▶Figure 314–34

Installation within walls or ceilings constructed of wood or other combustible material must have the front edge of the box, plaster ring, extension ring, or listed extender extend to or project out from the finished surface. ▶Figure 314–35

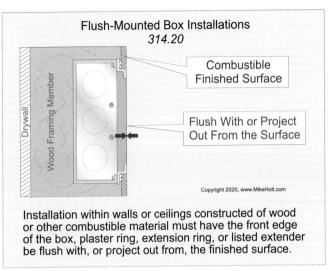

Flush-Mounted Box Installations
314.20

Combustible Finished Surface

Flush With or Project Out From the Surface

Installation within walls or ceilings constructed of wood or other combustible material must have the front edge of the box, plaster ring, extension ring, or listed extender be flush with, or project out from, the finished surface.

▶Figure 314–35

Author's Comment:

▶ Plaster rings and extension rings are available in a variety of depths to meet the above requirements.

▶ Final finished surfaces such as backsplashes and tile may need to be considered in order to meet the requirements of this section.

314.21 Repairing Noncombustible Surfaces

Gaps around boxes that are recessed in noncombustible surfaces (such as plaster, drywall, or plasterboard) must be repaired so there will be no gap more than ⅛ in. at the edge of the box. ▶Figure 314–36

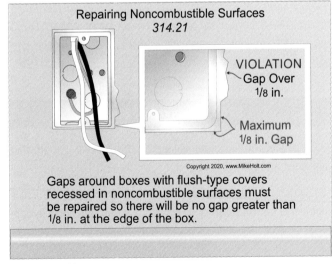

Repairing Noncombustible Surfaces
314.21

VIOLATION
Gap Over
1/8 in.

Maximum
1/8 in. Gap

Gaps around boxes with flush-type covers recessed in noncombustible surfaces must be repaired so there will be no gap greater than 1/8 in. at the edge of the box.

▶Figure 314–36

Author's Comment:

▸ Other examples of noncombustible surfaces include ceramic wall tile, ceramic or marble floor tile, brick, cinder block, and other types of masonry or stone; all of which are subject to the requirements of 314.20 and 314.21.

314.22 Surface Extensions

Surface extensions can only be made from an extension ring installed over a box. ▸Figure 314–37

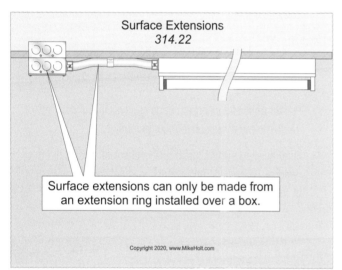

▸Figure 314–37

Ex: A surface extension can be made from the cover of a box if the cover is designed so it is unlikely to fall off if the mounting screws become loose. The surface extension wiring method must be flexible to permit the removal of the cover and provide access to the box interior, and the equipment grounding continuity must be independent of the connection between the box and the cover. ▸Figure 314–38

314.23 Support of Boxes

(A) Surface. Boxes can be fastened to any surface that provides adequate support.

(B) Structural Mounting. An enclosure supported from a structural member or from grade must be rigidly supported either directly or by using a metal, polymeric, or wood brace.

(2) Braces. Boxes can be supported from any structural member or by a metal, plastic, or wood brace. ▸Figure 314–39

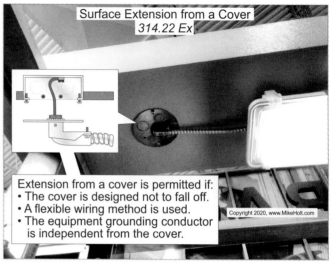

Extension from a cover is permitted if:
• The cover is designed not to fall off.
• A flexible wiring method is used.
• The equipment grounding conductor is independent from the cover.

▸Figure 314–38

Boxes can be supported from grade by a metal brace.

▸Figure 314–39

Metal braces no less than 0.02 in. thick and wood braces not less than a nominal 1 in. × 2 in. are permitted. ▸Figure 314–40

(C) Finished Surface Support. Boxes can be secured to a finished surface (drywall, plaster walls, or ceilings) by clamps or fittings identified for the purpose. ▸Figure 314–41

(D) Suspended-Ceiling Support. Outlet boxes can be supported to the structural or supporting elements of a suspended ceiling, if they are securely fastened by any of the following methods:

(1) Ceiling Framing Members. An outlet box can be secured to suspended-ceiling framing members by bolts, screws, rivets, clips, or other means identified for the suspended-ceiling framing member(s). ▸Figure 314–42

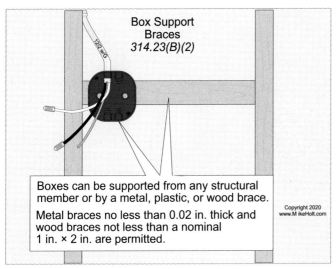

Box Support
Braces
314.23(B)(2)

Boxes can be supported from any structural member or by a metal, plastic, or wood brace.

Metal braces no less than 0.02 in. thick and wood braces not less than a nominal 1 in. × 2 in. are permitted.

Copyright 2020
www.MikeHolt.com

▶Figure 314–40

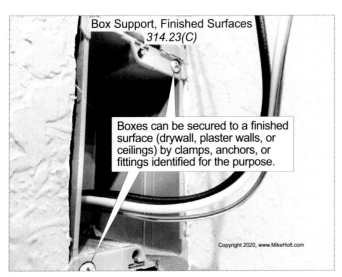

Box Support, Finished Surfaces
314.23(C)

Boxes can be secured to a finished surface (drywall, plaster walls, or ceilings) by clamps, anchors, or fittings identified for the purpose.

Copyright 2020, www.MikeHolt.com

▶Figure 314–41

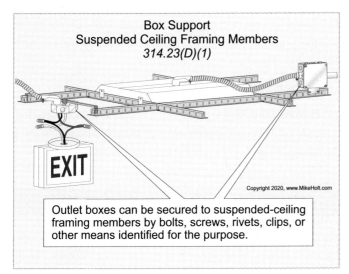

Box Support
Suspended Ceiling Framing Members
314.23(D)(1)

EXIT

Copyright 2020, www.MikeHolt.com

Outlet boxes can be secured to suspended-ceiling framing members by bolts, screws, rivets, clips, or other means identified for the purpose.

▶Figure 314–42

(2) Independent Support Wires. Outlet boxes can be secured with identified fittings to independent support wires in accordance with 300.11(B). ▶Figure 314–43

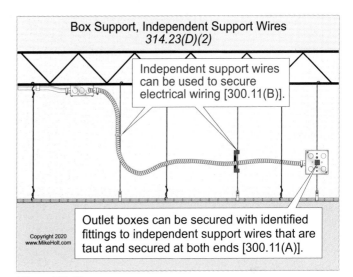

Box Support, Independent Support Wires
314.23(D)(2)

Independent support wires can be used to secure electrical wiring [300.11(B)].

Copyright 2020
www.MikeHolt.com

Outlet boxes can be secured with identified fittings to independent support wires that are taut and secured at both ends [300.11(A)].

▶Figure 314–43

(E) Threaded Raceway-Supported Boxes Without Devices or Luminaires. Two intermediate metal or rigid metal conduits, threaded wrenchtight into the enclosure, can be used to support an outlet box that does not contain a device or luminaire if each raceway is supported within 36 in. of the box, or within 18 in. of the box if all conduit entries are on the same side. ▶Figure 314–44

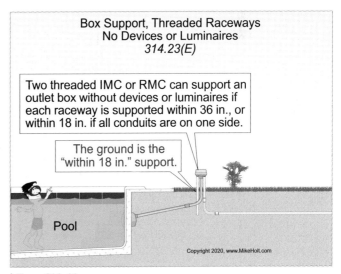

Box Support, Threaded Raceways
No Devices or Luminaires
314.23(E)

Two threaded IMC or RMC can support an outlet box without devices or luminaires if each raceway is supported within 36 in., or within 18 in. if all conduits are on one side.

The ground is the "within 18 in." support.

Pool

Copyright 2020, www.MikeHolt.com

▶Figure 314–44

Ex: The following wiring methods are permitted to support a conduit body of any size, including a conduit body constructed with only one conduit entry, provided the trade size of the conduit body is not larger than the largest trade size of the conduit or tubing: ▶Figure 314–45

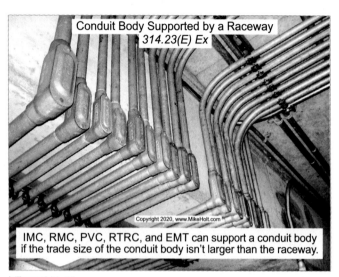

Conduit Body Supported by a Raceway
314.23(E) Ex

IMC, RMC, PVC, RTRC, and EMT can support a conduit body if the trade size of the conduit body isn't larger than the raceway.

▶Figure 314–45

Box Support, Threaded Raceways to Boxes With Devices
314.23(F)

VIOLATION: A free-standing outlet box with a device must be supported by two threaded IMC or RMC raceways within 18 in. of the box.

▶Figure 314–47

(1) Intermediate metal conduit, Type IMC

(2) Rigid metal conduit, Type RMC

(3) Rigid polyvinyl chloride conduit, Type PVC

(4) Reinforced thermosetting resin conduit, Type RTRC

(5) Electrical metallic tubing, Type EMT

(F) Threaded Raceway-Supported Boxes with Devices or Luminaires. Two intermediate metal or rigid metal conduits, threaded wrenchtight into the enclosure, can be used to support an outlet box containing devices or luminaires if each raceway is supported within 18 in. of the box. ▶Figure 314–46, ▶Figure 314–47, and ▶Figure 314–48

Box Support, Threaded Raceways to Boxes With Luminaires
314.23(F)

VIOLATION: A free-standing outlet box with a luminaire must be supported by two threaded IMC or RMC raceways within 18 in. of the box.

▶Figure 314–48

(G) Boxes in Concrete or Masonry. Boxes must be identified as suitably protected from corrosion and be securely embedded in concrete or masonry.

(H) Pendant Boxes.

(1) Flexible Cord. Boxes containing a hub can be supported from a flexible cord connected to fittings that prevent tension from being transmitted to joints or terminals [400.10]. ▶Figure 314–49

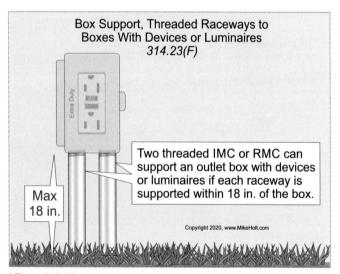

Box Support, Threaded Raceways to Boxes With Devices or Luminaires
314.23(F)

Two threaded IMC or RMC can support an outlet box with devices or luminaires if each raceway is supported within 18 in. of the box.

Max 18 in.

▶Figure 314–46

314.25 Covers and Canopies

When the installation is complete, each outlet box must be provided with a cover, faceplate, fixture canopy, or similar device. ▶Figure 314–50

Pendant Box Support
Flexible Cords
314.23(H)(1)

Boxes containing a hub can be supported from a flexible cord connected to fittings that prevent tension from being transmitted to joints or terminals [400.14].

▶Figure 314–49

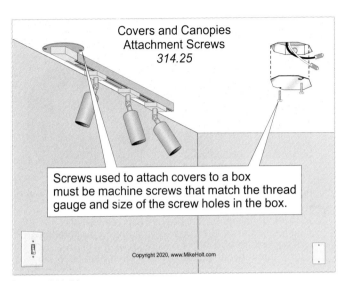

Covers and Canopies
Attachment Screws
314.25

Screws used to attach covers to a box must be machine screws that match the thread gauge and size of the screw holes in the box.

▶Figure 314–51

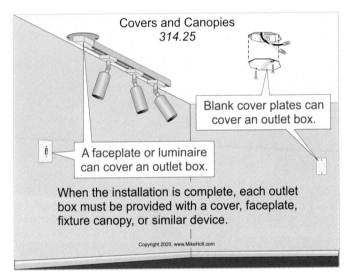

Covers and Canopies
314.25

Blank cover plates can cover an outlet box.

A faceplate or luminaire can cover an outlet box.

When the installation is complete, each outlet box must be provided with a cover, faceplate, fixture canopy, or similar device.

▶Figure 314–50

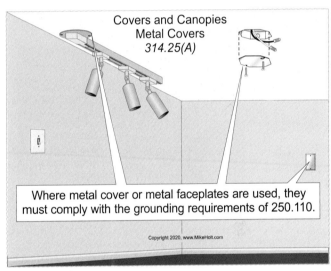

Covers and Canopies
Metal Covers
314.25(A)

Where metal cover or metal faceplates are used, they must comply with the grounding requirements of 250.110.

▶Figure 314–52

Screws used for attaching covers to the box must be machine screws that match the thread gage and size of the screw holes in the box.
▶Figure 314–51

(A) Metal Covers. Metal covers are only permitted if they can be connected to the circuit equipment grounding conductor [250.110].
▶Figure 314–52

Author's Comment:

▶ Metal switch cover plates are connected to the circuit equipment grounding conductor in accordance with 404.9(B), and metal receptacle cover plates are connected to the circuit equipment grounding conductor in accordance with 406.6(B).

314.27 Outlet Box Requirements

(A) Boxes at Luminaire Outlets.

(1) Luminaire Outlets in or on Vertical Surfaces. Boxes or fittings designed for the support of luminaires in or on a wall or other vertical surface must be identified and marked on the interior of the box to indicate the maximum weight of the luminaire that can be supported by the box if other than 50 lb. ▶Figure 314–53

Ex: A vertically mounted luminaire weighing no more than 6 lb can be supported to a device box or plaster ring secured to a device box, provided the luminaire or its supporting yoke is secured to the box with no fewer than two No. 6 or larger screws. ▶Figure 314–54

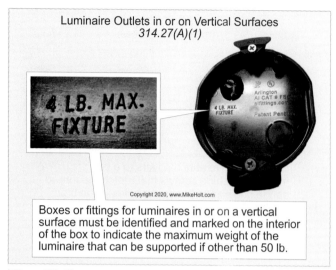

Luminaire Outlets in or on Vertical Surfaces
314.27(A)(1)

Boxes or fittings for luminaires in or on a vertical surface must be identified and marked on the interior of the box to indicate the maximum weight of the luminaire that can be supported if other than 50 lb.

▶Figure 314–53

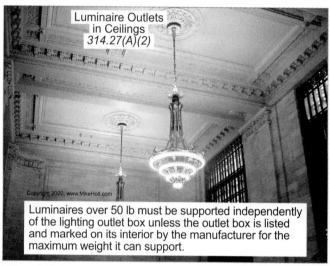

Luminaire Outlets in Ceilings
314.27(A)(2)

Luminaires over 50 lb must be supported independently of the lighting outlet box unless the outlet box is listed and marked on its interior by the manufacturer for the maximum weight it can support.

▶Figure 314–55

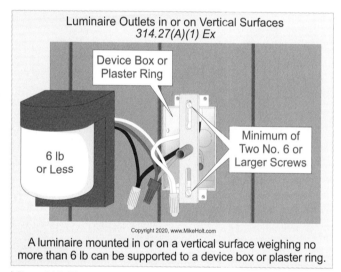

Luminaire Outlets in or on Vertical Surfaces
314.27(A)(1) Ex

A luminaire mounted in or on a vertical surface weighing no more than 6 lb can be supported to a device box or plaster ring.

▶Figure 314–54

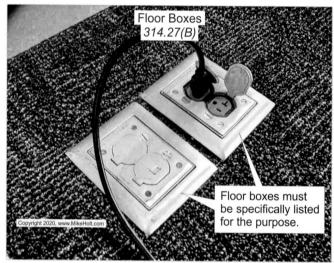

Floor Boxes
314.27(B)

Floor boxes must be specifically listed for the purpose.

▶Figure 314–56

(2) Luminaire Outlets in a Ceiling. Boxes for ceiling luminaires must be listed and marked to support a luminaire weighing a minimum of 50 lb. Luminaires weighing more than 50 lb must be supported independently of the outlet box unless it is listed and marked on the interior of the box by the manufacturer for the maximum weight it can support. ▶Figure 314–55

(B) Floor Box. Floor boxes must be specifically listed for the purpose. ▶Figure 314–56

(C) Ceiling Paddle Fan Box. Outlet boxes for a ceiling paddle fan must be listed and marked as suitable for the purpose and are not permitted to support a fan weighing more than 70 lb. Outlet boxes for a ceiling paddle fan that weighs more than 35 lb must include the maximum weight to be supported in the required marking. ▶Figure 314–57

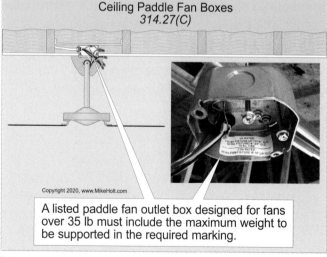

Ceiling Paddle Fan Boxes
314.27(C)

A listed paddle fan outlet box designed for fans over 35 lb must include the maximum weight to be supported in the required marking.

▶Figure 314–57

Ceiling-mounted outlet boxes in a habitable room of a dwelling unit where a ceiling-suspended (paddle) fan could be installed must comply with one of the following: ▶Figure 314–58

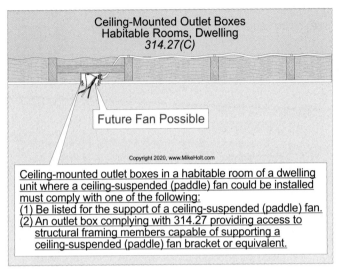

▶Figure 314–58

(1) Be listed for the support of a ceiling-suspended (paddle) fan.

(2) An outlet box complying with 314.27 providing access to structural framing members capable of supporting a ceiling-suspended (paddle) fan bracket or equivalent.

(D) Utilization Equipment. Boxes used for the support of utilization equipment must be designed to support equipment that weighs a minimum of 50 lb [314.27(A)].

Ex: Utilization equipment weighing 6 lb or less can be supported by any box or plaster ring secured to a box, provided the equipment is secured with no fewer than two No. 6 or larger screws. ▶Figure 314–59

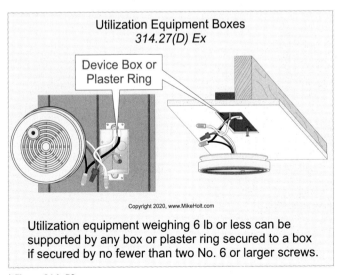

Utilization equipment weighing 6 lb or less can be supported by any box or plaster ring secured to a box if secured by no fewer than two No. 6 or larger screws.

▶Figure 314–59

(E) Separable Attachment Fittings. Outlet boxes required in 314.27 are permitted to support listed locking support and mounting receptacles used in combination with compatible attachment fittings. The combination must be identified for the support of equipment within the weight and mounting orientation limits of the listing. Where the supporting receptacle is installed within a box, it must be included in the fill calculation in accordance with 314.16(B)(4). ▶Figure 314–60

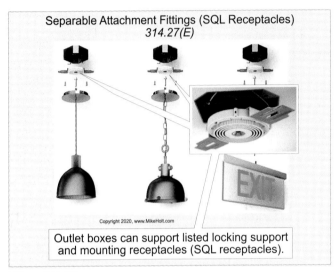

Outlet boxes can support listed locking support and mounting receptacles (SQL receptacles).

▶Figure 314–60

314.28 Sizing Pull and Junction Boxes

Boxes containing conductors 4 AWG and larger must be sized so the conductor insulation will not be damaged. ▶Figure 314–61 and ▶Figure 314–62

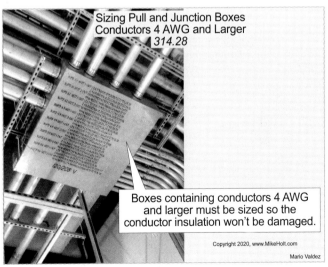

Boxes containing conductors 4 AWG and larger must be sized so the conductor insulation won't be damaged.

▶Figure 314–61

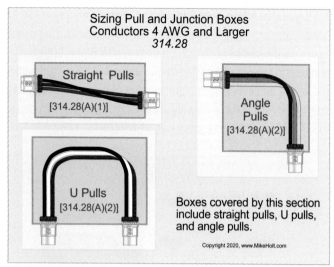

▶Figure 314–62

Author's Comment:

▸ The requirements for sizing boxes containing conductors 6 AWG and smaller are contained in 314.16.

▸ If conductors 4 AWG and larger enter a box or other enclosure, a fitting that provides a smooth, rounded, insulating surface (such as a bushing or adapter) is required to protect them from abrasion during and after installation [300.4(G)].

(A) Minimum Size. For raceways containing conductors 4 AWG and larger, the minimum dimensions of boxes must comply with the following:

(1) Straight Pulls. The distance from where the raceway enters the box to the opposite wall must not be less than eight times the trade size of the largest raceway. ▶Figure 314–63

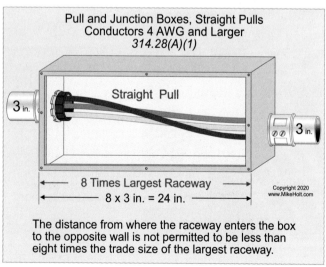

The distance from where the raceway enters the box to the opposite wall is not permitted to be less than eight times the trade size of the largest raceway.

▶Figure 314–63

(2) Angle Pulls, U Pulls, or Splices

Angle Pulls. The distance from the raceway entry of the box to the opposite wall must not be less than six times the trade size of the largest raceway, plus the sum of the trade sizes of the remaining raceways on the same wall and row. ▶Figure 314–64

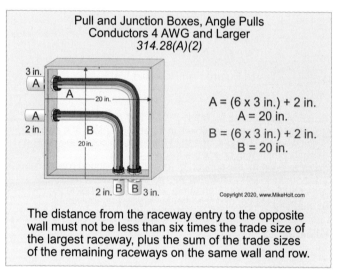

The distance from the raceway entry to the opposite wall must not be less than six times the trade size of the largest raceway, plus the sum of the trade sizes of the remaining raceways on the same wall and row.

▶Figure 314–64

U Pulls. When a conductor enters and leaves from the same wall of the box, the distance from the raceway entry of the box to the opposite wall must not be less than six times the trade size of the largest raceway, plus the sum of the trade sizes of the remaining raceways on the same wall and row. ▶Figure 314–65

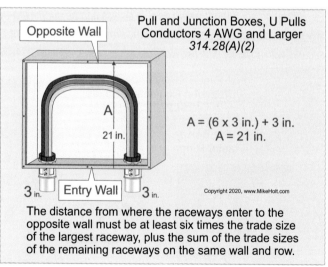

The distance from where the raceways enter to the opposite wall must be at least six times the trade size of the largest raceway, plus the sum of the trade sizes of the remaining raceways on the same wall and row.

▶Figure 314–65

Splices. When conductors are spliced, the distance from the raceways' entry of the box to the opposite wall must not be less than six times the trade size of the largest raceway, plus the sum of the trade sizes of the remaining raceways on the same wall and row. ▶Figure 314–66

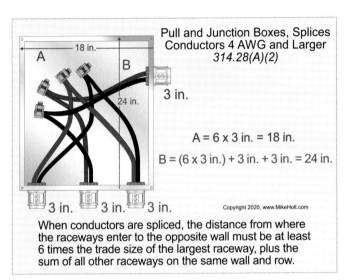

Pull and Junction Boxes, Splices
Conductors 4 AWG and Larger
314.28(A)(2)

A = 6 x 3 in. = 18 in.

B = (6 x 3 in.) + 3 in. + 3 in. = 24 in.

When conductors are spliced, the distance from where the raceways enter to the opposite wall must be at least 6 times the trade size of the largest raceway, plus the sum of all other raceways on the same wall and row.

▶Figure 314–66

Rows. If there are multiple rows of raceway entries, each row is calculated individually and the row with the largest distance must be used. ▶Figure 314–67

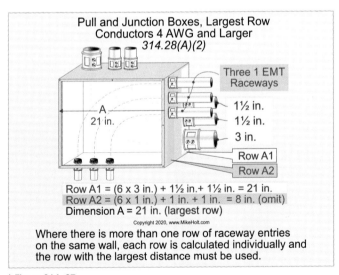

Pull and Junction Boxes, Largest Row
Conductors 4 AWG and Larger
314.28(A)(2)

Three 1 EMT Raceways

1½ in.
1½ in.
3 in.

Row A1
Row A2

Row A1 = (6 x 3 in.) + 1½ in. + 1½ in. = 21 in.
Row A2 = (6 x 1 in.) + 1 in. + 1 in. = 8 in. (omit)
Dimension A = 21 in. (largest row)

Where there is more than one row of raceway entries on the same wall, each row is calculated individually and the row with the largest distance must be used.

▶Figure 314–67

Distance Between Raceways. The distance between raceway entries enclosing the same conductor must not be less than six times the trade size of the largest raceway, measured between the raceway entry openings. ▶Figure 314–68 and ▶Figure 314–69

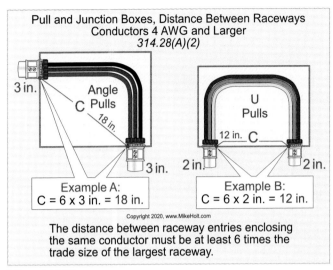

Pull and Junction Boxes, Distance Between Raceways
Conductors 4 AWG and Larger
314.28(A)(2)

Angle Pulls

U Pulls

Example A:
C = 6 x 3 in. = 18 in.

Example B:
C = 6 x 2 in. = 12 in.

The distance between raceway entries enclosing the same conductor must be at least 6 times the trade size of the largest raceway.

▶Figure 314–68

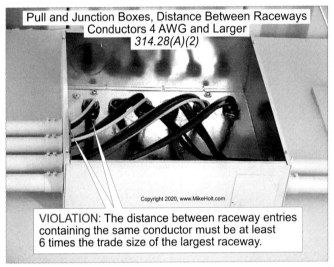

Pull and Junction Boxes, Distance Between Raceways
Conductors 4 AWG and Larger
314.28(A)(2)

VIOLATION: The distance between raceway entries containing the same conductor must be at least 6 times the trade size of the largest raceway.

▶Figure 314–69

Ex: When conductors enter an enclosure with a removable cover, the distance from where the conductors enter to the removable cover is not permitted to be less than the bending distance as contained in Table 312.6(A) for one conductor per terminal. ▶Figure 314–70

(B) Conductors in Pull or Junction Boxes. Pull boxes or junction boxes with any dimension over 6 ft must have all conductors cabled or racked in an approved manner.

(C) Covers. Metal covers must be connected to an equipment grounding conductor of a type recognized in 250.118, in accordance with 250.110 [250.4(A)(3)]. ▶Figure 314–71

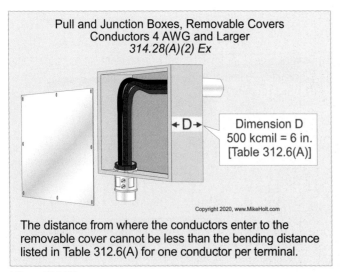

Pull and Junction Boxes, Removable Covers
Conductors 4 AWG and Larger
314.28(A)(2) Ex

◄─D─►

Dimension D
500 kcmil = 6 in.
[Table 312.6(A)]

The distance from where the conductors enter to the removable cover cannot be less than the bending distance listed in Table 312.6(A) for one conductor per terminal.

▶Figure 314–70

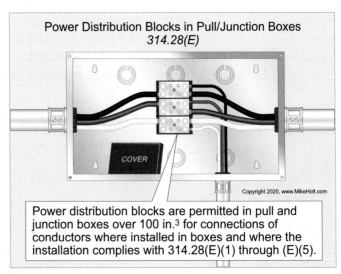

Power Distribution Blocks in Pull/Junction Boxes
314.28(E)

COVER

Power distribution blocks are permitted in pull and junction boxes over 100 in.³ for connections of conductors where installed in boxes and where the installation complies with 314.28(E)(1) through (E)(5).

▶Figure 314–72

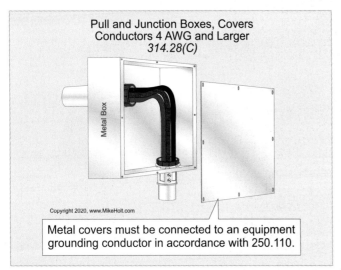

Pull and Junction Boxes, Covers
Conductors 4 AWG and Larger
314.28(C)

Metal Box

Metal covers must be connected to an equipment grounding conductor in accordance with 250.110.

▶Figure 314–71

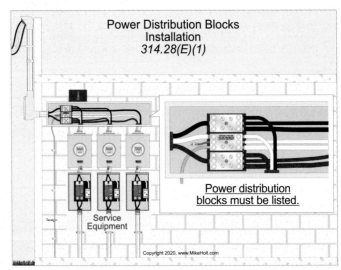

Power Distribution Blocks
Installation
314.28(E)(1)

Service
Equipment

Power distribution
blocks must be listed.

▶Figure 314–73

(E) Power Distribution Blocks. Power distribution blocks are permitted in pull and junction boxes over 100 in.³ for connections of conductors where installed in boxes and where the installation complies with 314.28(E)(1) through (E)(5). ▶Figure 314–72

Ex: Equipment grounding terminal bars are permitted in smaller enclosures.

(1) Installation. Power distribution blocks installed in boxes must be listed. ▶Figure 314–73

314.29 Wiring to be Accessible

(A) In Buildings and Other Structures. Boxes and conduit bodies must be installed so the wiring contained within is accessible without removing any part of the building or structure. ▶Figure 314–74

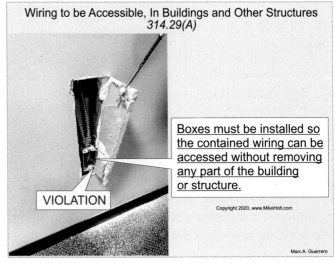

Wiring to be Accessible, In Buildings and Other Structures
314.29(A)

Boxes must be installed so the contained wiring can be accessed without removing any part of the building or structure.

VIOLATION

Marc A. Guerrero

▶Figure 314–74

(B) Underground. Underground boxes, conduit bodies, and hand-hole enclosures must be installed so the wiring contained within is accessible without removing any part of the excavating, sidewalks, paving, earth, or other substance used to establish the finished grade.

314.30 Handhole Enclosures

Handhole enclosures must be identified for underground use and be designed and installed to withstand all loads likely to be imposed on them. ▶Figure 314–75

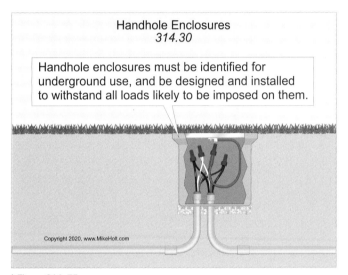

Handhole Enclosures
314.30

Handhole enclosures must be identified for underground use, and be designed and installed to withstand all loads likely to be imposed on them.

Copyright 2020, www.MikeHolt.com

▶Figure 314–75

(B) Wiring Entries. Underground raceways and cables entering a hand-hole are not required to be mechanically connected to the handhole. ▶Figure 314–76

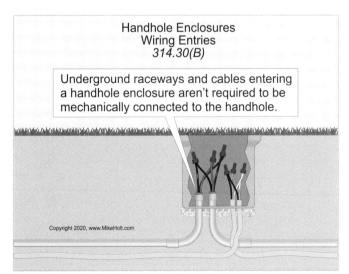

Handhole Enclosures
Wiring Entries
314.30(B)

Underground raceways and cables entering a handhole enclosure aren't required to be mechanically connected to the handhole.

Copyright 2020, www.MikeHolt.com

▶Figure 314–76

(C) Enclosure Wiring. Splices or terminations within a handhole must be listed for wet locations [110.14(B)].

(D) Covers. Handhole covers must have an identifying mark or logo that prominently identifies the function of the handhole, such as "electric." Handhole covers must require the use of tools to open, or they must weigh over 100 lb. ▶Figure 314–77

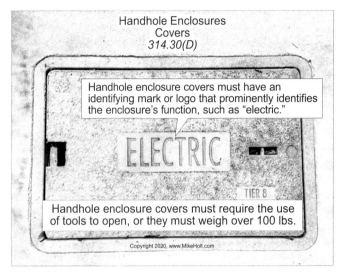

Handhole Enclosures
Covers
314.30(D)

Handhole enclosure covers must have an identifying mark or logo that prominently identifies the enclosure's function, such as "electric."

ELECTRIC

TIER 8

Handhole enclosure covers must require the use of tools to open, or they must weigh over 100 lbs.

Copyright 2020, www.MikeHolt.com

▶Figure 314–77

Metal covers and exposed conductive surfaces of handhole enclosures must be connected to an equipment grounding conductor sized in accordance with 250.122, based on the rating of the overcurrent protective device [250.102(D)]. ▶Figure 314–78

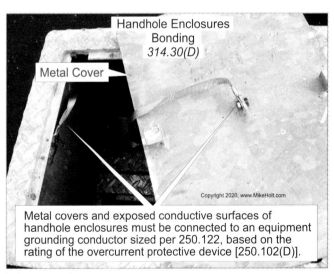

Handhole Enclosures
Bonding
314.30(D)

Metal Cover

Metal covers and exposed conductive surfaces of handhole enclosures must be connected to an equipment grounding conductor sized per 250.122, based on the rating of the overcurrent protective device [250.102(D)].

Copyright 2020, www.MikeHolt.com

▶Figure 314–78

ARTICLE
314

PRACTICE QUESTIONS

Please use the 2020 *Code* book to answer the following questions.

Article 314—Outlet, Pull, and Junction Boxes; Conduit Bodies; and Handhole Enclosures

1. The installation and use of all boxes and conduit bodies used as outlet, device, junction, or pull boxes, depending on their use, and handhole enclosures, are covered within _____.

   (a) Article 110
   (b) Article 200
   (c) Article 300
   (d) Article 314

2. Where internal _____ means are provided between all entries, nonmetallic boxes shall be permitted to be used with metal raceways or metal-armored cables.

   (a) grounding
   (b) bonding
   (c) connecting
   (d) splicing

3. Where a box is provided with _____ or more securely installed barriers, the volume shall be apportioned to each of the resulting spaces; each barrier, if not marked with its volume, shall be considered to take up ½ cu in. if metal, and 1 cu in. if nonmetallic.

   (a) one
   (b) two
   (c) three
   (d) four

4. The total volume occupied by two internal cable clamps, six 12 AWG conductors, and a single-pole switch is _____ cu in.

   (a) 2.00
   (b) 4.50
   (c) 14.50
   (d) 20.25

5. Equipment grounding conductor(s), and not more than _____ fixture wires smaller than 14 AWG shall be permitted to be omitted from the calculations where they enter the box from a domed luminaire or similar canopy and terminate within that box.

   (a) one
   (b) two
   (c) three
   (d) four

6. Where a luminaire stud or hickey is present in the box, _____ allowance in accordance with Table 314.16(B) shall be made for each type of fitting, based on the largest conductor present in the box.

   (a) a single volume
   (b) a double volume
   (c) a ¼ volume
   (d) no additional volume

7. Each strap containing one or more devices shall count as _____ allowance in accordance with Table 314.16(B), based on the largest conductor connected to a device(s) or equipment supported by the strap.

    (a) a single volume
    (b) a double volume
    (c) a ¼ volume
    (d) no additional volume

8. Where one or more equipment grounding conductors enter a box, _____ allowance in accordance with Table 314.16(B) shall be made based on the largest equipment grounding conductor.

    (a) a single volume
    (b) a double volume
    (c) a ¼ volume
    (d) no additional volume

9. Short-radius conduit bodies such as capped elbows and service-entrance elbows that enclose conductors 6 AWG or smaller shall not contain _____.

    (a) splices
    (b) taps
    (c) devices
    (d) any of these

10. When Type NM cable is used with nonmetallic boxes not larger than 2¼ in. x 4 in., securing the cable to the box shall not be required if the cable is fastened within _____ in. of that box.

    (a) 6
    (b) 8
    (c) 10
    (d) 12

11. In installations within walls or ceilings constructed of wood or other combustible surface material, boxes, plaster rings, extension rings, or listed extenders shall _____.

    (a) extend to the finished surface or project therefrom
    (b) not be permitted
    (c) be fire rated
    (d) be set back no more than ¼ in.

12. An outlet box or enclosure mounted on a building or other surface shall be _____.

    (a) rigidly and securely fastened in place
    (b) supported by cables that protrude from the box
    (c) supported by cable entries from the top and permitted to rest against the supporting surface
    (d) permitted to be supported by the raceway(s) terminating at the box

13. When mounting an enclosure in a finished surface, the enclosure shall be _____ secured to the surface by clamps, anchors, or fittings identified for the application.

    (a) temporarily
    (b) partially
    (c) never
    (d) rigidly

14. Support wire(s) used for enclosure support in suspended ceilings shall be fastened at _____ so as to be taut within the ceiling cavity.

    (a) each end
    (b) each corner
    (c) each ceiling support
    (d) the ceiling grid

15. Two intermediate metal or rigid metal conduits threaded wrenchtight into an enclosure can be used to support an outlet box containing devices or luminaires, if each raceway is supported within _____ in. of the box.

    (a) 12
    (b) 18
    (c) 24
    (d) 36

16. Screws used for the purpose of attaching covers or other equipment to the box shall be either machine screws matching the thread gauge and size that is integral to the box or be in accordance with the manufacturer

    (a) True
    (b) False

17. A vertically mounted luminaire weighing not more than _____ lb can be supported to a device box or plaster ring with no fewer than two No. 6 or larger screws.

    (a) 4
    (b) 6
    (c) 8
    (d) 10

18. A luminaire that weighs more than _____ lb can be supported by an outlet box that is listed for the weight of the luminaire to be supported.

    (a) 20
    (b) 30
    (c) 40
    (d) 50

19. Listed outlet boxes to support ceiling-suspended fans that weigh more than _____ lb shall have the maximum allowable weight marked on the box.

    (a) 35
    (b) 50
    (c) 60
    (d) 70

20. Utilization equipment weighing not more than 6 lb can be supported to any box or plaster ring secured to a box, provided the equipment is secured with at least two _____ or larger screws.

    (a) No. 6
    (b) No. 8
    (c) No. 10
    (d) any of these

21. Where splices, or, angle or U pulls are made and the conductor enters and leaves from the same wall and row of the box, the distance to the opposite wall may not be less than _____ the trade size of the largest raceway in the row plus the sum of the remaining trade sizes in the same row.

    (a) twice
    (b) 3 times
    (c) 6 times
    (d) 8 times

22. Where angle or U pulls are made, the distance between each raceway entry inside the box or conduit body and the opposite wall of the box or conduit body shall not be less than _____ times the trade size of the largest raceway in a row plus the sum of the trade sizes of the remaining raceways in the same wall and row.

    (a) six
    (b) eight
    (c) ten
    (d) twelve

23. All _____ shall be provided with covers compatible with the box or conduit body construction and suitable for the conditions of use.

    (a) pull boxes
    (b) junction boxes
    (c) conduit bodies
    (d) all of these

24. _____ shall be installed so that the wiring contained in them can be rendered accessible without removing any part of the building or structure or, in underground circuits, without excavating sidewalks, paving, or earth.

    (a) Boxes
    (b) Conduit bodies
    (c) Handhole enclosures
    (d) all of these

25. Underground raceways and cable assemblies entering a handhole enclosure shall extend into the enclosure, but they are not required to be _____.

    (a) bonded
    (b) insulated
    (c) mechanically connected to the handhole enclosure
    (d) below minimum cover requirements after leaving the handhole

26. Handhole enclosure covers shall have an identifying mark or logo that prominently identifies the function of the enclosure, such as "_____."

    (a) danger
    (b) utility
    (c) high voltage
    (d) electric

ARTICLE

320

ARMORED CABLE (TYPE AC)

Introduction to Article 320—Armored Cable (Type AC)

Armored cable (Type AC) is an assembly of insulated conductors, 14 AWG through 1 AWG, individually wrapped in wax paper (jute) and contained within a flexible spiral metal sheath. To the casual observer the outside appearance of armored cable is like flexible metal conduit and metal-clad cable (Type MC). Type AC cable has been referred to as "BX®" cable over the years.

Part I. General

320.1 Scope

This article covers the use, installation, and construction specifications of armored cable, Type AC. ▶Figure 320–1

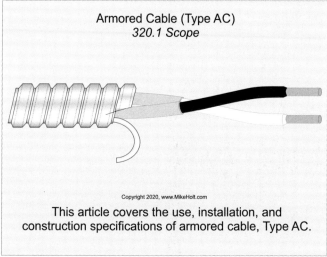

Armored Cable (Type AC)
320.1 Scope

Copyright 2020, www.MikeHolt.com

This article covers the use, installation, and construction specifications of armored cable, Type AC.

▶Figure 320–1

320.2 Definition

The definition in this section applies within this article and throughout the *Code*.

Armored Cable (Type AC). A fabricated assembly of conductors in a flexible interlocked metal armor with an internal bonding strip in intimate contact with the armor for its entire length. ▶Figure 320–2

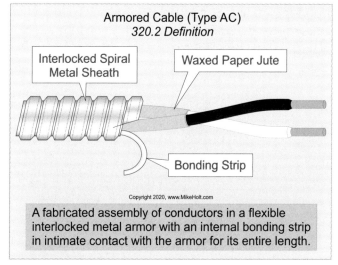

Armored Cable (Type AC)
320.2 Definition

Interlocked Spiral Metal Sheath

Waxed Paper Jute

Bonding Strip

Copyright 2020, www.MikeHolt.com

A fabricated assembly of conductors in a flexible interlocked metal armor with an internal bonding strip in intimate contact with the armor for its entire length.

▶Figure 320–2

Author's Comment:

▶ Type AC cable conductors are contained within a flexible metal sheath that interlocks at the edges with an internal aluminum bonding strip, giving the cable an outside appearance of flexible metal conduit. The advantages of any flexible cable, as compared to raceway wiring methods, are that there is no limit to the number of bends between terminations and the cable can be quickly installed.

Part II. Installation

320.10 Uses Permitted

Type AC cable can be used or installed as follows:

(1) For feeders and branch circuits in both exposed and concealed installations.

(2) In cable trays.

(3) In dry locations.

(4) Embedded in plaster in dry locations.

(5) In air voids where not exposed to excessive moisture or dampness.

Note: The "Uses Permitted" is not an all-inclusive list, which indicates other suitable uses are permitted if approved by the authority having jurisdiction.

Author's Comment:

▶ Type AC cable can also be installed in a plenum space in accordance with 300.22(C)(1).

320.12 Uses Not Permitted

Type AC cable is not permitted to be installed:

(1) Where subject to physical damage.

(2) In damp or wet locations.

(3) In air voids of masonry block or tile walls where such walls are exposed or subject to excessive moisture or dampness.

(4) Where exposed to corrosive conditions.

Please use the 2020 *Code* book to answer the following questions.

Article 320—Armored Cable (Type AC)

1. Article _____ covers the use, installation, and construction specifications for armored cable, Type AC.

   (a) 300
   (b) 310
   (c) 320
   (d) 334

2. Type _____ cable is a fabricated assembly of insulated conductors in a flexible interlocked metallic armor.

   (a) AC
   (b) TC
   (c) NM
   (d) MA

3. Type AC cable is permitted in _____.

   (a) wet locations
   (b) corrosive conditions
   (c) damp locations
   (d) cable trays

4. Armored cable shall not be installed _____.

   (a) in damp or wet locations
   (b) where subject to physical damage
   (c) where exposed to corrosive conditions
   (d) all of these

ARTICLE 330

METAL-CLAD CABLE (TYPE MC)

Introduction to Article 330—Metal-Clad Cable (Type MC)

Metal-clad cable (Type MC) is probably the most often used metal-protected wiring method. Type MC cable encloses insulated conductors in a metal sheath of either corrugated or smooth copper or aluminum tubing, or in spiral interlocked steel or aluminum. The physical characteristics of Type MC cable make it a versatile wiring method that can be used in almost any location, and for almost any application. The most commonly used Type MC cable is the interlocking kind, which looks like armored cable or flexible metal conduit. Traditional interlocked Type MC cable is not permitted to serve as an equipment grounding conductor; therefore, this cable must contain an equipment grounding conductor in accordance with 250.118(1). Another type of Type MC cable is called interlocked Type MC^AP® cable. It contains a bare aluminum grounding/bonding conductor running just below the metal armor, which allows the sheath to serve as an equipment grounding conductor [250.118(10)(b)].

Part I. General

330.1 Scope

Article 330 covers the use, installation, and construction specifications of metal-clad cable, Type MC. ▶Figure 330–1

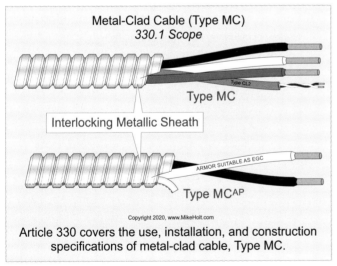

Metal-Clad Cable (Type MC)
330.1 Scope

Type MC

Interlocking Metallic Sheath

ARMOR SUITABLE AS EGC

Type MC^AP

Copyright 2020, www.MikeHolt.com

Article 330 covers the use, installation, and construction specifications of metal-clad cable, Type MC.

▶Figure 330–1

330.2 Definition

The definition in this section applies within this article and throughout the *NEC*.

Metal-Clad Cable (Type MC). A factory assembly of insulated circuit conductors, with or without optical fiber members, enclosed in an armor of interlocking metal tape; or a smooth or corrugated metallic sheath. ▶Figure 330–2

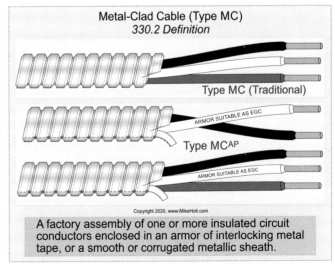

Metal-Clad Cable (Type MC)
330.2 Definition

Type MC (Traditional)

ARMOR SUITABLE AS EGC

Type MC^AP

ARMOR SUITABLE AS EGC

Copyright 2020, www.MikeHolt.com

A factory assembly of one or more insulated circuit conductors enclosed in an armor of interlocking metal tape, or a smooth or corrugated metallic sheath.

▶Figure 330–2

Part II. Installation

330.10 Uses Permitted

(A) General Uses. Type MC cable can be used:

(1) For branch circuits, feeders, and services.

(2) For power, lighting, control, and signaling circuits.

(3) For indoor or outdoor locations.

(4) Exposed or concealed.

(5) To be directly buried (if identified for the purpose).

(6) In a cable tray (if identified for the purpose).

(7) In a raceway.

(8) As aerial cable on a messenger.

(9) In hazardous (classified) locations as permitted in 501.10(B), 502.10(B), and 503.10.

(10) Embedded in plaster in dry locations.

(11) In wet locations, where a corrosion-resistant jacket is provided over the metallic sheath and any of the following conditions are met:

    a. The metallic covering is impervious to moisture.

    b. A jacket is provided under the metal covering that is moisture resistant. ▶Figure 330–4

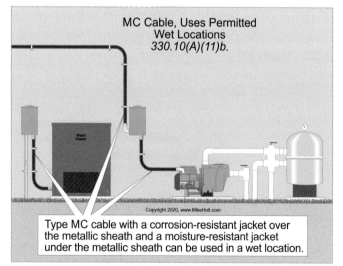

MC Cable, Uses Permitted
Wet Locations
330.10(A)(11)b.

Type MC cable with a corrosion-resistant jacket over the metallic sheath and a moisture-resistant jacket under the metallic sheath can be used in a wet location.

▶Figure 330–4

(B) Specific Uses.

(1) Cable Tray. Type MC cable can be installed in a cable tray in accordance with Article 392.

(2) Direct Buried. Direct-buried cables must be protected in accordance with 300.5.

(3) Installed as Service-Entrance Cable. Type MC cable is permitted to be used as service-entrance cable when installed in accordance with 230.43.

(4) Installed Outside Buildings. Type MC cable installed outside buildings must comply with 225.10, 396.10, and 396.12.

Note: The "Uses Permitted" is not an all-inclusive list, which indicates other suitable uses are permitted if approved by the authority having jurisdiction.

330.12 Uses Not Permitted

Type MC cable is not permitted to be used where:

(1) Subject to physical damage.

(2) Exposed to the destructive corrosive conditions in (a) or (b), unless the metallic sheath or armor is resistant to the conditions or protected by material resistant to the conditions:

    a. Direct burial in the earth or embedded in concrete unless identified for the application.

    b. Exposed to cinder fills, strong chlorides, caustic alkalis, or vapors of chlorine or hydrochloric acids.

ARTICLE
330

PRACTICE QUESTIONS

Please use the 2020 *Code* book to answer the following questions.

Article 330—Metal-Clad Cable (Type MC)

1. The use, installation, and construction specifications of metal-clad cable, Type MC are covered within Article _____.

   (a) 300
   (b) 310
   (c) 320
   (d) 330

2. Type _____ cable is a factory assembly of insulated circuit conductors within an armor of interlocking metal tape, or a smooth or corrugated metallic sheath.

   (a) AC
   (b) MC
   (c) NM
   (d) CMS

3. Type MC cable shall be permitted for _____.

   (a) branch circuits
   (b) feeders
   (c) services
   (d) any of these

4. Type MC cable shall not be used under which of the following conditions?

   (a) Where subject to physical damage.
   (b) Direct buried in the earth or embedded in concrete unless identified for direct burial.
   (c) Exposed to cinder fills, strong chlorides, caustic alkalis, or vapors of chlorine or of hydrochloric acids.
   (d) all of these

ARTICLE
334

NONMETALLIC-SHEATHED CABLE (TYPE NM)

Introduction to Article 334—Nonmetallic-Sheathed Cable (Type NM)

Nonmetallic-sheathed cable (Type NM) provides very limited physical protection for the conductors inside, so the installation restrictions are stringent. Its low cost and relative ease of installation make it a common wiring method for residential and commercial branch circuits.

Part I. General

334.1 Scope

Article 334 covers the use, installation, and construction specifications of nonmetallic-sheathed cable, Type NM. ▶Figure 334–1

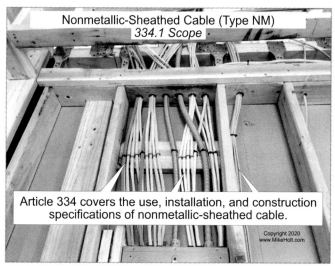

Nonmetallic-Sheathed Cable (Type NM)
334.1 Scope

Article 334 covers the use, installation, and construction specifications of nonmetallic-sheathed cable.

Copyright 2020
www.MikeHolt.com

▶Figure 334–1

334.2 Definition

Nonmetallic-Sheathed Cable (Type NM). A wiring method that encloses two or more insulated conductors within a nonmetallic jacket.
▶Figure 334–2

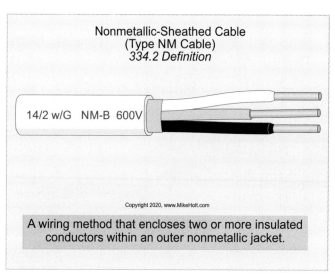

Nonmetallic-Sheathed Cable
(Type NM Cable)
334.2 Definition

14/2 w/G   NM-B 600V

Copyright 2020, www.MikeHolt.com

A wiring method that encloses two or more insulated conductors within an outer nonmetallic jacket.

▶Figure 334–2

Author's Comment:

▶ It is the generally accepted practice in the electrical industry to call Type NM cable "Romex®," a registered trademark of the Southwire Company.

Part II. Installation

334.10 Uses Permitted

Type NM cables can be used in:

(1) One-family and two-family dwellings and their garages and storage buildings. ▶Figure 334–4

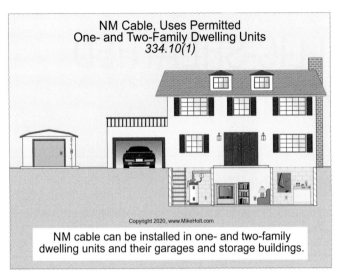

NM Cable, Uses Permitted
One- and Two-Family Dwelling Units
334.10(1)

NM cable can be installed in one- and two-family dwelling units and their garages and storage buildings.

▶Figure 334–4

(2) Multifamily dwellings of Types III, IV, and V construction. ▶Figure 334–5

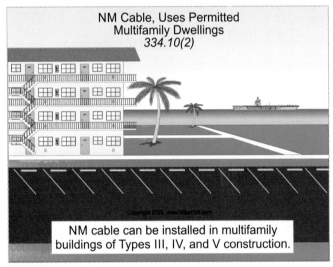

NM Cable, Uses Permitted
Multifamily Dwellings
334.10(2)

NM cable can be installed in multifamily buildings of Types III, IV, and V construction.

▶Figure 334–5

(3) Other buildings of Types III, IV, and V construction where the cable must be concealed within walls, floors, or ceilings that provide a thermal barrier of material with at least a 15-minute finish rating, as identified in listings of fire-rated assemblies. ▶Figure 334–6

Author's Comment:

▶ See the definition of "Concealed" in Article 100.

Note 1: Building constructions are defined in NFPA 220, *Standard on Types of Building Construction*.

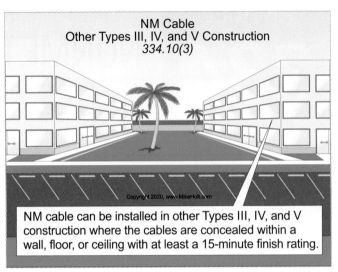

NM Cable
Other Types III, IV, and V Construction
334.10(3)

NM cable can be installed in other Types III, IV, and V construction where the cables are concealed within a wall, floor, or ceiling with at least a 15-minute finish rating.

▶Figure 334–6

Note 2: See Annex E of the *NEC* for the determination of building types [NFPA 220, Table 4.1.1].

334.12 Uses Not Permitted

(A) Type NM. Type NM cable is not permitted:

(1) In any dwelling or structure not specifically permitted in 334.10(1), (2), (3), and (5).

(2) Exposed within a dropped or suspended ceiling in other than dwelling units. ▶Figure 334–7

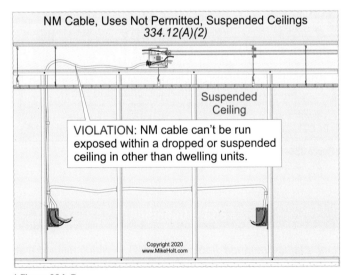

NM Cable, Uses Not Permitted, Suspended Ceilings
334.12(A)(2)

Suspended Ceiling

VIOLATION: NM cable can't be run exposed within a dropped or suspended ceiling in other than dwelling units.

▶Figure 334–7

(3) As service-entrance cable.

(4) In commercial garages having hazardous (classified) locations, as defined in 511.3.

(5) In theaters and similar locations, except where permitted in 518.4(B).

(6) In motion picture studios.

(7) In storage battery rooms.

(8) In hoistways, or on elevators or escalators.

(9) Embedded in poured cement, concrete, or aggregate.

(10) In any hazardous (classified) location, except where permitted by other sections in this *Code*.

(B) Type NM. Type NM cable is not permitted to be used under the following conditions, or in the following locations:

(1) If exposed to corrosive fumes or vapors.

(2) If embedded in masonry, concrete, adobe, fill, or plaster.

(3) In a shallow chase in masonry, concrete, or adobe and covered with plaster, adobe, or similar finish.

(4) In wet or damp locations. ▶Figure 334–8

Author's Comment:

▷ A raceway in a ground floor slab is considered a wet location [Article 100]. ▶Figure 334–9

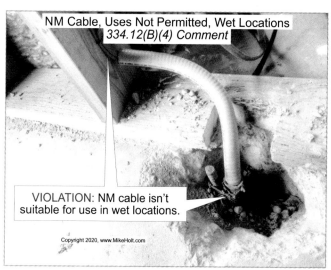

▶Figure 334–9

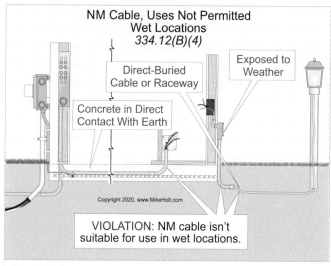

▶Figure 334–8

ARTICLE
334
PRACTICE QUESTIONS

Please use the 2020 *Code* book to answer the following questions.

Article 334—Nonmetallic-Sheathed Cable (Type NM)

1. The use, installation, and construction specifications of nonmetallic-sheathed cable are covered within Article _____.

   (a) 300
   (b) 334
   (c) 400
   (d) 410

2. Type _____ cable is a factory assembly that encloses two or more insulated conductors within a nonmetallic jacket.

   (a) AC
   (b) MC
   (c) NM
   (d) NMJ

3. Type NM cables shall not be used in one- and two-family dwellings exceeding three floors above grade.

   (a) True
   (b) False

4. Type NM and Type NMC cables shall be permitted in _____, except as prohibited in 334.12.

   (a) one- and two-family dwellings and their attached/detached garages and storage buildings
   (b) multifamily dwellings permitted to be of Types III, IV, and V construction
   (c) other structures permitted to be of Types III, IV, and V construction
   (d) any of these

5. Type NM cable can be installed as open runs in dropped or suspended ceilings in other than one- and two-family and multi-family dwellings.

   (a) True
   (b) False

6. Type NM cable shall not be used _____.

   (a) in other than dwelling units
   (b) in the air void of masonry block not subject to excessive moisture
   (c) for exposed work
   (d) embedded in poured cement, concrete, or aggregate

ARTICLE
336

POWER AND CONTROL TRAY CABLE (TYPE TC)

Introduction to Article 336—Power and Control Tray Cable (Type TC)

Power and control tray cable (Type TC) is flexible, inexpensive, and easily installed. It provides very limited physical protection for the conductors, so the installation restrictions are stringent. Its low cost and relative ease of installation make it a common wiring method for industrial applications.

Part I. General

336.1 Scope

This article covers the use and installation for power and control tray cable, Type TC. ▶Figure 336–1

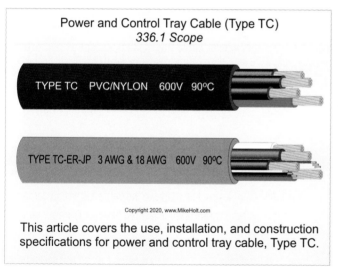

Power and Control Tray Cable (Type TC)
336.1 Scope

TYPE TC   PVC/NYLON   600V   90°C

TYPE TC-ER-JP   3 AWG & 18 AWG   600V   90°C

Copyright 2020, www.MikeHolt.com

This article covers the use, installation, and construction specifications for power and control tray cable, Type TC.

▶Figure 336–1

336.2 Definition

Power and Control Tray Cable (Type TC). A factory assembly of two or more insulated conductors, <u>with or without associated bare or covered equipment grounding conductors,</u> under a nonmetallic jacket. ▶Figure 336–2

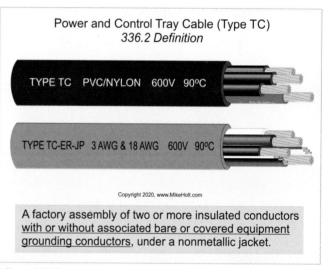

Power and Control Tray Cable (Type TC)
336.2 Definition

TYPE TC   PVC/NYLON   600V   90°C

TYPE TC-ER-JP   3 AWG & 18 AWG   600V   90°C

Copyright 2020, www.MikeHolt.com

A factory assembly of two or more insulated conductors <u>with or without associated bare or covered equipment grounding conductors,</u> under a nonmetallic jacket.

▶Figure 336–2

336.6 Listing Requirements

Type TC cable and associated fittings must be listed. ▶Figure 336–3

Part II. Installation

336.10 Uses Permitted

Type TC cable is permitted to be used:

(1) For power, lighting, control, and signaling circuits.

(2) In cable trays including those with mechanically discontinuous segments up to 1 ft.

▶Figure 336–3

(3) In raceways.

(4) In outdoor locations supported by a messenger wire.

(5) For Class 1 circuits in accordance with Article 725.

(7) Between a cable tray and equipment if it complies with 336(10)(7).

(8) In wet locations where the cable is resistant to moisture and corrosive agents.

(9) In one- and two-family dwellings, Type TC-ER-JP cable is permitted for branch circuits and feeders where installed in accordance with Part II of Article 334 for interior wiring, and Part II of Article 340 for exterior wiring. ▶Figure 336–4

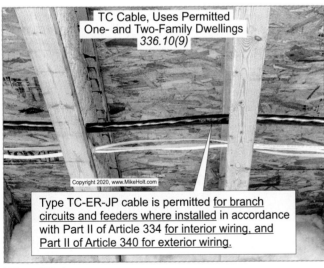

▶Figure 336–4

Author's Comment:

▶ The "ER" marking on Type TC-ER cable identifies it as suitable for exposed run use in accordance with UL and the suffix "-JP identifies it as being suitable for pulling through wood framing members.

Ex: Where Type TC-ER-JP cable is used to connect a generator and its associated equipment, the cable ampacity limitations of 334.80 and 340.80 do not apply.

Author's Comment:

▶ The "JP" marking on Type TC-ER-JP cable identifies it as suitable to be pulled through wood framing members because the cable has met the joist pull testing requirements of UL.

(10) Direct buried where identified for direct burial.

336.12 Uses Not Permitted

Type TC cables are not permitted:

(1) Where exposed to physical damage.

(2) Outside a raceway or cable tray system, except as permitted in 336.10(4), 336.10(7), 336.10(9), and 336.10(10).

(3) Exposed to the direct rays of the sun, unless identified as sunlight resistant.

336.24 Bending Radius

Bends in Type TC cable must be made so the cable will not be damaged. Type TC cable without metal shielding must have a minimum bending radius as follows:

(1) Four times the overall diameter for cables 1 in. or less in diameter.

(2) Five times the overall diameter for cables larger than 1 in. but not more than 2 in. in diameter.

NFPA 70
National
Electrical
Code
2020
nec
NFPA

Please use the 2020 *Code* book to answer the following questions.

Article 336—Power and Control Tray Cable (Type TC)

1. Article _____ covers the use, installation, and construction specifications for power and control tray cable, Type TC.

   (a) 326
   (b) 330
   (c) 334
   (d) 336

2. Type _____ cable is a factory assembly of two or more insulated conductors, with or without associated bare of covered grounding conductors, under a nonmetallic jacket.

   (a) NM
   (b) TC
   (c) SE
   (d) UF

3. Type TC cable and associated fittings shall be _____.

   (a) identified
   (b) approved
   (c) listed
   (d) labeled

4. Type TC cable can be used _____.

   (a) for power, lighting, control, and signal circuits
   (b) in cable trays including those with mechanically discontinuous segments up to 1 ft
   (c) for Class 1 control circuits as permitted in Parts II and III of Article 725
   (d) all of these

5. In _____, type TC-ER-JP cable containing both power and control conductors that is identified for pulling through structural members shall be permitted.

   (a) multifamily dwellings
   (b) one- and two- family dwelling units
   (c) only duplexes
   (d) none of these

6. Where Type TC-ER cable is used to connect a generator and associated equipment having terminals rated _____ degrees C or higher, the cable shall not be limited in ampacity by 334.80 or 340.80.

   (a) 60
   (b) 75
   (c) 90
   (d) 100

7. Type TC-ER-JP cable shall be permitted for branch circuits and feeders in one and two family dwelling units.

   (a) True
   (b) False

8. Where Type TC cable is installed in one- and two-family dwelling units, 725.136 provides rules for limitations on Class 2 or 3 circuits contained within the same cable with conductors of electric light, power, or Class 1 circuits.

   (a) True
   (b) False

9. Type TC cable shall be permitted to be direct buried, where _____ for such use.

   (a) identified
   (b) approved
   (c) listed
   (d) labeled

10. Type TC cable shall be permitted for use in hazardous (classified) locations where specifically _____ by other articles in this *Code*.

    (a) required
    (b) permitted
    (c) approved
    (d) identified

11. Type TC cable shall not be used where _____.

    (a) it will be exposed to physical damage
    (b) installed outside of a raceway or cable tray system, unless permitted in 336.10(4), 336.10(7), 336.10(9), and 336.10(10)
    (c) exposed to direct rays of the sun, unless identified as sunlight resistant
    (d) all of these

12. Bends in Type TC cable shall be made so as not to damage the cable. For TC Cable larger than 1 in. and up to 2 in. in diameter, without metal shielding, the minimum bending radius shall be at least _____ times the overall diameter of the cable.

    (a) 2
    (b) 3
    (c) 5
    (d) 7

ARTICLE
338

SERVICE-ENTRANCE CABLE (TYPES SE AND USE)

Introduction to Article 338—Service-Entrance Cable (Types SE and USE)

Service-entrance (SE) and underground service-entrance (USE) cables, can be a single conductor or a multiconductor assembly within an overall nonmetallic outer jacket or covering. This cable is used primarily for services but is permitted for feeders and branch circuits. When used as a service conductor(s) or service entrance conductor(s), Type SE cable assemblies will contain insulated phase conductors and a bare neutral conductor. For feeders or branch circuits, you must use Type SE cable that contains insulated phase and neutral conductors with an uninsulated equipment grounding conductor.

Part I. General

338.1 Scope

Article 338 covers the use, installation, and construction specifications of service-entrance cable, Types SE and USE. ▶Figure 338–1

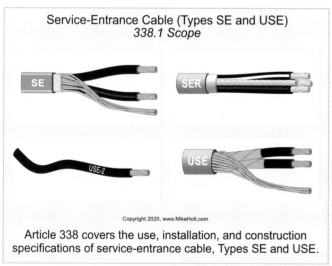

Service-Entrance Cable (Types SE and USE)
338.1 Scope

Copyright 2020, www.MikeHolt.com

Article 338 covers the use, installation, and construction specifications of service-entrance cable, Types SE and USE.

▶Figure 338–1

338.2 Definitions

Service-Entrance Cable (Types SE and USE). Service-entrance cable is a single or multiconductor <u>cable</u> with an overall covering. ▶Figure 338–2

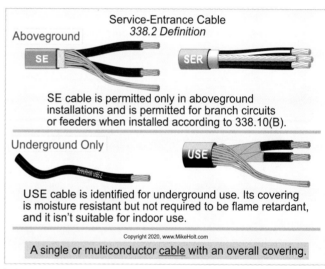

Service-Entrance Cable
338.2 Definition

Aboveground

SE cable is permitted only in aboveground installations and is permitted for branch circuits or feeders when installed according to 338.10(B).

Underground Only

USE cable is identified for underground use. Its covering is moisture resistant but not required to be flame retardant, and it isn't suitable for indoor use.

Copyright 2020, www.MikeHolt.com

A single or multiconductor <u>cable</u> with an overall covering.

▶Figure 338–2

Service-Entrance Conductor Assembly. Multiple single-insulated conductors twisted together without an overall covering, other than an optional binder intended only to keep the conductors together.

Author's Comment:

▶ "Triplex" and "Quadruplex" with an outer wire wrapped around them are examples of an SE conductor assembly.

Type SE. Type SE cables have a flame-retardant, moisture-resistant covering and are permitted only in aboveground installations. These cables are permitted for branch circuits or feeders when installed in accordance with 338.10(B).

Type USE. USE cable is identified as a wiring method permitted for underground use; its covering is moisture resistant, but not flame retardant.

> **Author's Comment:**
>
> ▸ Type USE cable is not permitted to be installed indoors [338.12(B)].

Part II. Installation

338.10 Uses Permitted

(A) Service-Entrance Conductors. Types SE and USE cable can be used as service-entrance conductors in accordance with Article 230.

(B) Branch Circuits or Feeders.

(2) Insulated Conductor. Type SE service-entrance cable is permitted for branch circuits and feeders where the neutral conductor is insulated, and the uninsulated conductor is only used for equipment grounding. ▸**Figure 338–4**

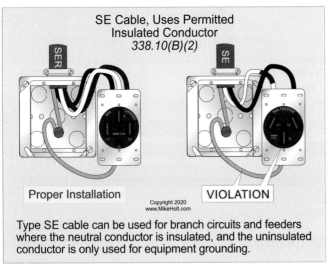

SE Cable, Uses Permitted
Insulated Conductor
338.10(B)(2)

Proper Installation   VIOLATION

Type SE cable can be used for branch circuits and feeders where the neutral conductor is insulated, and the uninsulated conductor is only used for equipment grounding.

▸Figure 338–4

(3) Temperature Limitations. SE cable is not permitted to be subjected to conductor temperatures exceeding its insulation rating.

(4) Installation Methods for Branch Circuits and Feeders. SE cable used for branch circuits or feeders must comply with (a) and (b).

(a) Interior Installations.

(1) SE cable used for interior branch-circuit or feeder wiring must be installed in accordance with the same requirements as Type NM cable in Part II of Article 334, excluding 334.80. ▸**Figure 338–5**

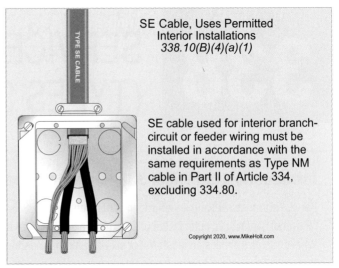

SE Cable, Uses Permitted
Interior Installations
338.10(B)(4)(a)(1)

SE cable used for interior branch-circuit or feeder wiring must be installed in accordance with the same requirements as Type NM cable in Part II of Article 334, excluding 334.80.

▸Figure 338–5

(2) If multiple cables pass through the same wood framing opening that is to be sealed with thermal insulation, caulking, or sealing foam, the ampacity of each conductor must be adjusted in accordance with Table 310.15(C)(1). ▸**Figure 338–6**

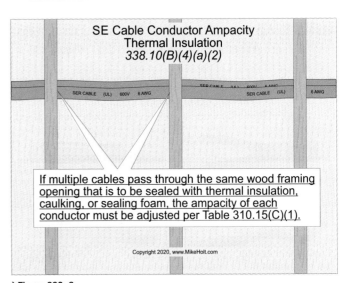

SE Cable Conductor Ampacity
Thermal Insulation
338.10(B)(4)(a)(2)

If multiple cables pass through the same wood framing opening that is to be sealed with thermal insulation, caulking, or sealing foam, the ampacity of each conductor must be adjusted per Table 310.15(C)(1).

▸Figure 338–6

(3) The ampacity of conductors 10 AWG and smaller, where installed in contact with thermal insulation, must be sized in accordance with 60°C (140°F) conductor temperature rating. For conductor ampacity correction and/or adjustment, the conductor temperature rating ampacity must be used.

(b) Exterior Installations.

(1) The cable must be installed in accordance with Part I of Article 225 and supported in accordance with 334.30. Where it is run underground, the cable must comply with Part II of Article 340.

338.12 Uses Not Permitted

(A) Service-Entrance Cable. Type SE cable is not permitted under the following conditions or locations:

(1) Where subject to physical damage.

(2) Underground with or without a raceway.

(B) Underground Service-Entrance Cable. Type USE cable is not permitted:

(1) For interior wiring.

(2) Above ground, except where protected against physical damage in accordance with 300.5(D).

ARTICLE
338 PRACTICE QUESTIONS

Please use the 2020 *Code* book to answer the following questions.

Article 338—Service-Entrance Cable (Types SE and USE)

1. Type _____ cable is an assembly primarily used for services.

   (a) NM
   (b) UF
   (c) SE
   (d) SEC

2. Type _____ cable is a single conductor or multiconductor cable identified for use as underground service-entrance cable.

   (a) SE
   (b) NM
   (c) UF
   (d) USE

3. Type SE cable shall be permitted to be used as _____.

   (a) branch circuits
   (b) feeders
   (c) underground service entrance conductors if in a raceway
   (d) branch circuits or feeders

4. Type SE cable can be used for interior wiring as long as it complies with the installation requirements of Part II of Article 334, excluding 334.80.

   (a) True
   (b) False

5. Where more than two Type SE cables are installed in contact with thermal insulations, caulk, or sealing foam without maintaining spacing between cables, the ampacity of each conductor shall be _____ in accordance with Table 310.15(C)(1).

   (a) increased
   (b) adjusted
   (c) corrected
   (d) multiplied

6. Where more than two Type SE cables are installed in contact with _____, the ampacity of each conductor shall be adjusted in accordance with Table 310.15(C)(1).

   (a) thermal insulation
   (b) caulk
   (c) sealing foam
   (d) any of these

7. For interior installations of Type SE cable with ungrounded conductor sizes _____ AWG and smaller, where installed in thermal insulation, the ampacity shall be in accordance with 60 degree C (140 degree F) conductor temperature rating.

   (a) 14
   (b) 12
   (c) 10
   (d) 8

8. Type USE cable is permitted for _____ wiring.

   (a) underground
   (b) interior
   (c) aerial
   (d) above ground installations

9. Type USE cable used for service laterals shall be permitted to emerge from the ground if terminated in an enclosure at an outside location and protected in accordance with 300.5(D).

   (a) True
   (b) False

ARTICLE 340

UNDERGROUND FEEDER AND BRANCH-CIRCUIT CABLE (TYPE UF)

Introduction to Article 340—Underground Feeder and Branch-Circuit Cable (Type UF)

UF cable (Type UF) is a moisture-, fungus-, and corrosion-resistant cable suitable for direct burial in the Earth. It comes in sizes 14 AWG through 4/0 AWG [340.104]. The covering of multiconductor Type UF cable is molded plastic that encases the insulated conductors. Because the covering of Type UF cable encloses the insulated conductors, it is difficult to strip off the outer jacket to gain access to them, but this covering provides excellent corrosion protection. Be careful not to damage the conductor insulation or cut yourself when you remove the outer cover.

Part I. General

340.1 Scope

Article 340 covers the use, installation, and construction specifications of underground feeder and branch-circuit cable, Type UF. ▶Figure 340–1

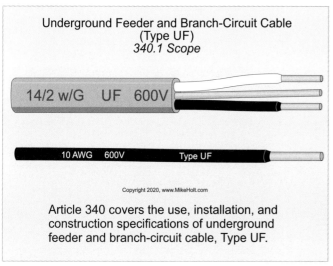

Underground Feeder and Branch-Circuit Cable (Type UF) 340.1 Scope

14/2 w/G   UF   600V

10 AWG   600V   Type UF

Copyright 2020, www.MikeHolt.com

Article 340 covers the use, installation, and construction specifications of underground feeder and branch-circuit cable, Type UF.

▶Figure 340–1

340.2 Definition

Underground Feeder and Branch-Circuit Cable (Type UF). A factory assembly of insulated conductors with an integral or an overall covering of nonmetallic material suitable for direct burial in the Earth.
▶Figure 340–2

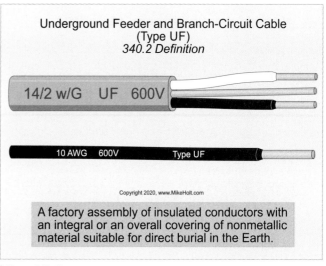

Underground Feeder and Branch-Circuit Cable (Type UF) 340.2 Definition

14/2 w/G   UF   600V

10 AWG   600V   Type UF

Copyright 2020, www.MikeHolt.com

A factory assembly of insulated conductors with an integral or an overall covering of nonmetallic material suitable for direct burial in the Earth.

▶Figure 340–2

Part II. Installation

340.10 Uses Permitted

Type UF cable is permitted:

(1) Underground in accordance with 300.5.

(2) As a single conductor in a trench or raceway with circuit conductors.

(3) For wiring in wet, dry, or corrosive locations.

(4) Where installed as nonmetallic-sheathed cable, the installation must comply with Parts II and III of Article 334.

340.12 Uses Not Permitted

Type UF cable is not permitted to be used:

(1) As service-entrance cable [230.43].

(2) In commercial garages [511.3].

(3) In theaters [520.5].

(4) In motion picture studios [530.11].

(5) In storage battery rooms [Article 480].

(6) In hoistways [Article 620].

(7) In hazardous (classified) locations, except as specifically permitted by other articles in this *Code*.

(8) Embedded in concrete.

(9) Exposed to direct sunlight unless identified.

Note: The sunlight-resistant marking on the outer jacket does not apply to the individual conductors.

(10) Where subject to physical damage. ▶Figure 340–3

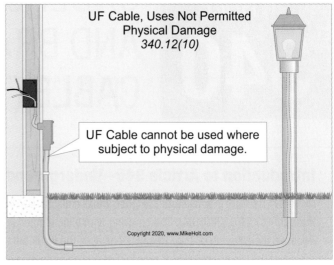

▶Figure 340–3

(11) As overhead cable, except where installed as messenger-supported wiring in accordance with Part II of Article 396.

Author's Comment:

▸ UF cable is not permitted in ducts or plenum spaces [300.22], or in patient care spaces of health care facilities [517.13].

ARTICLE
340 PRACTICE QUESTIONS

Please use the 2020 *Code* book to answer the following questions.

Article 340—Underground Feeder and Branch-Circuit Cable (Type UF)

1. Article 340 covers the use, installation, and construction specifications for underground feeder and branch-circuit cable, Type _____.

   (a) USE
   (b) UF
   (c) UFC
   (d) NMC

2. Type _____ cable is a factory assembly of conductors with an overall covering of nonmetallic material suitable for direct burial in the earth.

   (a) NM
   (b) UF
   (c) SE
   (d) TC

3. Type UF cable is permitted to be used for inside wiring.

   (a) True
   (b) False

4. Type UF cable can be used for service conductors.

   (a) True
   (b) False

5. Type UF cable can be used in commercial garages.

   (a) True
   (b) False

6. Type UF cable shall not be used in _____.

   (a) motion picture studios
   (b) storage battery rooms
   (c) hoistways
   (d) all of these

7. Type UF cable shall not be used _____.

   (a) in any hazardous (classified) location except as otherwise permitted in this *Code*
   (b) embedded in poured cement, concrete, or aggregate
   (c) where exposed to direct rays of the sun, unless identified as sunlight resistant
   (d) all of these

8. Type UF cable shall not be used where subject to physical damage.

   (a) True
   (b) False

ARTICLE
342

INTERMEDIATE METAL CONDUIT (TYPE IMC)

Introduction to Article 342—Intermediate Metal Conduit (Type IMC)

Intermediate metal conduit is a circular metal raceway with the same outside diameter as rigid metal conduit (Type RMC). The wall thickness of IMC is less than that of rigid metal conduit, so it has a larger interior cross-sectional area for holding conductors. IMC is lighter and less expensive than RMC and is approved by the *NEC* for use in the same applications. IMC also uses a different steel alloy, which makes it stronger than RMC even though the walls are thinner. Intermediate metal conduit is manufactured in both galvanized steel and aluminum; the steel type is much more common.

Part I. General

342.1 Scope

Article 342 covers the use, installation, and construction specifications of intermediate metal conduit (Type IMC) and associated fittings. ▶Figure 342–1

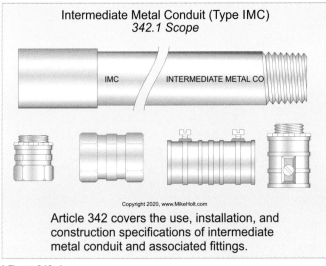

Intermediate Metal Conduit (Type IMC)
342.1 Scope

IMC
INTERMEDIATE METAL CO

Copyright 2020, www.MikeHolt.com

Article 342 covers the use, installation, and construction specifications of intermediate metal conduit and associated fittings.

▶Figure 342–1

342.2 Definition

Intermediate Metal Conduit (Type IMC). A steel raceway of circular cross section that can be threaded with integral or associated couplings listed for the installation of electrical conductors. ▶Figure 342–2

Intermediate Metal Conduit (Type IMC)
342.2 Definition

IMC
INTERMEDIATE METAL CONDUIT

A listed steel circular raceway that can be threaded with integral or associated couplings.

Copyright 2020, www.MikeHolt.com

▶Figure 342–2

Author's Comment:

▸ The type of steel from which intermediate metal conduit is manufactured, the process by which it is made, and the corrosion protection applied are all equal (or superior) to that of rigid metal conduit.

Part II. Installation

342.10 Uses Permitted

(A) Atmospheric Conditions and Occupancies. IMC is permitted in all atmospheric conditions and occupancies.

(B) Corrosive Environments. IMC, elbows, couplings, and fittings can be installed in concrete, in direct contact with the Earth, or in areas subject to severe corrosive influences if provided with supplementary corrosion protection approved for the condition.

(E) Severe Physical Damage. IMC is permitted where subject to severe physical damage.

ARTICLE
342

PRACTICE QUESTIONS

Please use the 2020 *Code* book to answer the following questions.

Article 342—Intermediate Metal Conduit (Type IMC)

1. Article _____ covers the use, installation, and construction specifications for intermediate metal conduit (IMC) and associated fittings.

   (a) 342
   (b) 348
   (c) 352
   (d) 356

2. IMC, elbows, couplings, and fittings shall be permitted to be installed in concrete, in direct contact with the earth, or in areas subject to severe corrosive influences where protected by corrosion protection _____ for the condition.

   (a) identified
   (b) approved
   (c) listed
   (d) suitable

3. Type IMC conduit shall be permitted to be installed where subject to severe physical damage.

   (a) True
   (b) False

ARTICLE
344

RIGID METAL CONDUIT (TYPE RMC)

Introduction to Article 344—Rigid Metal Conduit (Type RMC)

Rigid metal conduit (Type RMC), commonly called "rigid," has long been the standard raceway used to protect conductors from physical damage and from difficult environments. The outside diameter of rigid metal conduit is the same as intermediate metal conduit. However, the wall thickness is greater than IMC so the interior cross-sectional area is smaller. RMC is heavier and more expensive than intermediate metal conduit, and it can be used in any location. It is manufactured in both galvanized steel and aluminum; the steel type is much more common.

Part I. General

344.1 Scope

Article 344 covers the use, installation, and construction specifications of rigid metal conduit (Type RMC) and associated fittings. ▶Figure 344–1

▶Figure 344–1

344.2 Definition

Rigid Metal Conduit (Type RMC). A listed metal raceway of circular cross section with integral or associated couplings listed for the installation of electrical conductors. ▶Figure 344–2

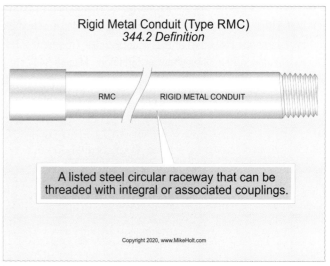

▶Figure 344–2

Author's Comment:

▸ When the mechanical and physical characteristics of rigid metal conduit are necessary, but the installation will be in an environment detrimental to the metal, a PVC-coated raceway system is commonly used. This variation of RMC is frequently used in the petrochemical industry. The common trade name of this coated raceway is "Plasti-Bond®," and is commonly referred to as "Rob Roy." The benefits of the improved corrosion protection can be achieved only when the system is properly installed. Joints must be sealed in accordance with the manufacturer's instructions and coated to prevent corrosion where damaged with tools such as benders, pliers, and pipe wrenches. Couplings are available with an extended skirt that can be properly sealed after installation.

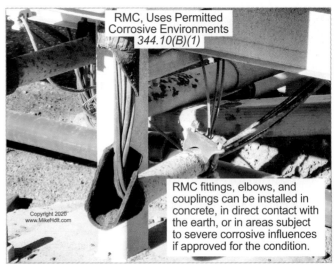

▸Figure 344–3

Part II. Installation

344.10 Uses Permitted

(A) Atmospheric Conditions and Occupancies.

(1) RMC is permitted in all atmospheric conditions and occupancies.

(B) Corrosive Environments.

(1) RMC fittings, elbows, and couplings can be installed in concrete, in direct contact with the Earth, or in areas subject to severe corrosive influences if approved for the condition. ▸Figure 344–3

(D) Wet Locations. Support fittings (such as screws, straps, and so forth) installed in a wet location must be made of corrosion-resistant material or protected by corrosion-resistant coatings in accordance with 300.6.

(E) Severe Physical Damage. RMC is permitted where subject to severe physical damage.

ARTICLE 344

PRACTICE QUESTIONS

Please use the 2020 *Code* book to answer the following questions.

Article 344—Rigid Metal Conduit (Type RMC)

1. Article 344 covers the use, installation, and construction specifications for _____ conduit and associated fittings.

   (a) intermediate metal
   (b) rigid metal
   (c) electrical metallic
   (d) aluminum metal

2. Galvanized steel, stainless steel, and red brass RMC elbows, couplings, and fittings shall be permitted to be installed in concrete, in direct contact with the earth, or in areas subject to severe corrosive influences when protected by _____ approved for the condition.

   (a) ceramic
   (b) corrosion protection
   (c) backfill
   (d) a natural barrier

3. Type RMC conduit shall be permitted to be installed where subject to severe physical damage.

   (a) True
   (b) False

348

FLEXIBLE METAL CONDUIT (TYPE FMC)

Introduction to Article 348—Flexible Metal Conduit (Type FMC)

Flexible metal conduit (Type FMC), commonly called "Greenfield" (after its inventor) or "flex," is an interlocked metal strip type of raceway made of either steel or aluminum. It is primarily used where flexibility is necessary or where equipment moves, shakes, or vibrates.

Part I. General

348.1 Scope

Article 348 covers the use, installation, and construction specifications for flexible metal conduit (FMC) and associated fittings. ▶Figure 348–1

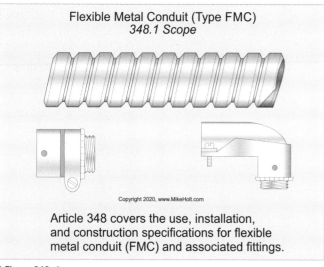

Flexible Metal Conduit (Type FMC)
348.1 Scope

Copyright 2020, www.MikeHolt.com

Article 348 covers the use, installation, and construction specifications for flexible metal conduit (FMC) and associated fittings.

▶Figure 348–1

348.2 Definition

Flexible Metal Conduit (Type FMC). A raceway of circular cross section made of a helically wound, formed, interlocked metal strip, listed for the installation of electrical conductors. ▶Figure 348–2

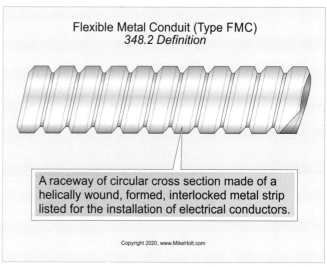

Flexible Metal Conduit (Type FMC)
348.2 Definition

A raceway of circular cross section made of a helically wound, formed, interlocked metal strip listed for the installation of electrical conductors.

Copyright 2020, www.MikeHolt.com

▶Figure 348–2

Part II. Installation

348.10 Uses Permitted

FMC is permitted to be installed exposed or concealed.

348.12 Uses Not Permitted

FMC is not permitted:

(1) In wet locations. ▶Figure 348–3

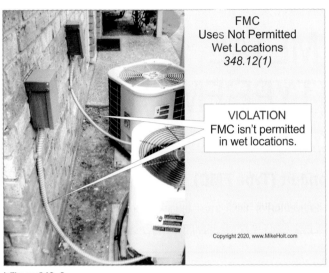

FMC
Uses Not Permitted
Wet Locations
348.12(1)

VIOLATION
FMC isn't permitted
in wet locations.

Copyright 2020, www.MikeHolt.com

▶Figure 348-3

(2) In hoistways, other than as permitted in 620.21(A)(1).

(3) In storage battery rooms.

(4) In any hazardous (classified) location, except as permitted by 501.10(B).

(5) Exposed to material having a deteriorating effect on the installed conductors.

(6) Underground or embedded in poured concrete.

(7) Where subject to physical damage.

ARTICLE 348 PRACTICE QUESTIONS

Please use the 2020 *Code* book to answer the following questions.

Article 348—Flexible Metal Conduit (Type FMC)

1. Article 348 covers the use, installation, and construction specifications for flexible metal conduit (FMC) and associated _____.

   (a) fittings
   (b) connections
   (c) terminations
   (d) rating

2. _____ is a raceway of circular cross section made of a helically wound, formed, interlocked metal strip.

   (a) Type MC cable
   (b) Type AC cable
   (c) LFMC
   (d) FMC

3. FMC can be installed exposed or concealed where not subject to physical damage.

   (a) True
   (b) False

4. FMC shall not be installed _____.

   (a) in wet locations
   (b) embedded in poured concrete
   (c) where subject to physical damage
   (d) all of these

ARTICLE 350

LIQUIDTIGHT FLEXIBLE METAL CONDUIT (TYPE LFMC)

Introduction to Article 350—Liquidtight Flexible Metal Conduit (Type LFMC)

Liquidtight flexible metal conduit (Type LFMC), with its associated connectors and fittings, is a flexible raceway commonly used for connections to equipment that vibrates or must be occasionally moved. Liquidtight flexible metal conduit is commonly called "Sealtite®" or "liquidtight." It is similar in construction to flexible metal conduit, but it has an outer liquidtight thermoplastic covering. LFMC has the same primary purpose as flexible metal conduit, but also provides protection from liquids and some corrosive effects.

Part I. General

350.1 Scope

Article 350 covers the use, installation, and construction specifications of liquidtight flexible metal conduit (Type LFMC) and associated fittings. ▶Figure 350–1

Liquidtight Flexible Metal Conduit (Type LFMC)
350.1 Scope

Article 350 covers the use, installation, and construction specifications of liquidtight flexible metal conduit and associated fittings.

▶Figure 350–1

350.2 Definition

Liquidtight Flexible Metal Conduit (Type LFMC). A raceway of circular cross section, having an outer liquidtight, nonmetallic, sunlight-resistant jacket over an inner flexible metal core, with associated connectors and fittings, listed for the installation of electrical conductors. ▶Figure 350–2

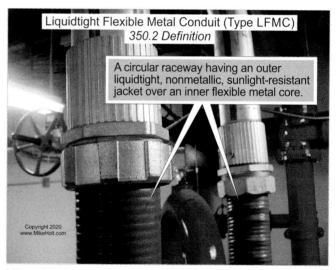

Liquidtight Flexible Metal Conduit (Type LFMC)
350.2 Definition

A circular raceway having an outer liquidtight, nonmetallic, sunlight-resistant jacket over an inner flexible metal core.

▶Figure 350–2

Part II. Installation

350.10 Uses Permitted

Listed LFMC is permitted, either exposed or concealed, at any of the following locations: ▶Figure 350–3

(1) If flexibility or protection from machine oils, liquids, vapors, or solids is required.

(2) In hazardous (classified) locations as permitted in Chapter 5.

(3) For direct burial if listed and marked for this purpose. ▶Figure 350–4

▶Figure 350-3

▶Figure 350-4

(4) Conductors or cables rated at a temperature higher than the listed temperature rating of LFMC conduit may be installed in LFMC, provided the conductors or cables are not operated at a temperature higher than the listed temperature rating of the LFMC per 110.14(C).

350.12 Uses Not Permitted

LFMC must not be used where subject to physical damage. ▶Figure 350-5

▶Figure 350-5

ARTICLE 350 PRACTICE QUESTIONS

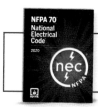

Please use the 2020 *Code* book to answer the following questions.

Article 350—Liquidtight Flexible Metal Conduit (Type LFMC)

1. The use, installation, and construction specifications for liquid-tight flexible metal conduit (LFMC) and associated fittings are covered within Article _____.

    (a) 300
    (b) 334
    (c) 350
    (d) 410

2. _____ is a raceway of circular cross section having an outer liquidtight, nonmetallic, sunlight-resistant jacket over an inner flexible metal core.

    (a) FMC
    (b) LFNMC
    (c) LFMC
    (d) Vinyl-clad Type MC

3. The use of LFMC shall be permitted for direct burial where listed and marked for the purpose.

    (a) True
    (b) False

ARTICLE
352
RIGID POLYVINYL CHLORIDE CONDUIT (TYPE PVC)

Introduction to Article 352—Rigid Polyvinyl Chloride Conduit (Type PVC)

Rigid polyvinyl chloride conduit (Type PVC) is a rigid nonmetallic conduit that provides many of the advantages of rigid metal conduit, while allowing installation in wet or corrosive areas. It is an inexpensive raceway and easily installed, lightweight, easily cut and glued together, and relatively strong. However, rigid polyvinyl chloride (PVC) is brittle when cold and will sag when hot. This type of conduit is commonly used as an underground raceway because of its low cost, ease of installation, and resistance to corrosion and decay.

Part I. General

352.1 Scope

Article 352 covers the use, installation, and construction specifications of polyvinyl chloride conduit (Type PVC) and associated fittings.
▶Figure 352–1

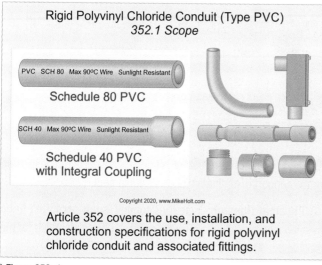

Rigid Polyvinyl Chloride Conduit (Type PVC)
352.1 Scope

PVC SCH 80 Max 90ºC Wire Sunlight Resistant
Schedule 80 PVC

SCH 40 Max 90ºC Wire Sunlight Resistant
Schedule 40 PVC
with Integral Coupling

Copyright 2020, www.MikeHolt.com

Article 352 covers the use, installation, and construction specifications for rigid polyvinyl chloride conduit and associated fittings.

▶Figure 352–1

352.2 Definition

Rigid Polyvinyl Chloride Conduit (Type PVC). A rigid nonmetallic raceway of circular cross section with integral or associated couplings, listed for the installation of electrical conductors. ▶**Figure 352–2**

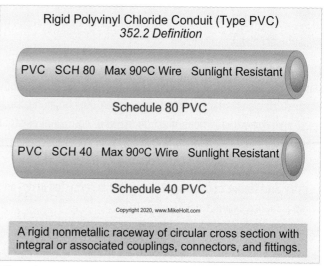

Rigid Polyvinyl Chloride Conduit (Type PVC)
352.2 Definition

PVC SCH 80 Max 90ºC Wire Sunlight Resistant
Schedule 80 PVC

PVC SCH 40 Max 90ºC Wire Sunlight Resistant
Schedule 40 PVC

Copyright 2020, www.MikeHolt.com

A rigid nonmetallic raceway of circular cross section with integral or associated couplings, connectors, and fittings.

▶Figure 352–2

Part II. Installation

352.10 Uses Permitted

Type PVC conduit is permitted in the following applications:

Note: In extreme cold, PVC conduit can become brittle and is more susceptible to physical damage.

(A) Concealed. PVC conduit can be concealed within walls, floors, or ceilings. ▶**Figure 352–3**

▶Figure 352–3

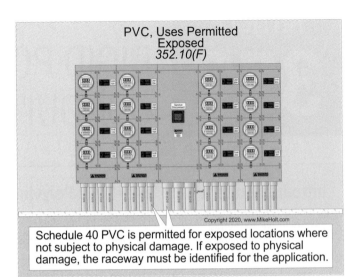

Schedule 40 PVC is permitted for exposed locations where not subject to physical damage. If exposed to physical damage, the raceway must be identified for the application.

▶Figure 352–4

(B) Corrosive Influences. PVC conduit is permitted in areas subject to severe corrosion for which the material is specifically approved by the authority having jurisdiction.

(D) Wet Locations. PVC conduit is permitted in wet locations such as dairies, laundries, canneries, car washes, and other areas frequently washed. It is also permitted in outdoor locations. Support fittings such as straps, screws, and bolts must be made of corrosion-resistant materials or must be protected with a corrosion-resistant coating in accordance with 300.6(A).

(E) Dry and Damp Locations. PVC conduit is permitted in dry and damp locations except where limited in 352.12.

(F) Exposed. Schedule 40 PVC conduit is permitted for exposed locations where not subject to physical damage. If the conduit is exposed to physical damage, the raceway must be identified for the application. ▶Figure 352–4

Note: PVC Schedule 80 conduit is identified for use in areas subject to physical damage. ▶Figure 352–5

(G) Underground. PVC conduit is permitted to be installed underground and in concrete and must comply with the burial requirements of 300.5.

352.12 Uses Not Permitted

PVC conduit is not permitted in the following environments:

(A) Hazardous (Classified) Locations. PVC conduit is not permitted to be used in hazardous (classified) locations except as permitted by 501.10(A)(1)(a) Ex, 501.10(B)(6),.503.10(A), 504.20, 514.8 Ex 2, and 515.8.

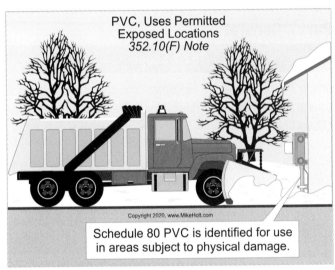

Schedule 80 PVC is identified for use in areas subject to physical damage.

▶Figure 352–5

(B) Support of Luminaires. PVC conduit is not permitted to be used for the support of luminaires or other equipment.

(C) Physical Damage. Type PVC conduit is not permitted to be installed where subject to physical damage unless identified for the application. ▶Figure 352–6

Author's Comment:

▶ PVC Schedule 40 conduit is not identified for use where subject to physical damage, but PVC Schedule 80 conduit is [352.10(F) Note].

(D) Ambient Temperature. PVC conduit is not permitted to be installed if the ambient temperature exceeds 50°C (122°F).

PVC, Uses Not Permitted
Physical Damage
352.12(C)

VIOLATION

Schedule 40 PVC
must not be used
where subject to
physical damage.

Schedule 80 PVC
is listed for use
where subject to
physical damage
[352.10(F) Note].

Copyright 2020, www.MikeHolt.com

▶Figure 352–6

Author's Comment:

▸ PVC conduit and fittings are not permitted to be installed in
environmental air spaces (plenums) [300.22(C)].

Notes

Please use the 2020 *Code* book to answer the following questions.

Article 352—Rigid Polyvinyl Chloride Conduit (Type PVC)

1. Article 352 covers the use, installation, and construction specifications for _____ and associated fittings.

   (a) ENT
   (b) RMC
   (c) IMC
   (d) PVC

2. A rigid nonmetallic raceway of circular cross section, with integral or associated couplings, connectors, and fittings for the installation of electrical conductors and cables describes _____.

   (a) ENT
   (b) RMC
   (c) IMC
   (d) PVC

3. Extreme _____ may cause PVC conduit to become brittle, and therefore more susceptible to damage from physical contact.

   (a) sunlight
   (b) corrosive conditions
   (c) heat
   (d) cold

4. PVC conduit is permitted in locations subject to severe corrosive influences and where subject to chemicals for which the materials are specifically _____.

   (a) approved
   (b) identified
   (c) listed
   (d) non-hazardous

5. PVC conduit shall be permitted for exposed work where subject to physical damage if identified for such use.

   (a) True
   (b) False

6. PVC conduit shall not be used _____, unless specifically permitted.

   (a) in hazardous (classified) locations
   (b) for the support of luminaires or other equipment
   (c) where subject to physical damage unless identified for such use
   (d) all of these

ARTICLE 356

LIQUIDTIGHT FLEXIBLE NONMETALLIC CONDUIT (TYPE LFNC)

Introduction to Article 356—Liquidtight Flexible Nonmetallic Conduit (Type LFNC)

Liquidtight flexible nonmetallic conduit (Type LFNC) is a listed raceway of circular cross section with an outer liquidtight, nonmetallic, sunlight-resistant jacket over an inner flexible core with associated couplings, connectors, and fittings. It is commonly referred to as "Carflex®."

Part I. General

356.1 Scope

Article 356 covers the use, installation, and construction specifications of liquidtight flexible nonmetallic conduit (Type LFNC) and associated fittings. ▶Figure 356–1

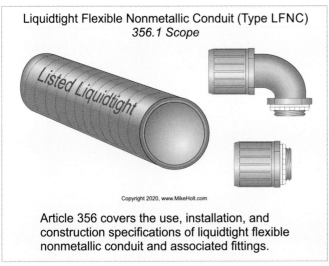

Liquidtight Flexible Nonmetallic Conduit (Type LFNC)
356.1 Scope

Copyright 2020, www.MikeHolt.com

Article 356 covers the use, installation, and construction specifications of liquidtight flexible nonmetallic conduit and associated fittings.

▶Figure 356–1

356.2 Definition

Liquidtight Flexible Nonmetallic Conduit (Type LFNC). A raceway of circular cross section, with an outer liquidtight, nonmetallic, sunlight-resistant jacket over a flexible inner core, with associated couplings, connectors, and fittings, listed for the installation of electrical conductors. ▶Figure 356–2

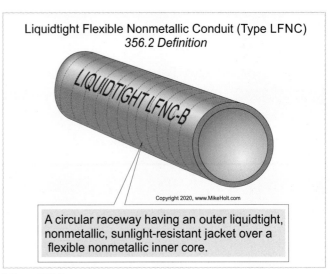

Liquidtight Flexible Nonmetallic Conduit (Type LFNC)
356.2 Definition

Copyright 2020, www.MikeHolt.com

A circular raceway having an outer liquidtight, nonmetallic, sunlight-resistant jacket over a flexible nonmetallic inner core.

▶Figure 356–2

Part II. Installation

356.10 Uses Permitted

Listed LFNC is permitted, either exposed or concealed, at any of the following locations:

(1) If flexibility is required.

(2) If protection from liquids, vapors, <u>machine oils, and</u> solids is required.

(3) Outdoors, if listed and marked for this purpose.

(4) Directly buried in the Earth if listed and marked for this purpose. ▶Figure 356–3

LFNC, Uses Permitted
Direct Burial
356.10(4)

Listed liquidtight flexible nonmetallic conduit is permitted to be directly buried if listed and marked for this purpose.

▶Figure 356–3

(5) LFNC-B (gray color) is permitted in lengths over 6 ft if secured in accordance with 356.30.

(6) LFNC-C (black color) is permitted as a listed manufactured prewired assembly.

(7) Encasement in concrete if listed for direct burial.

(8) Conductors or cables rated at a temperature rating of LFNC conduit are permitted to be installed in LFNC, provided the conductors or cables are not operated at a temperature higher than the listed temperature rating of the LFNC.

Note: Extreme cold can cause some types of nonmetallic conduits to become brittle and therefore more susceptible to damage from physical contact.

356.12 Uses Not Permitted

(1) Where subject to physical damage.

(2) If the ambient temperature and/or conductor temperature is in excess of its listing.

(3) Longer than 6 ft, except if approved by the authority having jurisdiction as essential for a required degree of flexibility.

(4) In any hazardous (classified) location except as permitted by 501.10(B), 502.10(A) and (B), and 504.20.

ARTICLE
356
PRACTICE QUESTIONS

Please use the 2020 *Code* book to answer the following questions.

Article 356—Liquidtight Flexible Nonmetallic Conduit (Type LFNC)

1. Article _____ covers the use, installation, and construction specifications for liquidtight flexible nonmetallic conduit (LFNC) and associated fittings.

    (a) 300
    (b) 334
    (c) 350
    (d) 356

2. LFNC shall be permitted for _____.

    (a) direct burial where listed and marked for the purpose
    (b) exposed work
    (c) outdoors where listed and marked for this purpose
    (d) all of these

3. Extreme cold can cause some types of nonmetallic conduits to become _____ and therefore more susceptible to damage from physical contact.

    (a) stiff
    (b) larger
    (c) weak
    (d) brittle

4. Liquidtight nonmetallic flexible conduit is not permitted to be used where _____.

    (a) subject to physical damage
    (b) ambient temperatures exceed its listing
    (c) in lengths greater than 6 ft unless approved
    (d) all of these

ARTICLE
358

ELECTRICAL METALLIC TUBING (TYPE EMT)

Introduction to Article 358—Electrical Metallic Tubing (Type EMT)

Electrical metallic tubing (Type EMT) is perhaps the most commonly used raceway in commercial and industrial installations. It is a lightweight raceway that is relatively easy to bend, cut, and ream. Because EMT is not threaded, all connectors and couplings are of the threadless type (either set screw or compression) and provide for quick, easy, and inexpensive installations as compared to other metallic raceway systems; all of which make it very popular. Electrical metallic tubing is manufactured in both galvanized steel and aluminum; the steel type is used most often.

Part I. General

358.1 Scope

Article 358 covers the use, installation, and construction specifications of electrical metallic tubing (Type EMT) and associated fittings. ▶Figure 358–1

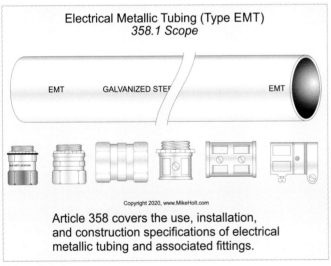

Electrical Metallic Tubing (Type EMT)
358.1 Scope

EMT   GALVANIZED STE[...]   EMT

Copyright 2020, www.MikeHolt.com

Article 358 covers the use, installation, and construction specifications of electrical metallic tubing and associated fittings.

▶Figure 358–1

358.2 Definition

Electrical Metallic Tubing (Type EMT). An unthreaded thinwall circular metallic raceway used for the installation of electrical conductors. When joined together with listed fittings and enclosures as a complete system, it is a reliable wiring method providing both physical protection for conductors as well an effective ground-fault current path. ▶Figure 358–2

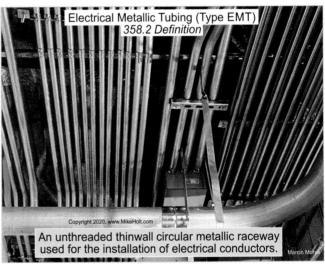

Electrical Metallic Tubing (Type EMT)
358.2 Definition

Copyright 2020, www.MikeHolt.com

An unthreaded thinwall circular metallic raceway used for the installation of electrical conductors.

▶Figure 358–2

Part II. Installation

358.10 Uses Permitted

(A) Exposed and Concealed. EMT is permitted to be used exposed and concealed for the following applications: ▶Figure 358–3

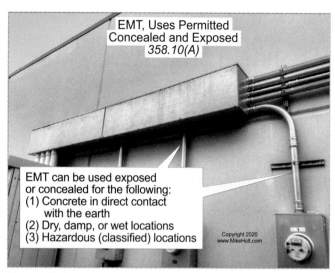

▶Figure 358-3

(1) In concrete in direct contact with the earth in accordance with 358.10(B).

(2) In dry, damp, or wet locations.

(3) In any hazardous (classified) location as permitted by other articles in this *Code*.

(B) Corrosive Environments.

(1) Galvanized Steel. Galvanized steel EMT, elbows, and fittings can be installed in concrete, in direct contact with the Earth, or in areas subject to severe corrosive influences if protected by corrosion protection and approved as suitable for the condition [300.6(A)].

(D) Wet Locations. Support fittings such as screws, straps, and so on, installed in a wet location must be made of corrosion-resistant material.

Author's Comment:

▶ If installed in wet locations, fittings for EMT must be listed for use in wet locations and prevent moisture or water from entering or accumulating within the enclosure in accordance with 314.15 [358.42].

358.12 Uses Not Permitted

EMT is not permitted to be used under the following conditions:

(1) Where subject to severe physical damage. ▶Figure 358-4

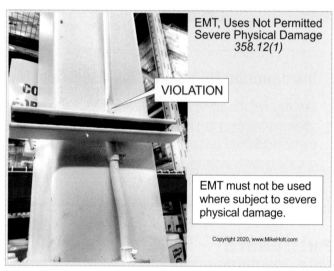

▶Figure 358-4

(2) For the support of luminaires or other equipment. ▶Figure 358-5

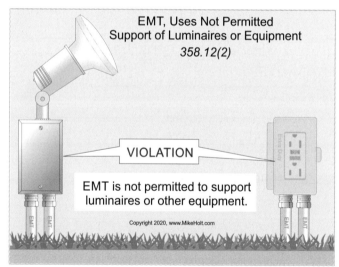

▶Figure 358-5

ARTICLE 358 PRACTICE QUESTIONS

Please use the 2020 *Code* book to answer the following questions.

Article 358—Electrical Metallic Tubing (Type EMT)

1. Article _____ covers the use, installation, and construction specifications for electrical metallic tubing (EMT) and associated fittings.

   (a) 334
   (b) 350
   (c) 356
   (d) 358

2. _____ is an unthreaded thinwall metallic raceway of circular cross section designed for the routing and physical protection of electrical conductors and cables when joined together with listed fittings.

   (a) LFNC
   (b) EMT
   (c) NUCC
   (d) RTRC

3. The use of EMT shall be permitted for both exposed and concealed work in _____.

   (a) concrete, in direct contact with the earth, or in areas subject to severe corrosive influences where installed in accordance with 358.10(B)
   (b) dry, damp, and wet locations
   (c) any hazardous (classified) location as permitted by other articles in this *Code*
   (d) all of these

4. Galvanized steel and stainless steel EMT, elbows, couplings, and fittings can be installed in concrete, in direct contact with the earth, or in areas subject to severe corrosive influences where _____.

   (a) protected by corrosion protection
   (b) made of aluminum
   (c) made of stainless steel
   (d) listed for wet locations

5. When EMT is installed in wet locations, all supports, bolts, straps, and screws shall be _____.

   (a) made of aluminum
   (b) protected against corrosion
   (c) made of stainless steel
   (d) of nonmetallic materials only

6. EMT shall not be used where _____.

   (a) subject to severe physical damage
   (b) embedded in concrete
   (c) used for the support of luminaires except conduit bodies no larger than the largest trade size of the tubing
   (d) installed in wet locations

ARTICLE

362

ELECTRICAL NONMETALLIC TUBING (TYPE ENT)

Introduction to Article 362—Electrical Nonmetallic Tubing (Type ENT)

Electrical nonmetallic tubing is a pliable, corrugated, circular raceway. It resembles the flexible tubing you might see used at swimming pools and is often referred to as "Smurf Pipe" or "Smurf Tube" (as a reference to the children's cartoon characters "The Smurfs") because it was only available in blue when it first came out. It can now be purchased in additional colors such as red and yellow.

Part I. General

362.1 Scope

Article 362 covers the use, installation, and construction specifications of electrical nonmetallic tubing (Type ENT) and associated fittings. ▶Figure 362–1

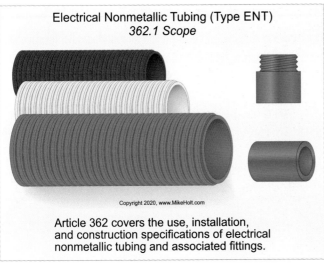

Electrical Nonmetallic Tubing (Type ENT)
362.1 Scope

Copyright 2020, www.MikeHolt.com

Article 362 covers the use, installation, and construction specifications of electrical nonmetallic tubing and associated fittings.

▶Figure 362–1

362.2 Definition

Electrical Nonmetallic Tubing (Type ENT). A pliable corrugated raceway of circular cross section, with integral or associated couplings, connectors, and fittings that are listed for the installation of electrical conductors. It is composed of a material that is resistant to moisture and chemical atmospheres and is flame retardant. ▶Figure 362–2

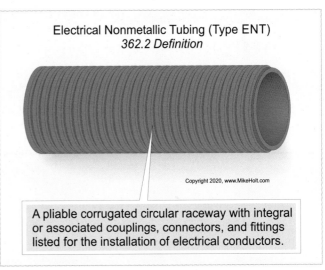

Electrical Nonmetallic Tubing (Type ENT)
362.2 Definition

Copyright 2020, www.MikeHolt.com

A pliable corrugated circular raceway with integral or associated couplings, connectors, and fittings listed for the installation of electrical conductors.

▶Figure 362–2

Electrical nonmetallic tubing can be bent by hand with reasonable force but without other assistance.

362.6 Listing

ENT and its associated fittings must be listed.

Part II. Installation

362.10 Uses Permitted

Electrical nonmetallic tubing is permitted as follows:

(1) In buildings not exceeding three floors. ▶Figure 362–3

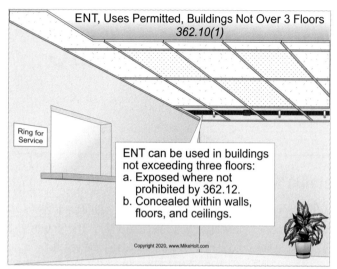

▶Figure 362–3

a. Exposed, where not prohibited by 362.12.

b. Concealed within walls, floors, and ceilings.

(2) In buildings exceeding three floors, where installed concealed in walls, floors, or ceilings that provide a thermal barrier having a 15-minute finish rating, as identified in listings of fire-rated assemblies. ▶Figure 362–4

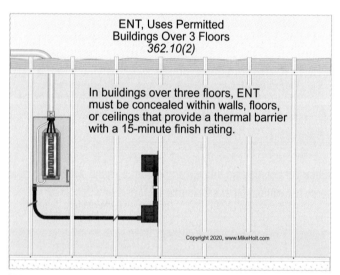

▶Figure 362–4

Ex to (2): If a fire sprinkler system is installed on all floors in accordance with NFPA 13, Standard for the Installation of Sprinkler Systems, electrical nonmetallic tubing is permitted exposed or concealed in buildings of any height. ▶Figure 362–5

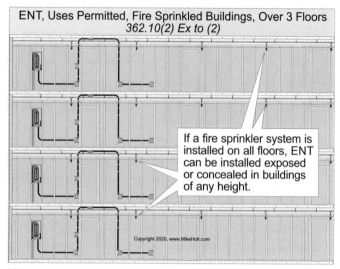

▶Figure 362–5

Author's Comment:

▸ ENT is not permitted above a suspended ceiling used as a plenum space [300.22(C)].

(3) In severe corrosive and chemical locations when identified for this use.

(4) In dry and damp concealed locations if not prohibited by 362.12.

(5) Above a suspended ceiling if the suspended ceiling provides a thermal barrier having a 15-minute finish rating, as identified in listings of fire-rated assemblies. ▶Figure 362–6

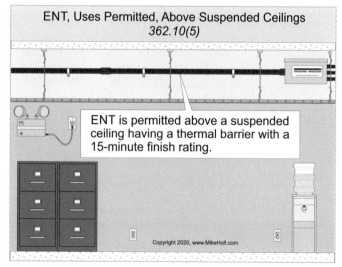

▶Figure 362–6

Ex to (5): If a fire sprinkler system is installed on all floors in accordance with NFPA 13, Standard for the Installation of Sprinkler Systems, ENT is permitted above a suspended ceiling that does not have a 15-minute finish rated thermal barrier. ▶Figure 362–7

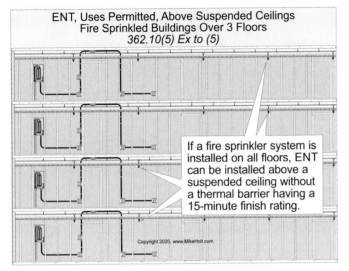

▶Figure 362–7

(6) Encased or embedded in a concrete slab provided fittings identified for the purpose are used.

(7) In wet locations indoors, or in a concrete slab on or below grade, with fittings that are listed for the purpose.

362.12 Uses Not Permitted

ENT is not permitted to be used in the following applications:

(1) In any hazardous (classified) location, except as permitted by 504.20 and 505.15(A)(1).

(2) For the support of luminaires or equipment. See 314.23.

(3) If the ambient temperature exceeds 50°C (122°F).

(4) For direct Earth burial.

Author's Comment:

▷ Electrical nonmetallic tubing is permitted to be encased in concrete [362.10(6)].

(5) Exposed in buildings over three floors, except as permitted by 362.10(1) and (5) Ex.

(6) In assembly occupancies or theaters, except as permitted by 518.4 and 520.5.

(7) Exposed to the direct rays of the sun. ▶Figure 362–8

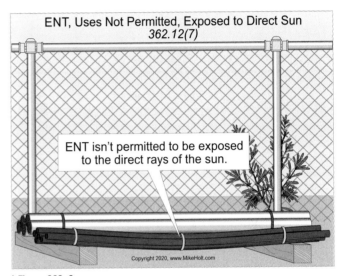

▶Figure 362–8

Author's Comment:

▷ Exposing electrical nonmetallic tubing to the direct rays of the sun for an extended time may result in the product becoming brittle, unless it is listed to resist the effects of ultraviolet (UV) radiation.

(8) Where subject to physical damage.

Author's Comment:

▷ Electrical nonmetallic tubing is prohibited in ducts, plenum spaces [300.22(C)], and patient care space circuits in health care facilities [517.13(A)].

ARTICLE 362 PRACTICE QUESTIONS

Please use the 2020 *Code* book to answer the following questions.

Article 362—Electrical Nonmetallic Tubing (Type ENT)

1. Article _____ covers the use, installation, and construction specifications for electrical nonmetallic tubing (ENT) and associated fittings.

   (a) 358
   (b) 362
   (c) 366
   (d) 392

2. ENT is composed of a material resistant to moisture and chemical atmospheres and is _____.

   (a) rigid
   (b) flame retardant
   (c) fireproof
   (d) flammable

3. When a building is supplied with a(an) _____ fire sprinkler system, ENT shall be permitted to be used within walls, floors, and ceilings, exposed or concealed, in buildings exceeding three floors above grade.

   (a) listed
   (b) identified
   (c) NFPA 13
   (d) NFPA 72

4. When a building is supplied with a fire sprinkler system, ENT can be installed above any suspended ceiling.

   (a) True
   (b) False

5. ENT and fittings can be _____, provided fittings identified for this purpose are used.

   (a) encased in poured concrete
   (b) embedded in a concrete slab on grade where the tubing is placed on sand or approved screenings
   (c) for wet locations indoors
   (d) any of these

6. ENT is not permitted in hazardous (classified) locations, unless permitted in other articles of the *Code*.

   (a) True
   (b) False

7. ENT shall be permitted for direct earth burial unless used with fittings listed for this purpose.

   (a) True
   (b) False

8. ENT shall not be used where exposed to the direct rays of the sun, unless identified as _____.

   (a) high-temperature rated
   (b) sunlight resistant
   (c) Schedule 80
   (d) suitable

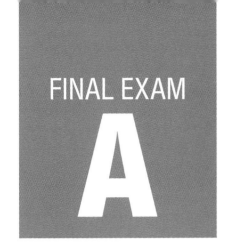

FINAL EXAM

Please use the 2020 *Code* book to answer the following questions.

1. Compliance with the *Code* and proper maintenance result in an installation that is essentially _____.

   (a) free from hazards
   (b) not necessarily efficient or convenient
   (c) not necessarily adequate for good service or future expansion
   (d) all of these

2. Installations supplying _____ power to ships and watercraft in marinas and boatyards are covered by the *NEC*.

   (a) shore
   (b) primary
   (c) secondary
   (d) auxiliary

3. The *Code* covers underground mine installations and self-propelled mobile surface mining machinery and its attendant electrical trailing cable.

   (a) True
   (b) False

4. Chapters 5, 6, and 7 apply to special occupancies, special equipment, or other special conditions and may supplement or modify the requirements in Chapters 1 through 7.

   (a) True
   (b) False

5. The _____ has the responsibility for deciding on the approval of equipment and materials.

   (a) manufacturer
   (b) authority having jurisdiction
   (c) testing agency
   (d) the owner of the premises

6. An arc-fault circuit interrupter is a device intended to de-energize the circuit when a(an) _____ is detected.

   (a) overcurrent condition
   (b) arc fault
   (c) ground fault
   (d) harmonic fundamental

7. An accessory, such as a locknut, intended primarily to perform a mechanical function rather than an electrical function best describes _____.

   (a) a part
   (b) equipment
   (c) a device
   (d) a fitting

8. A service drop is defined as the overhead conductors between the utility electric supply system and the _____.

   (a) service equipment
   (b) service point
   (c) grounding electrode
   (d) equipment grounding conductor

9. Conductor sizes are expressed in American Wire Gage (AWG) or in _____.

   (a) inches
   (b) circular mils
   (c) square inches
   (d) cubic inches

10. Connectors and terminals for conductors more finely stranded than Class B and Class C, as shown in Table 10 of Chapter 9, shall be _____ for the specific conductor class or classes.

   (a) listed
   (b) approved
   (c) identified
   (d) all of these

11. The *NEC* requires tested series-rated installations of circuit breakers or fuses to be legibly marked in the field to indicate the equipment has been applied with a series combination rating.

   (a) True
   (b) False

12. The working space in front of the electric equipment shall not be less than _____ in. wide, or the width of the equipment, whichever is greater.

   (a) 15
   (b) 30
   (c) 40
   (d) 60

13. Illumination shall be provided for all working spaces about service equipment, switchboards, switchgear, panelboards, or motor control centers _____.

   (a) over 600V
   (b) installed indoors
   (c) rated 1,200A or more
   (d) using automatic means of control

14. In order for a metal underground water pipe to be used as a grounding electrode, it shall be in direct contact with the earth for _____.

   (a) 5 ft
   (b) 10 ft or more
   (c) less than 10 ft
   (d) 20 ft or more

15. Where the resistance-to-ground of 25 ohms or less is not achieved for a single rod electrode, _____.

   (a) other means besides electrodes shall be used in order to provide grounding
   (b) the single rod electrode shall be supplemented by one additional electrode
   (c) additional electrodes must be added until 25 ohms is achieved
   (d) any of these

16. Where the supplemental electrode is a rod, that portion of the bonding jumper that is the sole connection to the supplemental grounding electrode shall not be required to be larger than _____ AWG copper wire.

   (a) 8
   (b) 6
   (c) 4
   (d) 1

17. Type MC cable provides an effective ground-fault current path and is recognized by the *NEC* as an equipment grounding conductor when _____.

   (a) it contains an insulated or uninsulated equipment grounding conductor in compliance with 250.118(1)
   (b) the cable assembly contains a bare copper conductor
   (c) only when it is hospital grade Type MC cable
   (d) it is terminated with bonding bushings

18. The structural metal frame of a _____ shall not be used as an equipment grounding conductor.

   (a) roof or crawl space
   (b) wall or ceiling
   (c) building or structure
   (d) floor or window

19. The provisions of Article 300 apply to the conductors that form an integral part of equipment or listed utilization equipment.

   (a) True
   (b) False

20. A cable, raceway, or box installed under metal-corrugated sheet roof decking shall be supported so the top of the cable, raceway, or box is not less than _____ in. from the lowest surface of the roof decking to the top of the cable, raceway, or box.

    (a) ½
    (b) 1
    (c) 1½
    (d) 2

21. _____ is defined as the shortest distance measured between a point on the top surface of direct-burial cable and the top surface of the finished grade.

    (a) Notch
    (b) Cover
    (c) Gap
    (d) Spacing

22. Where independent support wires of a suspended ceiling assembly are used to support raceways, cable assemblies, or boxes above a ceiling, they shall be secured at _____ end(s).

    (a) one
    (b) both
    (c) the line and load
    (d) at the attachment to the structural member

23. The number and size of conductors permitted in a raceway is limited to _____.

    (a) permit heat to dissipate
    (b) prevent damage to insulation during installation
    (c) prevent damage to insulation during removal of conductors
    (d) all of these

24. Wiring methods that are permitted to be installed in ducts fabricated for environmental air include _____.

    (a) MC cable without an overall nonmetallic covering
    (b) EMT (electrical metallic tubing)
    (c) RMC (rigid metal conduit)
    (d) all of these

25. Where installed in raceways, conductors _____ AWG and larger shall be stranded, unless specifically permitted or required elsewhere in the *NEC*.

    (a) 10
    (b) 8
    (c) 6
    (d) 4

26. Where internal _____ means are provided between all entries, nonmetallic boxes shall be permitted to be used with metal raceways or metal-armored cables.

    (a) grounding
    (b) bonding
    (c) connecting
    (d) splicing

27. Where a luminaire stud or hickey is present in the box, _____ allowance in accordance with Table 314.16(b) shall be made for each type of fitting, based on the largest conductor present in the box.

    (a) a single volume
    (b) a double volume
    (c) a ¼ volume
    (d) no additional volume

28. When Type NM cable is used with nonmetallic boxes not larger than 2¼ in. x 4 in., securing the cable to the box shall not be required if the cable is fastened within _____ in. of that box.

    (a) 6
    (b) 8
    (c) 10
    (d) 12

29. A luminaire that weighs more than _____ lb can be supported by an outlet box that is listed for the weight of the luminaire to be supported.

    (a) 20
    (b) 30
    (c) 40
    (d) 50

30. Where angle or U pulls are made, the distance between each raceway entry inside the box or conduit body and the opposite wall of the box or conduit body shall not be less than _____ times the trade size of the largest raceway in a row plus the sum of the trade sizes of the remaining raceways in the same wall and row.

    (a) six
    (b) eight
    (c) ten
    (d) twelve

31. Handhole enclosure covers shall have an identifying mark or logo that prominently identifies the function of the enclosure, such as "_____."

(a) danger
(b) utility
(c) high voltage
(d) electric

32. Type _____ cable is a fabricated assembly of insulated conductors in a flexible interlocked metallic armor.

(a) AC
(b) TC
(c) NM
(d) MA

33. The use, installation, and construction specifications of nonmetallic-sheathed cable are covered within Article _____.

(a) 300
(b) 334
(c) 400
(d) 410

34. Type NM cable can be installed as open runs in dropped or suspended ceilings in other than one- and two-family and multi-family dwellings.

(a) True
(b) False

35. Article _____ covers the use, installation, and construction specifications for power and control tray cable, Type TC.

(a) 326
(b) 330
(c) 334
(d) 336

36. In _____, type TC-ER-JP cable containing both power and control conductors that is identified for pulling through structural members shall be permitted.

(a) multifamily dwellings
(b) one- and two- family dwelling units
(c) only duplexes
(d) none of these

37. Type TC cable shall be permitted to be direct buried, where _____ for such use.

(a) identified
(b) approved
(c) listed
(d) labeled

38. Type SE cable shall be permitted to be used as _____.

(a) branch circuits
(b) feeders
(c) underground service entrance conductors if in a raceway
(d) branch circuits or feeders

39. For interior installations of Type SE cable with ungrounded conductor sizes _____ AWG and smaller, where installed in thermal insulation, the ampacity shall be in accordance with 60°C (140°F) conductor temperature rating.

(a) 14
(b) 12
(c) 10
(d) 8

40. Type UF cable can be used for service conductors.

(a) True
(b) False

41. Type UF cable shall not be used where subject to physical damage.

(a) True
(b) False

42. IMC, elbows, couplings, and fittings shall be permitted to be installed in concrete, in direct contact with the earth, or in areas subject to severe corrosive influences where protected by corrosion protection _____ for the condition.

(a) identified
(b) approved
(c) listed
(d) suitable

43. Article 344 covers the use, installation, and construction specifications for _____ conduit and associated fittings.

(a) intermediate metal
(b) rigid metal
(c) electrical metallic
(d) aluminum metal

44. FMC shall not be installed _____.

    (a) in wet locations
    (b) embedded in poured concrete
    (c) where subject to physical damage
    (d) all of these

45. Article 352 covers the use, installation, and construction specifications for _____ and associated fittings.

    (a) ENT
    (b) RMC
    (c) IMC
    (d) PVC

46. PVC conduit shall be permitted for exposed work where subject to physical damage if identified for such use.

    (a) True
    (b) False

47. Extreme cold can cause some types of nonmetallic conduits to become _____ and therefore more susceptible to damage from physical contact.

    (a) stiff
    (b) larger
    (c) weak
    (d) brittle

48. The use of EMT shall be permitted for both exposed and concealed work in _____.

    (a) concrete, in direct contact with the earth, or in areas subject to severe corrosive influences where installed in accordance with 358.10(B)
    (b) dry, damp, and wet locations
    (c) any hazardous (classified) location as permitted by other articles in this *Code*
    (d) all of these

49. ENT and fittings can be _____, provided fittings identified for this purpose are used.

    (a) encased in poured concrete
    (b) embedded in a concrete slab on grade where the tubing is placed on sand or approved screenings
    (c) for wet locations indoors
    (d) any of these

50. ENT shall not be used where exposed to the direct rays of the sun, unless identified as _____.

    (a) high-temperature rated
    (b) sunlight resistant
    (c) Schedule 80
    (d) suitable

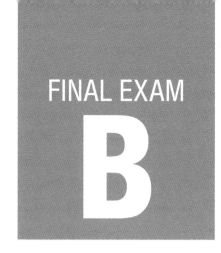

Please use the 2020 *Code* book to answer the following questions.

1. Compliance with the *Code* and proper maintenance result in an installation that is essentially _____.

    (a) free from hazards
    (b) not necessarily efficient or convenient
    (c) not necessarily adequate for good service or future expansion
    (d) all of these

2. Installations supplying _____ power to ships and watercraft in marinas and boatyards are covered by the *NEC*.

    (a) shore
    (b) primary
    (c) secondary
    (d) auxiliary

3. A device that provides a means to connect intersystem bonding conductors for _____ systems to the grounding electrode system is an intersystem bonding termination.

    (a) limited-energy
    (b) low-voltage
    (c) communications
    (d) power and lighting

4. A(An) _____ is a point on the wiring system at which current is taken to supply utilization equipment.

    (a) box
    (b) receptacle
    (c) outlet
    (d) device

5. General requirements for the examination and approval, installation and use, access to and spaces about electrical conductors and equipment; enclosures intended for personnel entry; and tunnel installations are within the scope of _____.

    (a) Article 800
    (b) Article 300
    (c) Article 110
    (d) Annex J

6. The *NEC* requires that electrical equipment be _____.

    (a) installed in a neat and workmanlike manner
    (b) installed under the supervision of a licensed person
    (c) completed before being inspected
    (d) all of these

7. Conductors shall have their ampacity determined using the _____ column of Table 310.16 for circuits rated over 100A, or marked for conductors larger than 1 AWG, unless the equipment terminals are listed for use with higher temperature-rated conductors.

    (a) 30
    (b) 60
    (c) 75
    (d) 90

8. Reconditioned equipment shall be marked with the _____ by which the organization responsible for reconditioning the electrical equipment can be identified, along with the date of the reconditioning.

    (a) name
    (b) trademark
    (c) descriptive marking
    (d) any of these

9. A minimum working space depth of _____ ft to live parts of equipment operating at 277 volts-to-ground is required where there are exposed live parts on one side and no live or grounded parts on the other side.

    (a) 2
    (b) 3
    (c) 4
    (d) 6

10. Working space shall not be used for _____.

    (a) storage
    (b) raceways
    (c) lighting
    (d) accessibility

11. All switchboards, switchgear, panelboards, and motor control centers shall be located in dedicated spaces and protected from damage and the working clearance space for outdoor installations shall include the zone described in _____.

    (a) 110.26(a)
    (b) 110.26(b)
    (c) 110.26(c)
    (d) 110.26(D)

12. Equipment grounding conductors, grounding electrode conductors, and bonding jumpers shall be connected by _____.

    (a) listed pressure connectors
    (b) terminal bars
    (c) exothermic welding
    (d) any of these

13. An electrode encased by at least 2 in. of concrete, located horizontally near the bottom or vertically and within that portion of a concrete foundation or footing that is in direct contact with the earth, shall be permitted as a grounding electrode when it consists of _____.

    (a) bare copper conductor not smaller than 8 AWG
    (b) bare copper conductor not smaller than 6 AWG
    (c) bare copper conductor not smaller than 4 AWG
    (d) bare copper conductor not smaller than 1/0 AWG

14. _____ shall not be used as grounding electrodes.

    (a) Metal underground gas piping systems
    (b) Aluminum
    (c) Metal well casings
    (d) Metal underground gas piping systems and aluminum

15. Where rock bottom is encountered at an angle up to 45 degrees when driving a rod or pipe electrode, the electrode shall be permitted to be buried in a trench _____ deep.

    (a) 30 in.
    (b) 6 ft
    (c) 8 ft
    (d) 10 ft

16. Listed FMC can be used as the equipment grounding conductor if the length in any ground return path does not exceed 6 ft and the circuit conductors contained in the conduit are protected by overcurrent devices rated at _____ amperes or less.

    (a) 15
    (b) 20
    (c) 30
    (d) 60

17. An insulated or covered conductor _____ AWG and larger shall be permitted, at the time of installation, to be permanently identified as an equipment grounding conductor at each end and at every point where the conductor is accessible.

    (a) 8
    (b) 6
    (c) 4
    (d) 1/0

18. Where cables or nonmetallic raceways are installed through bored holes in joists, rafters, or wood members, holes shall be bored so that the edge of the hole is _____ the nearest edge of the wood member.

    (a) not less than 1¼ in. from
    (b) immediately adjacent to
    (c) not less than ¹⁄₁₆ in. from
    (d) 90 degrees away from

19. What is the minimum cover requirement for direct burial Type UF cable installed outdoors that supplies a 120V, 30A circuit?

    (a) 6 in.
    (b) 12 in.
    (c) 18 in.
    (d) 24 in.

20. Backfill used for underground wiring shall not damage _____ or prevent adequate compaction of fill or contribute to corrosion.

    (a) raceways
    (b) cables
    (c) conductors
    (d) all of these

21. Raceways shall be provided with expansion, expansion-deflection, or deflection fittings where necessary to compensate for thermal expansion, deflection, and contraction.

    (a) True
    (b) False

22. In multiwire branch circuits, the continuity of the _____ shall not be dependent upon the device connections.

    (a) ungrounded conductor
    (b) grounded conductor
    (c) grounding electrode
    (d) raceway

23. Conductors in ferrous metal raceways or enclosures shall be arranged so as to avoid heating the surrounding ferrous metal by alternating-current induction. To accomplish this, the _____ conductor(s) shall be grouped together.

    (a) phase
    (b) grounded
    (c) equipment grounding
    (d) all of these

24. Wiring methods permitted in the ceiling areas used for environmental air include _____.

    (a) electrical metallic tubing
    (b) FMC of any length
    (c) RMC without an overall nonmetallic covering
    (d) all of these

25. The minimum size copper conductor permitted for voltage ratings up to 2,000V _____ AWG.

    (a) 14
    (b) 12
    (c) 10
    (d) 8

26. The total volume occupied by two internal cable clamps, six 12 AWG conductors, and a single-pole switch is _____ cu in.

    (a) 2
    (b) 4.5
    (c) 14.5
    (d) 20.25

27. Where one or more equipment grounding conductors enter a box, _____ allowance in accordance with Table 314.16(b) shall be made based on the largest equipment grounding conductor.

    (a) a single volume
    (b) a double volume
    (c) a ¼ volume
    (d) no additional volume

28. An outlet box or enclosure mounted on a building or other surface shall be _____.

    (a) rigidly and securely fastened in place
    (b) supported by cables that protrude from the box
    (c) supported by cable entries from the top and permitted to rest against the supporting surface
    (d) permitted to be supported by the raceway(s) terminating at the box

29. Screws used for the purpose of attaching covers or other equipment to the box shall be either machine screws matching the thread gauge and size that is integral to the box or be in accordance with the manufacturer

    (a) True
    (b) False

30. Utilization equipment weighing not more than 6 lb can be supported to any box or plaster ring secured to a box, provided the equipment is secured with at least two _____ or larger screws.

    (a) No. 6
    (b) No. 8
    (c) No. 10
    (d) any of these

31. _____ shall be installed so that the wiring contained in them can be rendered accessible without removing any part of the building or structure or, in underground circuits, without excavating sidewalks, paving, or earth.

    (a) Boxes
    (b) Conduit bodies
    (c) Handhole enclosures
    (d) all of these

32. Armored cable shall not be installed _____.

    (a) in damp or wet locations
    (b) where subject to physical damage
    (c) where exposed to corrosive conditions
    (d) all of these

33. The use, installation, and construction specifications of metal-clad cable, Type MC are covered within Article _____.

    (a) 300
    (b) 310
    (c) 320
    (d) 330

34. Type NM cables shall not be used in one- and two-family dwellings exceeding three floors above grade.

    (a) True
    (b) False

35. Type TC cable and associated fittings shall be _____.

    (a) identified
    (b) approved
    (c) listed
    (d) labeled

36. Type TC-ER-JP cable shall be permitted for branch circuits and feeders in one and two family dwelling units.

    (a) True
    (b) False

37. Type TC cable shall not be used where _____.

    (a) it will be exposed to physical damage
    (b) installed outside of a raceway or cable tray system, unless permitted in 336.10(4), 336.10(7), 336.10(9), and 336.10(10)
    (c) exposed to direct rays of the sun, unless identified as sunlight resistant
    (d) all of these

38. Type _____ cable is an assembly primarily used for services.

    (a) NM
    (b) UF
    (c) SE
    (d) SEC

39. Where more than two Type SE cables are installed in contact with thermal insulations, caulk, or sealing foam without maintaining spacing between cables, the ampacity of each conductor shall be _____ in accordance with Table 310.15(C)(1).

    (a) increased
    (b) adjusted
    (c) corrected
    (d) multiplied

40. Type USE cable used for service laterals shall be permitted to emerge from the ground if terminated in an enclosure at an outside location and protected in accordance with 300.5(D).

    (a) True
    (b) False

41. Type _____ cable is a factory assembly of conductors with an overall covering of nonmetallic material suitable for direct burial in the earth.

    (a) NM
    (b) UF
    (c) SE
    (d) TC

42. Type UF cable shall not be used in _____.

    (a) motion picture studios
    (b) storage battery rooms
    (c) hoistways
    (d) all of these

43. Type RMC conduit shall be permitted to be installed where subject to severe physical damage.

    (a) True
    (b) False

44. _____ is a raceway of circular cross section made of a helically wound, formed, interlocked metal strip.

    (a) Type MC cable
    (b) Type AC cable
    (c) LFMC
    (d) FMC

45. _____ is a raceway of circular cross section having an outer liquidtight, nonmetallic, sunlight-resistant jacket over an inner flexible metal core.

    (a) FMC
    (b) LFNMC
    (c) LFMC
    (d) Vinyl-clad Type MC

46. Extreme _____ may cause PVC conduit to become brittle, and therefore more susceptible to damage from physical contact.

    (a) sunlight
    (b) corrosive conditions
    (c) heat
    (d) cold

47. Article _____ covers the use, installation, and construction specifications for liquidtight flexible nonmetallic conduit (LFNC) and associated fittings.

    (a) 300
    (b) 334
    (c) 350
    (d) 356

48. Article _____ covers the use, installation, and construction specifications for electrical metallic tubing (EMT) and associated fittings.

    (a) 334
    (b) 350
    (c) 356
    (d) 358

49. When EMT is installed in wet locations, all supports, bolts, straps, and screws shall be _____.

    (a) made of aluminum
    (b) protected against corrosion
    (c) made of stainless steel
    (d) of nonmetallic materials only

50. When a building is supplied with a(an) _____ fire sprinkler system, ENT shall be permitted to be used within walls, floors, and ceilings, exposed or concealed, in buildings exceeding three floors above grade.

    (a) listed
    (b) identified
    (c) NFPA 13
    (d) NFPA 72

ABOUT THE AUTHOR

Mike Holt—Author

Founder and President
Mike Holt Enterprises
Groveland, Florida

Mike Holt is an author, businessman, educator, speaker, publisher and *National Electrical Code* expert. He has written hundreds of electrical training books and articles, founded three successful businesses, and has taught thousands of electrical *Code* seminars across the US and internationally. His electrical training courses have set the standard for trade education, enabling electrical professionals across the country to take their careers to the next level.

Mike's approach to electrical training is based on his own experience as an electrician, contractor, inspector and teacher. Because of his struggles in his early education, he's never lost sight of how hard it can be for students who are intimidated by school, by their own feelings towards learning, or by the complexity of the *NEC*. As a result of that, he's mastered the art of explaining complicated concepts in a straightforward and direct style. He's always felt a responsibility to his students and to the electrical industry to provide education beyond the scope of just passing an exam. This commitment, coupled with the lessons he learned at the University of Miami's MBA program, have helped him build one of the largest electrical training and publishing companies in the United States.

Mike's one-of-a-kind presentation style and his ability to simplify and clarify technical concepts explain his unique position as one of the premier educators and *Code* experts in the country. In addition to the materials he's produced, and the extensive list of companies around the world for whom he's provided training, Mike has written articles that have been seen in numerous industry magazines including, *Electrical Construction & Maintenance (EC&M), CEE News, Electrical Design and Installation (EDI), Electrical Contractor (EC), International Association of Electrical Inspectors (IAEI News), The Electrical Distributor (TED), Power Quality (PQ),* and *Solar Pro*.

Mike's ultimate goal has always been to increase electrical safety and improve lives and he is always looking for the best ways for his students to learn and teach the *Code* and pass electrical exams. His passion for the electrical field continues to grow and today he is more committed than ever to serve this industry.

His commitment to pushing boundaries and setting high standards extends into his personal life. Mike's an eight-time Overall National Barefoot Waterski Champion with more than 20 gold medals, and many national records, and he has competed in three World Barefoot Tournaments. In 2015, at the tender age of 64, he started a new adventure—competitive mountain bike racing. Every day he continues to find ways to motivate himself, both mentally and physically.

Mike and his wife, Linda, reside in New Mexico and Florida, and are the parents of seven children and six grandchildren. As his life has changed over the years, a few things have remained constant: his commitment to God, his love for his family, and doing what he can to change the lives of others through his products and seminars.

Special Acknowledgments

My Family. First, I want to thank God for my godly wife who's always by my side and also for my children.

My Staff. A personal thank you goes to my team at Mike Holt Enterprises for all the work they do to help me with my mission of changing peoples' lives through education. They work tirelessly to ensure that in addition to our products meeting and exceeding the educational needs of our customers, we stay committed to building life-long relationships with them throughout their electrical careers.

The National Fire Protection Association. A special thank you must be given to the staff at the National Fire Protection Association (NFPA), publishers of the *NEC*—in particular, Jeff Sargent for his assistance in answering my many *Code* questions over the years. Jeff, you're a "first class" guy, and I admire your dedication and commitment to helping others understand the *NEC*. Other former NFPA staff members I would like to thank include John Caloggero, Joe Ross, and Dick Murray for their help in the past.

ABOUT THE
MIKE HOLT TEAM

Mike Culbreath—Illustrator

Mike Culbreath
Graphic Illustrator
Alden, Michigan

Mike Culbreath has devoted his career to the electrical industry and worked his way up from apprentice electrician to master electrician. He started working in the electrical field doing residential and light commercial construction, and later did service work and custom electrical installations. While working as a journeyman electrician, he suffered a serious on-the-job knee injury. As part of his rehabilitation, Mike completed courses at Mike Holt Enterprises, and then passed the exam to receive his Master Electrician's license. In 1986, with a keen interest in continuing education for electricians, he joined the staff to update material and began illustrating Mike Holt's textbooks and magazine articles.

Mike started with simple hand-drawn diagrams and cut-and-paste graphics. Frustrated by the limitations of that style of illustrating, he took a company computer home to learn how to operate some basic computer graphics software. Realizing that computer graphics offered a lot of flexibility for creating illustrations, Mike took every computer graphics class and seminar he could to help develop his skills. He's worked as an illustrator and editor with the company for over 30 years and, as Mike Holt has proudly acknowledged, has helped to transform his words and visions into lifelike graphics.

Originally from south Florida, Mike now lives in northern lower Michigan where he enjoys hiking, kayaking, photography, gardening, and cooking; but his real passion is his horses. He also loves spending time with his children Dawn and Mac and his grandchildren Jonah, Kieley, and Scarlet.

Mike Culbreath-Special Acknowledgments

I would like to thank Eric Stromberg, an electrical engineer and super geek (and I mean that in the most complimentary manner, this guy is brilliant), for helping me keep our graphics as technically correct as possible. I would also like to thank all our students for the wonderful feedback to help improve our graphics.

A special thank you goes to Cathleen Kwas for making me look good with her outstanding layout design and typesetting skills; to Toni Culbreath who proofreads all of my material; and to Dawn Babbitt who has assisted me in the production and editing of our graphics. I would also like to acknowledge Belynda Holt Pinto, our Executive Vice-President, Brian House for his input (another really brilliant guy), and the rest of the outstanding staff at Mike Holt Enterprises, for all the hard work they do to help produce and distribute these outstanding products.

And last but not least, I need to give a special thank you to Mike Holt for not firing me over 30 years ago when I "borrowed" one of his computers and took it home to begin the process of learning how to do computer illustrations. He gave me the opportunity and time needed to develop my computer graphics skills. He's been an amazing friend and mentor since I met him as a student many years ago. Thanks for believing in me and allowing me to be part of the Mike Holt Enterprises family.

Brian House—V.P. of Digital and Technical Writing

Daniel Brian House
Mike Holt Enterprises
Leesburg, Florida

Brian House is Vice President of Digital and Technical Training at Mike Holt Enterprises, and a Certified Mike Holt Instructor. Starting in the 1990s Brian owned and ran a contracting firm that did everything from service work to designing energy-efficient lighting retrofits, exploring "green" biomass generators, and partnering with residential PV companies.

He began teaching seminars in 2000 after joining the elite group of instructors who attended Mike Holt's Train the Trainer boot camp. Brian was personally selected for development by Mike Holt after being named as one of the top presenters in that class. He now travels around the country to teach Mike Holt seminars to groups that include electricians, instructors, the military, and engineers. His first-hand experience as an electrical contractor, along with Mike Holt's instructor training, gave him a teaching style that is practical, straightforward, and refreshing.

Brian is high-energy, with a passion for doing business the right way. He expresses his commitment to the industry and his love for its people whether he's teaching, working on books, or developing instructional programs. Brian also leads the Mike Holt Enterprises apprenticeship and digital products teams. They're creating cutting-edge training tools and partnering with apprenticeship programs nation-wide to help them take their curriculum to the next level.

Brian and his wife Carissa have shared the joy of their four children and many foster children during 22 years of marriage. When not mentoring youth at work or church, he can be found racing mountain bikes with his kids or fly fishing on Florida's Intracoastal Waterway. He's passionate about helping others and regularly engages with the youth of his community to motivate them into exploring their future.

Editorial and Production

A special thanks goes to **Toni Culbreath** for her outstanding contribution to this project. She worked tirelessly to proofread and edit this publication. Her attention to detail and her dedication is irreplaceable.

Dan Haruch is the newest member of our technical team. His skillset and general knowledge of the *NEC*, combined with his work ethic and ability to work with other members of the production team, were a major part of the successful publication of this textbook.

Many thanks to **Cathleen Kwas** who did the design, layout, and production of this textbook. Her desire to create the best possible product for our customers is greatly appreciated.

Also, thanks to **Paula Birchfield** who was the Production Coordinator for this product. She helped keep everything flowing and tied up all the loose ends. She, **Jeff Crandall** and **Kirsten Shea** did a great job proofing the final files prior to printing.